In Defense of Single-Parent Families

In Defense of Single-Parent Families

NANCY E. DOWD

NEW YORK UNIVERSITY PRESS

NEW YORK AND LONDON

NEW YORK UNIVERSITY PRESS
New York and London

Library of Congress Cataloging-in-Publication Data
Dowd, Nancy E., 1949–
In defense of single-parent families / Nancy E. Dowd.
p.   cm.
Includes bibliographical references and index.
Contents: the stories of stigma : what we say about single-parent
families — The realities : what we know about single-parent
families. The poverty justification. The developmental
justification. The morality justification. Implicit justifications :
race and gender stories — Divorced single parents. The context of
work and family. Family law. Employment law. Welfare. Conclusion :
law, stigma, equality, and choice — Nonmarital single-parent
families. The context : nonmarital single parents. Nonmarital
families and the law — Single parents as positive role models.
Black single mothers and their families. General characteristics of
single-parent families — Policies for single-parent families.
Lessons from where we are now. Elements of changed policy toward
single-parent families — Legal strategies. Defining family. Family
support.
ISBN 0-8147-1869-8 (alk. paper)
1. Single-parent family—United States.   2. Single mothers—United
States.   3. Single fathers—United States.   4. Single parents—Legal
status, laws, etc.—United States.   I. Title.
HQ759.915.D69   1997
306.85'6—dc20   96-25268
                        CIP

Manufactured in the United States of America
10 9 8 7 6 5 4 3 2 1

To Zoe and Zachary

Contents

Acknowledgments

Many people made this book possible. I would like to acknowledge their help and thank them for their support.

I have been blessed with extraordinary research assistants who have shared their intellectual gifts as well as their friendship: Rosemary Howard, Craig Williams, Teresa Drake, Linnea Schram, Judy Erwin, Lisa Osborne, and Terry Bradford. While all of them contributed in significant ways, Rosemary Howard's work on the book was especially critical to completing the project. Her dedication and tireless effort were extraordinary.

Pam Smith, my secretary, has seen this project through with humor, compassion, and continual support.

The multidisciplinary research could not have been done without the expertise and diligence of the staff of the Law Library of the University of Florida College of Law. Rosalie Sanderson in particular was unfailingly helpful. In the last stages of the revisions of the manuscript, Julia McMahon O'Higgins of the Davis Law Library of the Auckland University School of Law provided invaluable support which enabled me to complete my revisions. I am also grateful for the financial support which enabled me to write that was provided by the University of Florida College of Law.

My thinking about single parents has been enriched and challenged by many. They include Elizabeth McCulloch, Marty Peters, Sharon Rush, Jan Perea, Martha Fineman, Paulette Caldwell, Elizabeth Bartholet, Wendy Fitzgerald, Walter Weyrauch, Lisette Burrows, Barbara Bennett Woodhouse, Dorothy Roberts, Patricia Bradford, Karen Blum, Larry Kalevitch, Michelle Jacobs, and Don Peters. I also benefited by presenting portions of the research in 1994 at meetings of the International Society of Family Law, and the Law and Society Association, as well as to the Conference on Feminism and Legal Theory at Columbia University in the summer of 1995. My students in the seminar on Nontraditional Families at the University of Florida in the fall of 1995 also challenged my thinking and conclusions.

Niko Pfund, my primary editor at New York University Press, has been an enthusiastic supporter and thoughtful contributor. One anonymous reader who reviewed the manuscript contributed valuable insights and feedback.

My friends and family have put up with me through the inevitable hard times of this project. Particular thanks go to Jane Pendergast, Dorota Hamen, and Patricia Bradford, and to my sister, Patricia McDermott, who has always been there for me.

My deepest love and appreciation go to my children, who have taught me more than they will ever know and tolerated so much so that mom could finish her book. I love you—higher than the moon, wider than the sky.

Introduction

"I am a single parent." The statement evokes admiration, sympathy, pity, disgust, uneasiness, skepticism. I never planned on being a single parent. Few do. I grew up with an ideal of parenting as something I would do with a husband, within a marriage. Choosing to parent alone was simply not an option. Unwed pregnancy was to be avoided at all costs. Divorce was rare and tragic. If it occurred, one remedied it as quickly as possible with remarriage, especially if one wanted to have children or raise existing children.

In my late thirties, divorced, childless, and still not remarried, I nevertheless so strongly wanted to parent that I reexamined these principles and decided, after much difficult soul-searching, that what was most important was my desire and my ability to parent. When I adopted my daughter, my family and friends greeted us without apprehension, with genuine support and joy.

But I remember the confusion of one friend, who after hearing my news looked at me, puzzled, and said, "So, does that make you — an unwed mother?" My high-school persona immediately rose to the surface and I wanted to say no, because unwed mothers were "bad" girls who had made a "mistake" and gotten pregnant, whom family and community shamed and rejected. It was a label laden with a clear cultural, moral, and religious message of stigma for me and for my child. I had made a conscious, reasoned, mature decision to become a parent that did not fit the stereotyped connotation of "unwed mother."

Yet I realized the answer was, in another sense, yes. I was a mother and unmarried, parenting alone. A complex set of social and cultural changes had given me a new label to claim, that of "single parent," which seemed free from the moralistic condemnation and gendered name-calling of "unwed mother." Indeed, during the homestudy process for my adoption, my social worker said he was comfortable with approving me as an adoptive parent despite the fact that I was single, because so many children were raised in single-parent families that my prospective child's family would not be "different."

Yet once I became a parent, virtually everything I read or saw about single-parent families indicated that it is a status still charged with negative connotations. Single-parent families are regularly equated with poverty, family breakdown, juvenile delinquency, and crime. We often blame single parents as the cause of these social ills. And while the connections are tied to a gender-neutral label, in reality we link these social problems to parenting by single *mothers*, because it is they who do most of the parenting in single-parent families.

The total absence of a father in my family is strangely unremarkable. Certainly it technically separates my children (I later also adopted a son) from most children in single-parent families, who by virtue of biology as well as legal status have both a mother and a father. But in reality my children experience family as the vast majority of children of single-parent families do, as sole parenting by their mother. Most single fathers are single parents in a different way from most single mothers: they are parents by virtue of a biological link or legal status as a noncustodial parent. They are expected to support their children economically, but only rarely are they caretakers of their children. It remains uncommon for men to have sole or primary custody of their children, or to maintain an ongoing significant caretaking relationship with them. We socially accept, indeed arguably support, a concept of fathering that expects men to separate from their children if they do not remain connected to the children's mother. This expected gendered allocation of care-taking either renders invisible those single fathers who parent like single mothers, or elevates them to near sainthood for their performance of the very role for which mothers seem inevitably subject to criticism, regardless of how well they perform.

Although I fit the norm of single parent as a single mother, I nevertheless became a single parent in an unconventional way. Typically, people become single parents by having a child without marrying or by divorcing after having children. Today, nearly one-third of American families with children under age eighteen are single-parent families, double the number less than two decades ago. Separation and divorce create most single-parent families, accounting for twice as many single-parent families (60 percent) as the failure to marry (30 percent), while the death of a parent creates less than 7 percent of such families. One of the odd byproducts of my adopting a child is that people imagine me as some sort of martyr doing a good deed, casting me in stark relief to someone perceived as making a selfish or misguided decision to have a child and raise it on her own as an unmarried single mother. I seem to be accorded a status closest to that of widows, the most honored and supported single parents, although I remain suspect because my single parenting is not associated with the death of a husband.

In another respect I also am an unconventional single mother in that I am not poor. Nearly 90 percent of children raised in single-parent families are raised by single mothers; half of those households are below the poverty line. My children will not suffer from the consequences of poverty simply because my income far exceeds that of most single mothers, although eight out of ten single mothers, like me, do wage work. Single fathers, whether with or without their children in their household, do not share this high poverty rate. An enormous proportion of single fathers contribute little or nothing economically to the support of their children. Public income supports do little to lessen these harsh economic realities. The consequences are profound. Poverty is indisputably a powerful and brutal detriment to opportunity and achievement, crippling to health, education, and employment, and strongly linked to crime and violence.

The stigma attached to single-parent families diverts attention from poverty while blaming single parents for the poverty of their families. It is a cruel Catch 22. By focusing on family form and status, society categorizes by marital status and by the number of people parenting a child in a household. Blaming parents for the poverty of the family presumes that there is a means or choice to avoid that poverty. It is a flaw of character or commitment by the parent that is perceived as resulting in poverty, either because they made a poor economic decision in choosing to become a single parent, or because they failed to work hard enough to avoid poverty once the choice was made. Assigning fault to the parent by stigmatizing single-parent families justifies the consequences of poverty as deserved. Not only the erring parent, but also children who have the bad luck to be connected to parents who make bad choices, are stuck with the consequences of this stigma.

To be clear: the economic circumstances of most single parents are not caused by family form but rather by the consequences of a complex combination of entrenched gender roles, failure to acknowledge and deal with dependency, and the debilitating consequences of ongoing racism. Most single parents cannot choose whether or not to live in poverty. The lack of choices is predetermined by a structure which penalizes these parents because of their status, and which refuses to recognize the legitimacy of any family other than a heterosexual, married, two-parent family. In addition, the difficulties suffered by many single-parent families simply expose more clearly the debilitating impact of conflicts between work and family responsibilities, conflicts that undermine all kinds of families.

The condemnation of single mothers for raising children without fathers is another basis for the stigmatizing of single-parent families. This hurts fathers as well as mothers because part of the underlying rationale—that two parents of opposite sexes are an essential, irreducible minimum for healthy child development—undermines support for single fathers just as it does support for single mothers. But the nearly exclusive concern with father absence as a corollary of this principle reflects both the dominance of mothers in caretaking in all family structures and an uneasiness with the implications of women successfully parenting alone. Although society sometimes presumes single-parent fathers with primary or sole custody of their children are inadequate as parents, more often we view fathers with sympathy rather than criticize them for failing to have a mother in the household. But we condemn single mothers for precisely that: the absence of a father and the presumed consequences of father absence. Single mothering is by definition deficient and inadequate.

Single fathers have been rightly criticized for their failure to support their children financially. But we do not condemn fathers for failing to parent their children socially or psychologically. The concern so evident in the critique of mothers is not paralleled by a critique of fathers or social conceptions of fatherhood. We rarely question how we as a society see fatherhood. Why is it difficult and unusual for men to nurture their children? Why do we expect them to separate emotionally from their children with an ease we would find callous and unnatural in mothers? We blame mothers for failing to have a man present, and we presume from that failure that their families are dysfunctional and psychologically harmful. We blame fathers for not fulfilling the role of economic provider, but we do not expect any broader fathering role.

Research simply does not support the view that single parenting is harmful to children because it prevents healthy child development. To the contrary, all that we know about families demonstrates that family form simply does not correlate with family function or developmental health. *Dysfunctional families come in all shapes and sizes; so do healthy families.* Furthermore, the processes of human development do not occur in isolation in a household incubator, but rather are a complex interaction of family, community, and educational institutions. No single form of family is essential, nor is it a guarantor of healthy, happy children.

By pointing the finger at family *form*, we deflect discussion away from the very real problems single-parent families face. Fixed on allocating blame, we obscure the choices we are making about children and our social future: that judgments about parents justify putting children at risk, by fostering an economic and social environment calculated to produce failure, frustration, and harm. Blaming single parents for the poverty of their families is not only wrong, it is social suicide. Presuming the inadequacy of single parenting is not only cruel, but self-defeating.

The stigmatizing of single parents informs popular culture, and, in so doing, justifies the structure of policies and institutions that have enormous impact on the lives of single parents and their families. The ideology of stigma pervades the law, underlying divorce laws and welfare structures, both of which weigh heavily on the lives of single-parent families. Through these structures law condemns rather than supports single-parent families, contributing to the impoverishment of these families and the predictable consequences of poverty.

The legal structure of divorce functions to perpetuate the economic impoverishment and asymmetric psychological relationships of *de facto* single-parent families that exist *within* intact marriages. Single parenting exists within marriage—indeed marriage *fosters* it—as the result of existing work-family structures and the persistence of gender roles and gender segregation, within and outside the family. Why are we not surprised that most children raised solely or primarily by one parent are raised by a single mother? And how is it that we find it unremarkable that men spend little or no time parenting their children? Indeed, why do we expect single fathers to emotionally separate from their children? Our acceptance of such strong gender imbalance in parenting springs from the persistence of outdated stereotypes of women parenting and men working, and the absence of any new, well-articulated gender roles. To the extent that there is a new gender ideal of equality in parenting and work, neither family life nor work fully supports it. The consequence is that single parenting, with its characteristic distinctive pattern for single mothers and single fathers, is created within marriage. Mothers parent, physically and psychologically, to a far greater degree than fathers. Faced with a double shift at home and occupational segregation and low wages at work, mothers voluntarily or involuntarily trade parenting for job opportunity and income. Their spouse's income conceals their economic vulnerability during marriage, a vulnerability that becomes apparent with divorce. Fathers similarly trade off significant caretaking in order to provide economically, a role strongly supported in the workplace and the family.

The illusion of equality hides the economic and psychological imbalance of marriage. Our semantic and ideological commitment to equality constantly pushes us to deny inequality, or to minimize significant deviations, or to accept them as "choice." Our unwillingness to confront the consequences of children's dependency also contributes to a refusal to see this imbalance. Even in instances of near equality, we deny the evidence of inadequate care, refusing to confront the real needs of dependent children.

Yet, with divorce, the inequalities become clearly apparent; indeed, they get worse. Economic impoverishment and father absence are all too often characteristic of single parenthood created at divorce. The judgment that single-parent families are bad families, to be discouraged and avoided, or at best, grudgingly permitted, underlies the unwillingness to provide single-parent families with the postdivorce resources they need. Fathers' removal from the lives of their children is sanctioned, even encouraged. They are prepared for this by their role as secondary parents within marriage, and the construction of fathering as economic fatherhood makes them equate parenting with money. This encourages them to believe that their parenting ends when they do not or cannot pay child support.

The inadequacies of the divorce and employment structure are magnified for nonmarital single-parent families. The minimal, often ephemeral support authorized by child support statutes is simply unavailable for the vast majority of children of nonmarital single parents. The reason is simple: that entitlement is triggered only if paternity is established, and the paternity rate for nonmarital children is a mere 30 percent. The children of non-marital single parents are therefore doubly stigmatized, because they are being raised by a single mother and because they are legally fatherless.

The welfare system exacerbates the lack of meaningful support of single-parent families. A significant proportion of divorced parents, as well as never-married single parents, turn to welfare as a temporary, necessary evil. The dynamic of the welfare system even more explicitly condemns single parents, especially never-married single parents. Once again, the system perpetuates poverty. And to an even more perverse extent, it discourages fathering.

The addition of race exacerbates gender inequity. Most welfare mothers are not Black mothers, but Black mothers are disproportionately represented as compared to their proportion of the population. African Americans account for less than 40 percent of Aid to Families with Dependent Children (AFDC) recipients, whites 38 percent, Hispanics 17 percent. Single-parent never-married families are far more predominant in the Black community than in the white community. Marriage is the most common, indeed for most women the only, way out of the poverty of single parenthood. For Black women, however, the economic gain of marriage is often absent or insignificant due to the poor economic position of Black men.

Race and gender have much to do with the stigma of single-parent families. We have long been willing to consign the vast majority of children of Black families to harshly unequal family circumstances that contribute significantly to perpetuating inequality. Our sensitivity to men's issues and our fear of supporting women has resulted in our labeling any support of single mothers as an attack on men, and silencing critical evaluation and redefinition of fatherhood.

Children have lost the most from our stigmatizing of single-parent families. Seventy percent of all children will spend all or part of their lives in a single-parent household. The lack of support and condemnation of single parents, based on the stigma associated with them, bears most heavily on children.

When I adopted my second child, some of my friends wondered if I had gone crazy. They feared that two children would be beyond my psychological and physical resources. Yet at the same time, I recalled those who had said, after I adopted my first child, that I was lucky to be parenting alone, without another adult.

Concern about resources, of course, is entirely legitimate. Single-parent families experience the stress of inadequate resources, financial and psychological, to a greater degree than do two-parent households. We must not ignore the very real problems that they face. They include economic needs as well as problems of time and energy, and needs for social support. Removing the stigma against single-parent families should not, *must* not, keep us from recognizing the problems they confront.

At the same time, recognition of the value of single-parent families is also crucial. It had never occurred to me that being a single parent could be a *benefit*; I merely saw myself as able to overcome and compensate for the absence of another parent in the household. I viewed my role as consciously compensating for a loss. I did not see my family as an alternative, different form with its own dynamic. In the process of evaluating the assumptions underlying the stigma attached to single-parent families, the data expose several fascinating benefits. Single-parent families are models of networking and extended family systems. The family dynamic also seems to produce children who are independent, self-reliant, and who believe and practice gender respect and equality.

My hope is that this book will reorient the debate about single-parent families and shift entrenched assumptions away from stigma and toward support of such families. The commonplace assumption that single-parent families are dysfunctional and bad *because* of inherent, fatal flaws in their structure is unsupported rhetoric. To the contrary, all we know about families indicates that structure does not dictate family function or success. Children need love, care, and parenting; structure neither precludes nor insures that those things will be present. We need to put children first, structure second. It makes no sense to punish children or separate them from their families as the consequence of structures that they had no hand in creating and that are unconnected to their well-being.

Powerful incentives remain—and should remain—for raising children in two-parent families. Supporting single-parent families need not translate into destabilizing two- or multiple-parent families. The value of particular families is not defined by blackballing others. We need not choose a single paradigm. By supporting single parents, we may learn ways family and work structures must be changed to support all families. By learning from single parents, we may better understand how to achieve our ideal of gender equality. Partnership must find a new basis; otherwise we are moving to only more subtle support for calcified gender roles. Supporting single-parent families also does not mean a rejection of fathers. To the contrary, supporting single parents must include reorienting the concept and support of fatherhood.

Rethinking fatherhood is one of the challenges to reorienting policy toward single-parent families. Since so many single parents raising children are mothers, any support of single-parent families, it might be argued, undermines the role of fathers in families. The perversity of patriarchy is such that any defense or support of women is often read as an attack on men. This red herring of male-bashing hides the perpetuation of a constrained, narrow role of fathering.

Teenage single parents also seem to confound changing policy toward single parents. It is easy to attack any suggestion of support for single-parent families with the argument that to do so encourages immature teenagers to have children. The alarming rate of teenage pregnancy and parenthood cannot be ignored. At the same time, it makes no sense to follow a policy that punishes any positive step to improve the lives of their children.

The difficulties with respect to teenagers and fathers reflect the changes that have occurred since the sixties, when the moral and cultural condemnation of single parenthood was so clear. Concepts of sexuality have changed. Premarital sex is more widely accepted. At the same time, sex education and birth control remain controversial and not universally available. Unwed motherhood has shifted from a status of shame to one of honor among some teenagers and adults; this shift in values affects the incentives to have children and to raise them, rather than to place them for adoption. There has been a sea change in attitudes about divorce, exemplified by the shift from fault to no-fault divorce.

All of these changes have created the illusion of more freedom and choice with respect to parenting, but the consequences remain remarkably similar to those I was taught as a teenager in the sixties. Successful single parenting is often limited to those with resources; for those without, it is a status fraught with negative consequences. The strongest disincentive then was moral and social; today economic realities would seem to be a disincentive. Ironically, however, even harsh economic consequences have had little effect on the rate of single parenthood. The increase in single parenting is not, it seems, economically linked. Thus, the economic consequences that we accept as justified by our stigmatized view of single parents are particularly perverse, as they are unlikely to discourage single parenting, but very likely to create long-term problems for the children in these families.

Viewed through the lens of race, the perversity of stigmatizing single-parent families, one might cynically conclude, makes sense as part of an ongoing assault upon Black families. Race pervades all policy making because of the high proportion of single-parent families among African Americans. The stories of stigma that blame parents fit neatly into a desire to blame the victims rather than confront racial hierarchy.

Where might the exposure of this unjustified, unnecessary, and harmful stigmatization of single parents lead? Obviously, it points toward the need for significant reform of the divorce and welfare structures. We need to insure economic independence and support for caregiving and caretaking of children within a framework of meaningful gender and race equality. We need to rethink both the economic and relationship aspects of parenting if equality is to have real meaning.

We must reconsider whether we have a working model of family which strikes a healthy balance between wage work and family work. The traditional marital contract and work-family structure purported to provide economic support and caregiving on gendered lines, often limited by race privilege to white families. Women sacrificed independence, power and opportunity; men sacrificed love, nurturing, and giving. Under this model, children were assured of the caretaking of one parent, with a backup, secondary caregiver in the second parent.

The goal of economic independence means the economic self-sufficiency of each parent and an economic minimum for households with children, regardless of family form. Wages, private support, and public family-income support allowances, either singly or in combination, are needed to achieve this goal. Economic independence also means thinking of marriage as a truly volitional, committed relationship independent of an economic contract. It means reconceiving marriage in a nondominating, coequal way. If economic independence is assured, then marriage presumes people partner for reasons largely apart from economics. It also means that partnership in the same household, whether married or otherwise, is not the only model of parenting, but that economic contribution is a responsibility of being a parent. At the same time, we cannot treat unmarried single parents as equivalent to previously married single parents, assuming or forcing a relationship that never was.

In addition to the economic side of parenting, we need to reconceive the status of caregiving work which lies at the heart of parenting. This means a commitment to the nurture of children and support of those who nurture. We can encourage the biological, adoptive, or foster parents to do so under the same roof, in a committed relationship of their own, but can also encourage the support of single parents and their networks of caregivers. Particularly, we must value the care of children at least as much as we impose economic responsibility on those who become parents. And we must rethink and reorient single fatherhood, while we also acknowledge and value single mothers.

To achieve this we must stop ignoring the intersections of family and work. We have ignored the impact on family structure of the lack of support of family responsibilities, as well as the insidious impact on family dynamics of ongoing sex and race discrimination in the workforce. We treat husbands and wives as equals, interchangeable, when their respective labor market positions are usually highly unequal. On the work side, we continue to pretend that family responsibilities do not exist, or virtually ignore them, while at the same time, those who take parenting seriously often face severe, long-term detriments at work. We demand that parents be invisible in the workplace, but single parents stick out like sore thumbs. Their conflicts between work and family, however, are simply more evident and difficult to avoid than those of two-parent families. They are harbingers of the dilemmas all families face.

Finally, the challenge is to create an ideology of diversity and acceptance, rather than exalting a single family form and, as a necessary correlation of that preference, denigrating any variation from that ideal. We sometimes idolize and idealize single parents, but far too often the best we give is grudging acceptance.

When my daughter entered preschool, one of the first drawings she brought home was her picture of our "family," a dazzling array of colors, lines, and shapes. When I asked who they were, she named everyone she knew who loved her. They were all in her circle of family. She now sometimes only draws me, her brother, and herself, but more often includes her current sense of the circle of people who love and care for her. She compares our family to the collections of people included in other families and knows families are different, but not because of shape or structure. I hope that this book may contribute to supporting that kind of acceptance of single-parent families, as well as focusing energy and resources on supporting children in all families.

PART I · MYTHS & REALITIES

CHAPTER 1

The Stories of Stigma: What We Say about Single-Parent Families

A remarkably consistent view of single-parent families dominates popular culture as well as public policy. " 'Single-parent family' is a euphemism . . . for 'problem family,' for some kind of social pathology" (Kamerman and Kahn 1988).[1] Single-parent families are characterized as part of the "underclass"; broken and deviant, as compared to the nuclear, traditional, patriarchal family. Some equate the rise in the numbers of single-parent families with social decline and the death of the "real" family.

Recent Republican welfare reform legislation mirrors this image of single-parent families, especially never-married single parents. The Personal Responsibility Act proclaims its goals as "restor[ing] the American family, [and] reduc[ing] illegitimacy" (House Report 1995). The act states that "marriage is the foundation of a successful society" and claims that "the negative consequences of an out-of-wedlock birth on the child, the mother, and the society are well

3

documented" (House Report 1995). Included in the act's data are bald statements that children of single-parent families are likely to have emotional or behavioral problems; are more likely themselves as teenagers to have children out of wedlock; are more likely to divorce; are more likely to have trouble at school and in peer adjustment; and are more likely to commit crime or to live in an area plagued by crime. The act also includes significant incentives for states to reduce out-of-wedlock births, dubbed the "illegitimacy bonus."

Blaming single parents for significant societal ills is by no means confined to partisan politics. Some leading advocates of communitarianism, one of the most dynamic intellectual movements of recent years, similarly condemn single parenting as a sign of social decline, and advocate the revival and support of two-parent families as one of the core structures of "community" (Etzioni 1993). In order to support two-parent families, some communitarians encourage strengthening premarital counseling, discouraging divorce, dissuading single women from childbearing, providing generous maternity and paternity leave, and improving childcare. Ironically, they also advocate incentives to permit *one* parent to stay at home to raise children (Anderson and Davey 1995, 18).

Stigmatizing single parents is not strange in light of dominant legal and social definitions of family, and the exalted place in those definitions given to the nuclear, marital, two-parent family. We as a society, through law, support nuclear marital families in significant material and ideological ways. We provide resources including financial support, fringe benefits, tax breaks, and housing. We facilitate the use of reproductive technology or adoption for favored families. We define our vision of family, ideologically and practically, by our construction of marriage and divorce, and by limiting recognition of nonmarital families.

Law values the nuclear, marital, two-parent family premised on its perceived essential role in the socialization of citizens as well as its presumed inherent worth as a form of intimate association. "[W]e protect the family because it contributes so powerfully to the happiness of individuals ... 'the ability independently to define one's identity that is central to any concept of liberty' cannot truly be exercised in a vacuum; we all depend on the 'emotional enrichment of close ties with others' " (*Bowers v. Hardwick* 1986, quoting *Rob-*

erts v. U.S. Jaycees 1984, 619).[2] "[T]he historic respect—indeed, sanctity would not be too strong a term—traditionally accorded to the relationships that develop with the unitary family . . . is typified, of course, by the marital family" (*Bowers v. Hardwick* 1986, n.3).

The veneration of the nuclear marital two-parent family as core social organization of society does not, however, reflect the reality of family structures. *It is estimated that 70 percent of children will spend some time in a single-parent family before reaching age eighteen; for women entering adulthood, the probability that they will maintain a single-parent family for some period of time is 40 percent* (Norton and Click 1986). Single-parent families now constitute 30 percent of all families with minor children and are the most rapidly growing family form in America (Ermisch 1990).

Divorced or separated single parents remain the largest group of single parents (nearly 60 percent), almost double the number of never-married single parents (just over 30 percent), while widowed single parents are a diminishing proportion of single-parent families (not quite 7 percent) (Bureau of the Census 1989; Norton and Click 1986). Most children experience living in a single-parent family as one of several family forms during their childhood; on average, most will spend one to six years in a single-parent family. Only a small minority, about 10 percent, will spend their entire childhood in a single-parent family (Duskin 1990).

The American picture mirrors international trends: one of three households in the world has a woman as the sole breadwinner (Snyder 1991). The proportion of single-parent families in postindustrial countries averages 10 to 15 percent of families with dependent children; the U.S. proportion of nearly 30 percent represents one of the highest percentages.

When family households are analyzed by race, single-parent households are the dominant family form for African Americans and a significant and growing alternative family form for Hispanics (33 percent) and whites (23 percent). Nearly two-thirds of single parents are white, but single-parent families are proportionately more prevalent among Blacks. Never-married single parents predominate among Blacks, while divorced single parents predominate among whites (Rawlings 1994).

Given their increasing numbers and their remarkable diversity, the vehemence of the stigma directed against single parents seems strange, in some respects. We exact a terrible price from many children and their parents because of the stigma attached to this form of family. Stigma is not limited to names and negative stereotypes in popular culture. We impose economic and psychic penalties as a matter of social policy and legal structure. In particular, we continue to consign large numbers of children to poverty who have the bad luck to be born into, or whose family becomes, what society deems the wrong kind of family.

Overwhelmingly, stigma is tied to the strongly negative images we have of single *mothers*. When we speak about single parents, we tend to mean an individual who is the sole or dominant caregiver and whose household is the place where their children live all or most of the time. By that definition of single parent, the ranks are disproportionately female, both from a historical and current perspective. The proportion of children living with their single mothers is 87 percent, compared with 13 percent who live with their single fathers (Rawlings 1994).[3] Divorced mothers, unmarried teenage mothers, welfare mothers, women of color—all of these categories of single mothers generate negative connotations. Those negative images and stories infect the law just as they infect other social institutions, acting as justifications for punitive legal outcomes.

Divorced mothers are frequently criticized as inadequate, incomplete mothers, particularly if they do wage work in addition to parenting. They fail as mothers because they do not mother enough; by definition they are second-rate parents. Single mothers' success at being economic providers may come at the price of losing custody of their children. Sharon Prost, for example, lost custody of her children to her former husband, Kenneth Greene, because of her career as a top Capitol Hill staffer. Prost, chief counsel for the Republicans on the Senate Judiciary Committee, was awarded six days of visitation per month and ordered to pay $23,000 per year in child support, while Greene, who also works full-time as a union administrator, was awarded custody of their two sons. Despite the limited visitation schedule granted in the custody order, Greene has permitted Prost to have the boys overnight twelve to fourteen times each month, and Prost continues to drive them to school daily, stays home with them when they are ill, does their laundry, attends soccer practices, and chaperones their school field trips.

The trial judge who determined custody found that Prost had

failed to make her children her first priority. "Her career choice of demanding jobs that require her to work late nights and many weekends necessarily cuts into the time available for her family . . . her devotion to her job and/or her personal pursuits often takes precedence over her family" (*Prost v. Greene* 1995, 624–25). The court viewed Prost as "driven to succeed" and "absorbed by her work," citing as evidence Prost's return to work immediately after the birth of her second child.

The court's conclusion that Greene was the more nurturing parent relied heavily on the testimony of the couple's au pair, who testified that Prost rarely cooked dinner or ate dinner with her children. By contrast, the court made little of Greene's insistence that the couple retain an au pair rather than care for his children himself when he was unemployed for two years in the early 1990s.

On appeal, the appellate court rejected arguments that the trial court's conclusions were based on gender stereotypes. The court remanded the custody decision only because the trial court had failed to consider evidence of domestic violence by Greene against Prost.

Similar cases are common. For example, in New York, Renee B.'s mother lost custody of her eight-year-old daughter to her unemployed ex-husband on the basis that the father, despite his repeated refusal to pay child support, was better able to care for his daughter because he was at home while his ex-wife was employed in an office (Steinbach 1995). In South Carolina, Ruth Parris lost custody of her son because a judge determined she was "not particularly family-oriented" (*Parris v. Parris* 1995). Parris, described by the trial court as an "aggressive, competitive" real estate agent, took a year off from work after her son's birth, was closely involved in his daily care, religious and secular education, music lessons, and other activities. Nevertheless, the judge gave great weight to the father's domesticity, evidenced by his cooking of weekend meals, attending his son's swim meets, and taking his son to doctor visits.

If there is an available stepmother who does not do wage work, that may further threaten the ability of a single working mother to retain custody. A two-parent marital family is viewed as a complete family; a single-parent family as presumptively inferior. A single mother may be required to replicate the time available to a mother working in the home, even if that undercuts the very wage work that she is required to do in order to carry her responsibility of economic support. So, for instance, Stephanie Orr was warned by a mediator that if she failed to rearrange her work schedule so as to be home each day by 3:30 P.M., she would risk losing custody of her eight-year-old daughter to her ex-husband, whose second wife was at home and could care for the girl after school (Creno 1995).

The stigma directed at single mothers increases dramatically when the mother has never married and even worse, if she is a teenager. Teenagers seem to epitomize all of the worst negatives of single parenting. They are viewed as socially, economically, and developmentally "at risk." Their perceived poor judgment and, for some, immorality in becoming pregnant justifies the greatest stigma as a necessary deterrence to others. Most teenage single mothers struggle against nearly insurmountable barriers deliberately placed in their path.

Overcoming those barriers may be met with alarm rather than congratulation. In the case of Jennifer Ireland, her efforts to obtain a college education nearly resulted in losing custody of her daughter. Ireland, who had her child when she was seventeen, was ordered to turn over custody of her three-year-old daughter to the child's father after she placed the toddler in day-care while she attended classes at the University of Michigan (Dateline 1994). Ireland had filed for child support from the father, Steven Smith, who countersued for custody, despite his lack of significant involvement in the child's life until the support action was brought.

Macomb County Circuit Judge Raymond R. Cashen awarded custody to the child's father because the father intended to have his mother, a homemaker, care for the child. The judge reasoned that the paternal grandmother would be the best caretaker of the child because of her maturity and availability, since she was not engaged in wage work. The young mother was characterized as uncaring and uninvolved, frequently pawning off her daughter on anyone willing to look after her. In November 1995, the decision was reversed and sent back to be retried by a different judge, with an order that day-care arrangements could not be taken into consideration in determining custody ("Mother Wins Custody" 1995).

The heightened stigma reserved for unmarried mothers is also evident in adoption cases (Dowd 1994). The adoption structure is designed to facilitate the transfer of children from stigmatized single mothers to, preferably, two-parent married couples. Recent high-profile adoption cases, such as the "Baby Jessica" and "Baby Rich-ard" cases, have not been litigated on the basis of the rights of single mothers, but rather as a contest between biological and adoptive couples (*DeBoer v. Schmidt* 1993; *In re Kirchner* 1995). The unwed mothers legitimated themselves, as well as their child, by marrying the biological fathers of their children, who then challenged the adoptions on the basis of the fathers' rights. Ironically, the recogni-tion of the fathers' rights to block the adoption is consistent with the devaluation of the judgments of the mothers, both with respect to the original surrender for adoption and subsequent rethinking of that decision.

One of the most public instances of stigma directed at unmarried single mothers was the furor over the decision to parent alone by the fictional television character Murphy Brown. Despite the relatively unusual circumstances of this single parent, that is, that she had an income sufficiently high that she could provide not only adequate but generous economic support for her child, the controversy over her decision to single parent reflects the stigma directed at real single parents of considerably less means and power. Then Vice President Dan Quayle strongly attacked the story line as an affront to "family values," with a clear understanding that "family" excluded those who do not parent in heterosexual pairs (Rosenthal 1992). Quayle's subsequent praise for divorced single parents served only to under-score the distinctive condemnation of unmarried single parents.[4] He continued to argue that the deliberate choice of parenting alone was irresponsible and morally reprehensible, as opposed to the presumed involuntary single parenting of divorced mothers. Furthermore, the prospect that economically independent single parents might view single parenting as a viable choice as a consequence of the very kind of work (high wages, full-time, demanding hours) that formal sexual equality guaranteed provoked strong moral condemnation.

The worst images of single mothers, however, are not those attached to atypical, privileged white women, but rather to women of color. These are women that we rarely name. The high-profile legal stories, which name and identify single mothers, concern more privileged, divorced (usually white) single mothers who have the resources to challenge unarticulated stereotypes. The powerfully negative images associated with Black single mothers and Black welfare mothers rarely identify individuals, but instead stigmatize the entire class of Black mothers. The courts are far more rarely used to vindicate the rights of these mothers by questioning underlying assumptions about their competency as parents.

"[I]deologues have continued to fashion from whole cloth the specter of the mythical Black welfare mother, complete with a prodigious reproductive capacity and a galling laziness, accompanied by the uncaring and equally lazy Black man in this life who will not work, will not marry her and will not support his family" (Bray 1992). The dominant culture's view of unwed Black single mothers continues to echo the 1965 Moynihan Report:

> Ours is a society which presumes male leadership in private and public affairs. The arrangements of society facilitate such leadership and reward it. A subculture, such as that of the Negro American, in which this is not the pattern, is placed at a distinct disadvantage. Fatherless families are the root of everything from poverty, violence, drug addiction, crime and declining standards in education and civility to teen pregnancy, sexually transmitted disease, narcissism and urban unrest. (Moynihan 1994)

According to this view, the predominance of single-parent families among African Americans is cultural in origin. The cultural explanation means that an additional layer of stigma is laid upon Black single mothers, the stigma of racial self-destruction.

The blame placed on single Black mothers for the violence of young Black men during the 1992 Los Angeles uprising reflects this strongly negative view of Black mothers (Buckley 1992a, 1992b; Rosenthal 1992). The target of Dan Quayle's speech that included a single reference to Murphy Brown was Black single mothers. "I believe the lawless social anarchy which we saw [in L.A.] is directly related to the breakdown of family structure, personal responsibility and social order in too many areas of our society. . . . Children need love and discipline. They need mothers and fathers. . . . Nature abhors a vacuum. When there are no mature, responsible men around to teach boys how to be good men, gangs serve in their place" (Rosenthal 1992). The most recent welfare reform debate as well is filled with negative images that presume the color of the typical welfare recipient is black, despite the fact that white, divorced women are the most numerous welfare recipients.

The scorn directed at single mothers has not insulated single fathers. Their failings simply are viewed remarkably differently from those of mothers. Although single fathers are praised, even lionized for parenting in a manner often taken for granted in the case of mothers, we nevertheless have more than our share of negative images of single fathers as well. We stigmatize single fathers as irresponsible reproducers and deadbeat dads, or render them invisible fathers.

The stereotype of men as irresponsible reproducers is particularly strong in recent high-profile adoption cases. When men assert parental rights in those cases, they rely on biology alone, not on caretaking, actual or potential, to assert their legal position. They also, generally, have succeeded only when they present themselves as willing not only to parent, but also to marry. Without the role of husband, fathers are seen as incapable caregivers, or, more strongly, as parents who routinely abandon their children.

Typical of this paradigm is the "Baby Emily" case, in which the Florida Supreme Court refused to reverse an adoptive placement in favor of a single father (*In re Adoption of Baby E.A.W.* 1995). In that case, the single birthmother supported the adoptive parents against the efforts by the biological father to block the adoption. The Court adopted a definition of fathering that required, in addition to genetic connection and economic support, emotional support of the mother during her pregnancy. In the absence of such parenting, the father was deemed to have abandoned the child, and as a consequence, to have forfeited his right to object to the adoption. While the Court certainly had adequate reasons to deny the father the right to block the adoption based on his emotionally abusive treatment of the mother, one can speculate whether the choice between an unmarried father and a two-parent married couple, supported by the wishes of the birthmother, also weighed in the court's decision.

Far more than women, men are viewed as parents who see their children as their biological property, and who are capable of the most horrifying abuse. In a tragic New Jersey case, an unmarried father, Alan Gubernat, began to establish a relationship with his son Scott seven months after his birth and after paternity was confirmed by a blood test (*Gubernat v. Deremer* 1995). When informal visitation broke down, the father filed for joint custody in 1992 and also requested that his son's last name be changed to Gubernat. The trial court granted joint legal custody and the name change. Just months before Scott's fourth birthday, the New Jersey Supreme Court reversed the name change. The court held that the common law rule giving fathers who legitimated their children this right could not be constitutionally upheld consistent with principles of gender equality and neutrality. Several days after the decision, Alan Gubernat killed his son, and then committed suicide. Although no one knows for sure what drove Gubernat to murder and suicide, the widely accepted explanation was that Gubernat killed his son because he could not give him his name, or obtain primary physical custody.

Among the strongest negative images attached to single fathers, however, is the image of the deadbeat dad. When fathers fail as economic providers, they are currently viewed, at least in theory, as being socially reprehensible. When economically capable of paying, their conduct is deemed especially immoral and justification for harsh criminal sanctions. A recent example is a 47–year-old investment advisor, Jeffrey Nichols, who owes over $500,000 back support for his three children. Nichols was jailed until he could raise at least $68,000 which he owed prior to his contempt conviction five years earlier (King 1995).

So widespread is the lack of economic support, or of full economic support, that the deadbeat dad is the presumed norm. In a 1995 Dear Abby column, a father who had consistently paid his child support bemoaned the negative image of single fathers, and gratefully thanked Abby for a Father's Day column in which she wrote "A 21–gun salute to the divorced father who has never uttered an unkind word about the mother of his children (at least to the children) and who has always been Johnny-on-the-spot with the support check" (Van Buren 1995a). Said the dad, "My morale has been worn down over the years by the stereotyping of divorced fathers as deadbeat dads—a particularly cruel label." Abby responded by again praising ex-husbands who pay child support, but also reinforced the deadbeat dad expectation. "It would be so easy [for fathers] to just walk away and not fulfill the responsibilities to their children. Yet you, and many like you, sacrifice to see that your children are fed, clothed and educated. You are to be commended for loving your children enough to be a responsible father" (Van Buren 1995a).

Two weeks later, in a follow-up column, Abby acknowledged that she had received much critical response to her column. "The common thread in the mail I received was that fathers who send their child support checks without fail are fulfilling their legal obligations—nothing else" (Van Buren 1995b). One reader composed a fantasy thank-you letter from her ex-husband, and concluded, "Compared to the monumental task of raising a child, how significant is writing a check? When my first husband thanks me for all (that I have done), I'll thank him for spending five minutes a month to provide child support" (Van Buren 1995b).

If fathers are not deadbeats, they are often simply invisible. They are stigmatized by not being noticed, by being treated as if they were not in the picture. That was literally the case in one story reported in the aftermath of the 1995 Oklahoma City bombing. In an issue of a popular weekly magazine devoted to stories about the families affected by the bombing, one story featured the single mother of two sons who died in the bombed-out daycare center. Identified beside the mother in a picture taken at the children's funeral, but otherwise unacknowledged in the article, was the father of the children, the mother's ex-husband.

Child development research did not study fathers *at all* until the 1970s, and studies of mothers continue to predominate even today. Paradoxically, other research presumed that single-parent families were detrimental to children, particularly boys, because of the absence of fathers.[5] According to one review of the sociological literature, studies of single-parent families rarely examined these families as functional systems. "The perspective of most research . . . appeared to be: when a marriage dissolves, the family dissolves; if a marriage never starts, a family never starts" (Gongla 1982, 6). The low economic status of single-parent families rarely appeared as a variable in these studies (14). Studies also rarely examined the nature or extent of ongoing relationships with fathers not in the household, and never-married fathers were studied even less than divorced fathers (17).

Similarly, until recently, psychological studies simply presumed that single-parent status explained psychological differences and negative traits, without examining the basis of this presumption (Mednick 1987). Strong views about appropriate gender roles infused much of the psychological research. "The values that have typically framed research in this area are that legitimate power and authority are the father's role, that the husband should be the sole or major economic provider, that marriage and family life must be structured in terms of separate roles and activities with a strict and proper division of labor, that all other family forms are deviant, and that single mothers are in a transitional state anyway" (187).

In some respects, of course, one could argue that the stigma associated with single parenting *has* declined—we have, after all, changed how we name and identify these parents. Until recently single-parent families were usually referred to as "broken" or "father-absent" families. Nonmarital families were not considered families at all; the only parent recognized was the mother, who was labeled an "unwed mother," while the children were called "bastards" or "illegitimates." We have largely shifted from this name-calling (although some conservatives continue to engage in it) to the more neutral "single parent" or "single-parent family," although no new terminology has emerged for children. This new name appears to remove the condemnation of family form and explicit gender reference, yet its meanings and connotations belie the persistence of stigma.

One meaning of "single parent" is that the parent is not married. "Single" conveys "unmarried," whether because the person never married or divorced (the death of a spouse entitles one to the more valued label of "widow" or "widower"). This meaning obscures, however, single parents who cannot marry, barred by the heterosexual limitation on marriage. At the same time, it clearly establishes the desired norm of parenting within marriage.

"Single" also means "sole" or "lone," and therefore the term "single parent" also means one who parents alone, without a marital partner. On the one hand, it suggests a parent functioning without a support network, literally alone and isolated. On the other hand, this definition connotes a person who is the primary or sole caretaker of children, as distinguished from the person with parental status who does little or no nurturing.

The more neutral "parent" terminology arguably hides men's and women's differing experiences, in general, of single parenting. One might also argue that, despite its neutrality, "single parent" is often understood as synonymous with "single mother." Single-parent fathers disappear under this presumption, while mothers' parenting is encoded.

But names are the least of it. The stigma we attach to single-parent families most significantly results in economic deprivation and social isolation. As a society, we continue to view that stigma and its results as appropriate and justified. Three core justifications are used to rationalize the view of single-parent families as sick families. First, single-parent families are poor; or, more strongly, many see single parenting as a structural form that *causes* poverty and its associated ills. Second, single-parent families are psychologically unhealthy. The children of single parents are developmentally at risk, so it is claimed, because children cannot develop normally without two opposite-sex parents in the household. Third, single-parent families are immoral. Religious in origin, but strongly reflected in secular views as well, this justification views single-parent families as sinful because they lack the blessing and validation of marriage. Finally, beneath these commonly articulated justifications are race and gender beliefs that further support the stigma attached to single-parent families as a necessary badge of social scorn and economic penalty.

What we know about single-parent families, however, is quite different from the myths we tell as "objective" justifications. It is to those realities that I now turn, juxtaposed against the myths underlying this powerful stigma.

CHAPTER 2

The Realities: What We Know about Single-Parent Families

Every time I have a school conference I worry about whether my children will be labeled. If there is anything bad to report, or improvement needed, our family status can be used as a convenient explanation. "She's from a single-parent family. Ah, that explains it." When my son has difficulty with the discipline at his preschool, I worry that he will be categorized by his family form, rather than evaluated and understood for himself. I am heartened by signs that the diversity of family forms are recognized and valued, and with every new teacher or doctor or child-care worker I discuss how important it is to me that our family be acknowledged and supported. But whenever the class assignment is about "family" I find myself watchful, wondering what messages will come home this time. And as my daughter learns how to read, I know I will constantly confront stereotypes about the type of family she lives in. Today, for example, the headline in the morning paper proclaims,

"Two-Parent Families Make Comeback, Census Says." In the article, it is noted that despite a modest increase in the percentage of two-parent families, the number of single-parent families continues to rise, especially among Black families. This is labeled by the expert quoted in the paper as a "disturbing" trend. There is a lot to be unpacked in that one word.

The common justifications for stigmatizing single parents—economic, developmental, and moral—together with underlying gender and racial beliefs, dictate harsh deterrents and punitive consequences for most single-parent families. What we know about single-parent families, however, contradicts the justifications for stigma. It is supreme irony, then, that some of what we know is used to justify these horrible end results. Real problems are blamed on single parents, on the structure of family, when in fact the structure of family should be irrelevant to function. What we blame on single parents instead has a great deal to do with other factors, especially poverty and its consequences. By blaming single parents for their families' problems, however, we as a society avoid responsibility for children.

It takes a powerful and complex mythology to misunderstand the real problems of single-parent families, and to sacrifice the well-being of children. The willingness to let children suffer, and indeed to *make* them suffer, is astounding. Seventy percent of all children will spend some or all of their childhood in single-parent families, and we know that the links between childhood environment and future success are strong. Punishing children in single-parent families is a sacrifice that is socially destabilizing as well as morally reprehensible.

We also ignore what is positive about single-parent families. Stigma walls off any recognition of insights from or alternative familial models exemplified by single-parent families. Single-parent families have much to tell us and teach us about the functioning of families and their interaction with broader communities.

What we perpetuate, then, are myths, undeniably powerful but manifestly false. In this chapter I address each of the primary justifications for stigmatizing single parents in light of the realities of what we know about single parents. I also expose the underlying race and gender myths that justify stigma as well.

THE POVERTY JUSTIFICATION

Myth: Single Parents Cause Poverty, Thus Harming Their Children

Single parents are often mentioned in the same breath as other leading causes of poverty. The 1991 report of the National Commission on Children states, for example, "If we measure success not just by how well most children do, but by how poorly some fare, America falls far short. One in four children is raised by just one parent. . . . Children living with their mothers are especially likely to be poor" (*Final Report* 1991, 24).[1] As one scholar has lamented, "poverty has been artfully reconfigured as a social/cultural/psychological pathology, corroborated by a public educational discourse of deficiency and remediation" (Polakow 1993). In other words, poverty is due to an individual lack of responsibility, motivation, and discipline.

Individual blame has shifted, over time, from men to women. Explanations of the causes of poverty have gone from blaming individual pathology, presumed to be male, to blaming the "culture of poverty," to blaming the culture of single motherhood (Thomas 1994). Poverty explanations began with notions of individual failure. Oscar Lewis popularized the notion of a culture of poverty, that is, that poverty was not merely an economic description but a way of life. Lewis worried that his description might be abused, that the poor would be blamed rather than helped by his analysis. He was right. Subsequent researchers focused on the means of transmission of this culture, and began to argue that although men were predisposed to poverty pathology, it was women who transmitted this pathology intergenerationally. From that observation it was an easy step to begin to attack the culture of single motherhood, which is now held accountable for poverty and its associated ills.

The assumption that underlies this view is that the choices of single mothers in poverty are freely made choices. If they made better choices (with the clearly preferred choice being marriage, not economic self-sufficiency), they would not be in this bind. The negative economic consequences of marriage for women are ignored. So too are structural problems that affect the marital choices of Black women particularly harshly. Single mothers, according to this view, are moral and economic hazards that produce developmentally impaired children.

There is no doubt that single-parent families are disproportionately poor. On average, single-parent family income is only 40 percent as much as the average income of two-parent families (Duncan and Rodgers 1990, 53). One of every two single mothers lives below the poverty line (McLanahan and Booth 1989, 558). Half of our poor children are in single-parent families (Ellwood 1988).

Although female-headed households constitute only about 10 percent of all households, they account for nearly one third of the poverty population (Handler 1994, 17). The majority of female-headed families (53 percent) are poor (Rawlings 1994; Handler 1994). Among Black single-parent families, nearly 60 percent are below the poverty line (National Research Council 1991). The differential in the poverty rates of white versus Black single mothers is attributed to the fact that white mothers are more likely to be employed, and when employed, better paid. But even at best, most female-headed families are low-income families, even if they are not below the poverty line; the average income of working single parents is less than half that of the average two-parent family and is lower still for nonworking single mothers, virtually all of whom are living below the poverty level (National Research Council 1990, 26). Median income in 1988 for unemployed mother-only families was $5,211; for employed mothers, it was approximately $15,000. The 1990 poverty line for a family of one adult and two children was $10,419; the average income of poor female-headed families in 1990 was roughly $4,500 (Burtless 1992).

If the economic circumstances of these families were assessed more realistically, the rate of poverty would be even worse. The federal poverty line is an inadequate reflection of real economic needs. Some economists have suggested that a basic needs budget (BNB), which takes into consideration expenditures for child care, transportation, and direct taxes, is a more accurate reflection of household needs (Renwick and Bergmann 1993). Based on this more comprehensive and sophisticated criterion, single parents who are working full-time year-round jobs (the single parents we would imagine to be doing well) have significantly higher-than-official poverty counts: the BNB rate is 23 percent, compared to the 9 percent official count.

The fixed costs of raising a family are expensive, and continue to rise as children remain dependent on their parents for longer periods of time in order to obtain the education and experience necessary to become self-sufficient. Housing is the largest expenditure for single-mother and married-couple families, ranging from 25 percent of income for married couples to 34 percent for never married mothers. The high cost of housing forces many single mothers to live in extended households. Food is the next largest expense for single-mother families (Lino 1994, 31). The cost of child care is another significant expense, and acts as a strong disincentive to doing wage work. An employed parent of two preschool-age children needs goods and services that cost 58 percent more than a parent who stays out of the labor force (Mednick 1987).

Despite these appalling statistics of poverty in single-parent families, more childhood poverty occurs within two-parent families (Duncan and Rodgers 1990, 53). Children are the fastest growing segment of the population in poverty. Nearly a quarter of all U.S. children are living below the poverty line, an increase of nearly one million since 1990 (Handler 1994). A significant proportion of two-parent families, including the working poor, are below the poverty line. Poverty for children has increased dramatically in *both* two- and one-parent families.

Furthermore, the economic plight of African American children confirms that a two-parent family structure does not preclude poverty. Black children on average are poorer than white children, whether in single- or two-parent families. The racial differential cannot be explained by family structure (Handler 1994).[2]

In order to make it economically, according to one 1990 study, a single parent working full time with preschool children and health benefits needed an hourly wage of about $8.70 (Duncan and Rodgers 1990). That is an unattainable goal for many wage workers. Almost one-third of all jobs do not pay wages sufficient to support a family above the poverty line (Mead 1988, 62). The problem facing single parents is inadequate income, not lack of or refusal to work. It is not bad choice-making, but rather a lack of viable choices.

The difficulty of supporting a family on one income is exacerbated for single mothers due to gender and race discrimination in the wage labor market. Like most women, single mothers most frequently work in service and blue-collar jobs. The low earning capacity of women's work, coupled with continuing job segregation, are fundamental sources of the problem. In 1990, median weekly earnings for women were $381, and for women maintaining families, $370 per week; for men, the corresponding figures were $505 for all men, and $451 for men maintaining families (Bureau of the Census 1993, 19). White women are more likely to obtain better-paying, more stable jobs than are women of color (Amott 1988, 99–102; Schultz 1990).

The impact of children on earning capacity also is strongly negative. Not only is the range of jobs compatible with child-rearing limited, but any absence from the workforce, whether a temporary full-time interruption, or a longer-term full- or part-time interruption, dramatically affects lifetime job opportunities and earnings (Dowd 1989a; Dowd 1990). In addition, many single mothers are younger women, because of the young average age of never-married mothers and the higher divorce rate among couples who marry young. Young single mothers are less likely to have a good education (many have not completed high school) or job experience, which relegates them to low paying jobs within the range of jobs available to women in general.

Single-parent poverty persists, then, despite strong labor force attachment. Nearly 80 percent of single mothers are in the paid workforce (Rawlings 1994). Approximately 16 percent of the female workforce is divorced, separated, or widowed. Up to a third of all employees may be single parents at some point in their work life (Burden 1986). In spite of this strong workforce commitment, single mothers are unable to translate employment into economic self-sufficiency (Mednick 1987, 187). The gender factor is evident when incomes are compared between mothers and fathers who have sole or primary custody: 57 percent of mother-only homes survive on incomes below $15,000, while only 30 percent of father-only homes do. Nearly 46 percent of father-only homes have an income between $15,000 and $40,000; only 39 percent of mother-only homes do (Bureau of Census 1994).

In addition, many single parents work only part-time or not at all due to insufficient child care and the failure of employers to provide health insurance benefits. Of the total number of employed mothers with children under age thirteen, approximately 70 percent work full time; 80 percent of single mothers with children in that age group work full-time, a higher proportion than married women (McLanahan and Booth 1989, 559; Chamallas 1986; National Research Council 1990, 21). The cost of child care is prohibitive for many single parents and a significant barrier to employment, particularly if it is partially offset only by a low-wage job. "The lack of child care clearly keeps some women from working at all and inhibits their ability to pursue education or job training. Poorly educated women with little work experience earn low wages, and unless they can find subsidized, affordable, or free child care, employment may not make economic sense to them" (National Research Council 1990, 34–35; Dowd 1993). For single mothers who qualify for Medicaid, the unavailability of health insurance, or the failure to insure dependents, is another critical deterrent to employment, since they will eventually lose Medicaid if they take a job. Health insurance is less likely to be available in low-wage jobs; half of workers with family incomes below the poverty level are uninsured (Pettit 1993).

Employment income could, of course, be supplemented with contributions from the other parent (not in all cases, but in many) and/ or public support administered by the state. The inadequacy of private and public income transfers, however, compound labor market problems. Private income transfers, redistributing income from one parent to another, consist primarily of child support, as alimony is rarely awarded. Child support plays a relatively minor role in the income structure of single-parent families. Nearly two-thirds of parents with custody receive no child support (Bergmann 1986, 245). Only six of ten eligible mothers have an award (Garfinkel et al. 1994, 85–86), and of those who do, a significant proportion receive no payments or less than full payment, despite conservative estimates that at least 60 percent of absent parents could afford to pay (Roberts 1991, 868). Even if full payment were made, however, the bulk of single-parent family poverty would remain untouched. As Irwin Garfinkel, the noted welfare expert, has concluded, "even if the maximum could be achieved, it would leave unsolved three-quarters of the poverty and dependency problem. Supplementing private support with an assured public, child-support benefit would solve only about half the problem. To come close to eliminating poverty and dependence requires going beyond child support alone" (Garfinkel and Wong 1990, 101).

Even to the extent that child support could assist single-parent families, however, the legal structure does not guarantee either an automatic right to such support (it must be legally sought, individually monitored, and collected), nor does the state guarantee, replace, or supplement any portion or the total of support unless the individual qualifies for welfare. Under the 1988 Family Support Act, states must provide for child support collection through immediate wage withholding *unless both parents agree to an alternative arrangement or a court finds good cause for not ordering it.* Allowing for private agreement to bypass mandatory wage withholding may prove to be only a new weapon in the divorce wars. Allowing court override may invite the abuse of judicial discretion so heavily criticized in divorce proceedings.

Public income transfers, redistributing tax revenues to those with economic needs, far outweigh private transfers as sources of single-parent income. Fifty-five percent of never-married mothers receive AFDC; 20 percent of divorced and separated mothers receive AFDC; and 65 percent of widows receive social security (Lino 1994, 31).

The highest proportion of single parents to receive public transfers are widows/widowers who receive Survivor's Insurance Benefits, the most generous benefits paid to single parents. White widows receive the largest share of benefits. Ninety percent of white widows, but only 70 percent of Black widows, receive Survivor's Insurance (Garfinkel and McLanahan 1986, 26). The spouse of a fully insured worker caring for an eligible child under the age of sixteen may collect benefits set at 75 percent of the amount the worker would have received had he retired. When the youngest child turns sixteen, the widow/widower's benefits are terminated, although the child will continue to collect benefits until eighteen or nineteen years of age. At age sixty, the widow/widower again has access to Social Security; the benefit is 100 percent of the amount which would have been paid had the deceased worker lived to the age of retirement. The amount of the benefit is based on the amount an employee earns through employment, so those who earn the most get the most, up to the benefit cap (O'Connell 1993, 1481, 1491).

Death benefits to children are substantially higher than AFDC benefits; on average, the death benefit is double the AFDC benefit.[3] Not surprisingly, the poverty rate among widows is approximately half that of single mothers on welfare. In 1994, the before-tax income of widows averaged $22,790; divorced or separated women $18,580; and never-married mothers $9,820 (Lino 1994, 31). Only one in fifty single-parent families are led by a single mother over age thirty with a before-tax income of more than $30,000.

Welfare benefits nevertheless are far more pervasive in the income structure of single-parent families than are widows' benefits. Twenty-three percent of white and 34 percent of Black divorced women receive welfare, while 40 percent of white and 59 percent of Black never-married women receive welfare (Garfinkel and McLanahan 1986, 26). Divorced women head the majority of households on welfare, which is not surprising in view of the larger number of single-parent households created by divorce. Roughly half of all children in female-headed households receive AFDC (Garfinkel and Wong 1990, 107). Just over 10 percent of households on AFDC receive financial support from absent parents.

Single parents who turn to welfare often do not escape poverty, however. In a large majority of states, the state does not provide benefits sufficient to meet its own definition of need. In most states, the combination of AFDC, Medicaid, and food stamps provides a benefit that is only 70 percent of the federal poverty level (Committee on Ways and Means 1992). The difference between the level of welfare benefits and a minimal level of need cannot be met by wage work beyond a minimal amount without sacrificing welfare benefits; in many households the difference is made up by work off the books, which jeopardizes benefits and constitutes welfare fraud.

Finding work that generates sufficient income to leave welfare, however, is daunting. Single mothers with jobs receive fewer non-cash benefits like food stamps and Medicaid than single mothers without jobs (Renwick and Bergmann 1993). Every dollar earned is deducted from welfare (Ellwood 1988). A minimum-wage job is not sufficient to replace welfare benefits. In even the best of programs to assist welfare recipients to find permanent work, participants did not make much more than if they had stayed on welfare. In a Florida study, participants earned only $157 more annually than if they had stayed on welfare (Stanfield 1994). In addition they may lose Medicaid, a critical benefit too important to sacrifice. Because wage work is not additive, and benefits available on AFDC, especially health insurance, may not be available in the workplace, the incentive is to remain on AFDC rather than become self-supporting through market work. Furthermore, expenses associated with working, such as transportation costs, clothing costs, and lost time available for other responsibilities associated with child rearing can be monumental. Without resources to pay for the additional expenses or a support structure in place, an income equivalent to or not much higher than

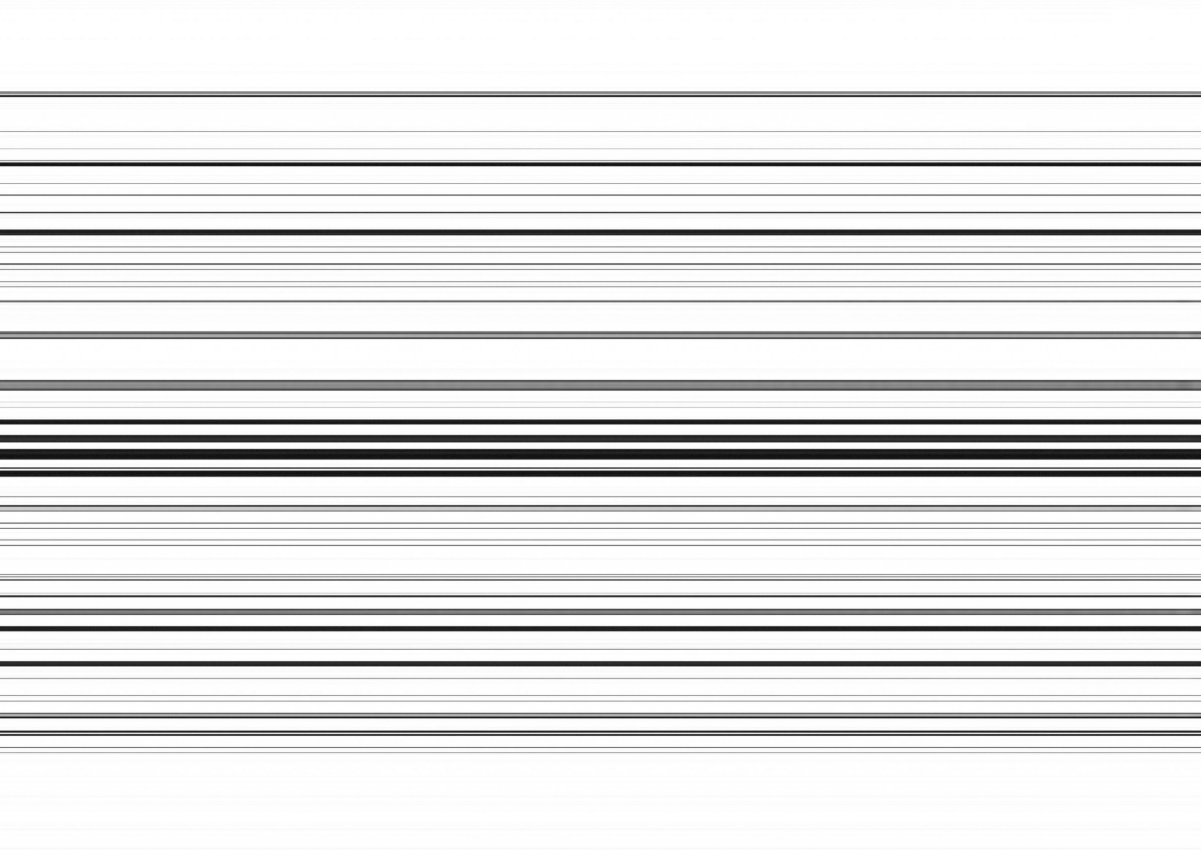

of these additional

ich seem designed to

nd on welfare, half of

ithin two years, and

dler 1994). However,

return, almost half

40 percent of single-

is fashion. However,

ned as dependent on

ilies who remain on

arket disadvantages

on, and lack of wage

long-term welfare is

ion, with little or no

children) under the

oyment earnings are

imarily in the form

collect, and inade-

em, are bedeviled by

oyment. The bulk of

nues to come from

59). Over time, the

ployment increases,

or welfare) decline,

changing economic

nt families are pre-

al effects on children

ng consequences for

ational class, health,

s the strongest pre-

rty begets a lack of

entrenches poverty

cz 1992). The corre-

behavioral conse-

scent problems, poor

ns, substance abuse,

delinquency, crime, early sex,
mance are all associated with po
puts it, "poverty is the number
Murder by malfeasance" (Funi
that children of poverty perceive
in problem behavior, including
al. 1984, 214).

A recent compilation of studi
McLanahan and Gary Sandefur
outcomes suffered by children in
associated with poverty. They e
fered by children in single-pare
from two-parent families is tied
equate parental guidance and at
nity resources," what in combi
responsible for most of the re
turns out to be a strong factor i
disruption is strongly tied to
income or a drop in income. Su
is also income-connected, in te
to afford quality paid caregivers
fur connect social capital defici
holds, the social deficits are stro
not surprisingly, while they ma
between fathers' absences and
argue family structure is the
living with just one parent incr
tive outcomes, it is not the only
han and Sandefur 1994, 2).

For parents, poverty affects
pacts upon the parent-child rela
correlates with greater parenta
sonal conflict, and more harsh a
1994). "Unemployment is ofte
pensity toward mental illness,
1985, 12). Poor parents are str
a constant succession of exter
retaining adequate housing, e
parents often take out their

delinquency, crime, early sex, pregnancy, and poor school performance are all associated with poverty. As one commentator bluntly
puts it, "poverty is the number one killer of children in the U.S.A.
Murder by malfeasance" (Funiciello 1990). There also is evidence
that children of poverty perceive their parents negatively and engage
in problem behavior, including delinquency (Siegal 1985; Adams et
al. 1984, 214).

A recent compilation of studies on single-parent families by Sara
McLanahan and Gary Sandefur (1994) concludes that the negative
outcomes suffered by children in single-parent families are strongly
associated with poverty. They estimate half of the disadvantage suffered by children in single-parent families as compared to children
from two-parent families is tied to low income. They identify "inadequate parental guidance and attention" and "lack of ties to community resources," what in combination they call "social capital," as
responsible for most of the remaining disadvantage. Yet income
turns out to be a strong factor in social capital as well. Community
disruption is strongly tied to residential moves triggered by low
income or a drop in income. Supervision and attention from parents
is also income-connected, in terms of parental stress and the ability
to afford quality paid caregivers. Thus, while McLanahan and Sandefur connect social capital deficits to fathers' absences from households, the social deficits are strongly economically determined. Thus,
not surprisingly, while they make a strong case for the *correlation*
between fathers' absences and children's disadvantages, they do not
argue family structure is the *cause* of the disadvantages. "While
living with just one parent increases the risk of each of these negative outcomes, it is not the only, or major, cause of them" (McLanahan and Sandefur 1994, 2).

For parents, poverty affects psychological well-being, which impacts upon the parent-child relationship in a variety of ways. Poverty
correlates with greater parental anxiety, emotional stress, interpersonal conflict, and more harsh and inconsistent punishment (Handler
1994). "Unemployment is often accompanied by a significant pro-
pensity toward mental illness, depression, and even suicide" (Siegal
1985, 12). Poor parents are stressed parents. Poverty translates into
a constant succession of external stresses, including managing and
retaining adequate housing, employment, and child care. Stressed
parents often take out their stress on their children (10). These

welfare benefits is no gain, precisely because of these additional expenses and taxes associated with wage work.

Despite flaws in the welfare structure which seem designed to maintain single-parent households in poverty and on welfare, half of the single-parent households on welfare leave within two years, and over 60 percent leave within three years (Handler 1994). However, three-quarters of those who leave eventually return, almost half within one year (DeParle 1994). Approximately 40 percent of single-parent families cycle on and off welfare in this fashion. However, only 18 percent are long-term recipients, defined as dependent on AFDC for five years or more. Single-parent families who remain on welfare over a longer period reflect the labor market disadvantages of immaturity, young children, lack of education, and lack of wage work experience. The most likely candidate for long-term welfare is a teenage mother, without a high school education, with little or no work experience, and with a young child (or children) under the age(s) of three (DeParle 1994).

In sum, income transfers to supplement employment earnings are wholly inadequate. Private income transfers, primarily in the form of child support, remain uncertain, difficult to collect, and inadequate. Public transfers, through the welfare system, are bedeviled by policy contradictions that seem to penalize employment. The bulk of family income in single-parent families continues to come from employment (McLanahan and Booth 1989, 559). Over time, the importance of income from (inadequate) paid employment increases, as alternative sources of income (child support or welfare) decline, due to lack of payment or lack of adjustment to changing economic conditions.[4]

The consequences of poverty for single-parent families are predictable. Poverty has well-established detrimental effects on children and parents. It has negative and often life-long consequences for children's future employment, education, occupational class, health, and self-satisfaction/self-esteem. Low income is the strongest predictor that a child will drop out of school. Poverty begets a lack of education, which, in Catch 22 fashion, further entrenches poverty from generation to generation (Li and Wojtkiewicz 1992). The correlation is high between poverty and negative behavioral consequences: early school failure, violence and adolescent problems, poor physical and mental health, brain dysfunctions, substance abuse, come structure of single-parent families than are widows' benefits. Twenty-three percent of white and 34 percent of Black divorced women receive welfare, while 40 percent of white and 59 percent of Black never-married women receive welfare (Garfinkel and McLanahan 1986, 26). Divorced women head the majority of households on welfare, which is not surprising in view of the larger number of single-parent households created by divorce. Roughly half of all children in female-headed households receive AFDC (Garfinkel and Wong 1990, 107). Just over 10 percent of households on AFDC receive financial support from absent parents.

Single parents who turn to welfare often do not escape poverty, however. In a large majority of states, the state does not provide benefits sufficient to meet its own definition of need. In most states, the combination of AFDC, Medicaid, and food stamps provides a benefit that is only 70 percent of the federal poverty level (Committee on Ways and Means 1992). The difference between the level of welfare benefits and a minimal level of need cannot be met by wage work beyond a minimal amount without sacrificing welfare benefits; in many households the difference is made up by work off the books, which jeopardizes benefits and constitutes welfare fraud.

Finding work that generates sufficient income to leave welfare, however, is daunting. Single mothers with jobs receive fewer non-cash benefits like food stamps and Medicaid than single mothers without jobs (Renwick and Bergmann 1993). Every dollar earned is deducted from welfare (Ellwood 1988). A minimum-wage job is not sufficient to replace welfare benefits. In even the best of programs to assist welfare recipients to find permanent work, participants did not make much more than if they had stayed on welfare. In a Florida study, participants earned only $157 more annually than if they had stayed on welfare (Stanfield 1994). In addition they may lose Medicaid, a critical benefit too important to sacrifice. Because wage work is not additive, and benefits available on AFDC, especially health insurance, may not be available in the workplace, the incentive is to remain on AFDC rather than become self-supporting through market work. Furthermore, expenses associated with working, such as transportation costs, clothing costs, and lost time available for other responsibilities associated with child rearing can be monumental. Without resources to pay for the additional expenses or a support structure in place, an income equivalent to or not much higher than

ual qualifies for welfare. Under the 1988 Family Support Act, states must provide for child support collection through immediate wage withholding *unless both parents agree to an alternative arrangement or a court finds good cause for not ordering it.* Allowing for private agreement to bypass mandatory wage withholding may prove to be only a new weapon in the divorce wars. Allowing court override may invite the abuse of judicial discretion so heavily criticized in divorce proceedings.

Public income transfers, redistributing tax revenues to those with economic needs, far outweigh private transfers as sources of single-parent income. Fifty-five percent of never-married mothers receive AFDC; 20 percent of divorced and separated mothers receive AFDC; and 65 percent of widows receive social security (Lino 1994, 31).

The highest proportion of single parents to receive public transfers are widows/widowers who receive Survivor's Insurance Benefits, the most generous benefits paid to single parents. White widows receive the largest share of benefits. Ninety percent of white widows, but only 70 percent of Black widows, receive Survivor's Insurance (Garfinkel and McLanahan 1986, 26). The spouse of a fully insured worker caring for an eligible child under the age of sixteen may collect benefits set at 75 percent of the amount the worker would have received had he retired. When the youngest child turns sixteen, the widow/widower's benefits are terminated, although the child will continue to collect benefits until eighteen or nineteen years of age. At age sixty, the widow/widower again has access to Social Security; the benefit is 100 percent of the amount which would have been paid had the deceased worker lived to the age of retirement. The amount of the benefit is based on the amount an employee earns through employment, so those who earn the most get the most, up to the benefit cap (O'Connell 1993, 1481, 1491).

Death benefits to children are substantially higher than AFDC benefits; on average, the death benefit is double the AFDC benefit.[3] Not surprisingly, the poverty rate among widows is approximately half that of single mothers on welfare. In 1994, the before-tax income of widows averaged $22,790; divorced or separated women $18,580; and never-married mothers $9,820 (Lino 1994, 31). Only one in fifty single-parent families are led by a single mother over age thirty with a before-tax income of more than $30,000.

Welfare benefits nevertheless are far more pervasive in the in-negative parenting consequences are also more often directed at younger children.

Studies indicate that impoverished men suffer worse mental health problems than women, because poverty means that they have failed to fulfill the stereotypical male role of economic provider (Siegal 1985, 9; Gilbert and Rachlin 1987, 15; Rodman and Safilios-Rothschild 1984, 63). Similarly, studies also indicate that boys are strongly affected by a father's inability to be a good breadwinner.[5]

Single-parent families face an array of real and significant economic problems. But the poverty of single-parent families is not a given; it is made. Family form is a cause of poverty only if we are willing to say that poverty is "chosen" when family form deviates from the standard of a two-parent heterosexual family. In practice, gender discrimination in the wage labor market, as well as insufficient and inefficient private and public support mechanisms disadvantage single mothers. The rate of labor force participation for single parents is high, but discriminatory wage rates, continuing sex segregation in jobs, and structural constraints against combining work and family prevalent in much of the wage labor market strongly disadvantage single-parent families. They are further disadvantaged by an unwillingness to mandate child support or provide meaningful family support outside patriarchal structures. The stigma perspective views irresponsible choice making as the source of poverty and its related social ills. This perspective conceals economic inequalities and deep structural problems for all families in the economy.

THE DEVELOPMENTAL JUSTIFICATION

Myth: Children Need a Father

Just as widespread as the myth that single parents cause poverty is the myth that single parents are by definition deviant, inadequate parents, unable to provide necessary parenting for the healthy development of their children. Every child needs two parents. Because women predominate as single-parent caretakers, this is often articulated in gender-specific terms: "every child needs a father." The developmental justification emphasizes the key role of two heterosexual parents in healthy child development. Researchers link father absence to poor academic performance, inappropriate sex-role behavior, juvenile delinquency, and mental illness.

The assumption that fathers are essential to healthy child development has had strong academic appeal. In the 1960s, social scientists published a wave of "father-absence" studies emphasizing the father's role and the detriment to sex-role development, academic performance, and moral development due to fathers' absences in single-parent families. Premised on the theories of sociologist Talcott Parsons, who believed that mothers and fathers played clear, distinct roles in the family, these studies viewed fathers as "instrumental," responsible for developing the family's relationships with the external world, in stark contrast to mothers' internal, "expressive" roles.

Critics of Parsons have pointed out that fathers can hardly be deemed critical when traditional fathers typically were formally present but functionally absent in many families. In addition, children in stepfather families do not do much better emotionally and developmentally than those raised in single-mother families (Bronstein et al. 1993, 268–76). The confounding troubles of stepfamilies directly contradict the two-is-better-than-one notion, or the belief that a father-in-the-house is essential to healthy development. Indeed, McLanahan and Sandefur's comparison of single-parent and two-parent families classified stepfamilies (and their negative outcomes) with single-parent families, implicitly acknowledging that a heterosexual married pair is not the key to successful child outcomes (McLanahan and Sandefur 1994). While some might argue that the lack of a direct genetic connection explains unsuccessful fathering (Blankenhorn 1995), I suspect that the difficulties of stepparenthood reflect the difficult and sensitive emotional interweavings of multiple parenthood as well as the balancing of partner and child ties in blended families.

Parsons's theories also ignored the impact of other factors, especially class and income, which might have equal or greater bearing on child development. But perhaps most significantly, Parsons' view of appropriate gender roles is contradicted by what we know about parenting. Good parenting is not sex-specific nor sex-related. Although the attributes of good parenting are more strongly associated with traditional and modern views of mothering, this connection is cultural, not biological. When men have been primary parents, by choice or by circumstances, they have parented as well as women, and similarly to women. As we move toward a more androgynous model of parenting, the notion that men *as men* are essential to healthy child development is unsupported. It is particularly absurd to claim that fathers are essential for parenting, apart from their income, when most parenting in two-parent families continues to be done by mothers.

Nevertheless, the claim that fathers are essential remains powerful. The empirical evidence supports correlation but not causation between father absence and children's difficulties or lack of success, and much of that, as I have already argued, connects economics, not the absence of a developmentally required father. Alternatively, proponents of the essential nature of fathers are forced to make increasingly tenuous arguments in the face of the accumulated evidence of how men father and how children develop. For example, David Blankenhorn (1995), one of the strongest advocates for the essential role of fathers, argues that fathers are the linchpin of families and therefore of society. Denying fathers their critical, unique roles, then, is tantamount to social suicide. Blankenhorn argues less, however, that fathers have something unique to offer *children*, than he argues that fatherhood is essential to a positive social role for *men*. Although he asserts that perhaps the most important thing that fathers contribute to their children is "paternal cultural transmission," which he describes as a father's "distinctive capacity to contribute to the identity, character, and competence of his children," he does little to support this bald assertion (25). Rather, Blankenhorn does much to argue the importance of a unique role for men, or a belief in their own uniqueness, so that men will be responsible for their children.

In Blankenhorn's own words,

> Fatherhood is a social role that obligates men to their biological offspring. For two reasons, it is society's most important role for men. First, fatherhood, more than any other male activity, helps men to become good men: more likely to obey the law, to be good citizens, and to think about the needs of others. Put more abstractly, fatherhood bends maleness—in particular, male aggression—toward prosocial purposes. Second, fatherhood privileges children. In this respect, fatherhood is a social invention designed to supplement maternal investment in children with paternal investment in children. . . .
>
> For society, the primary results of fatherhood are right-doing

males and better outcomes for children. Conversely, the primary consequences of fatherlessness are rising male violence and declining
child well-being. . . .

As a social role, the deepest purpose of fatherhood is to socialize
men by obligating them to their children . . . . The fatherhood story
is the irreplaceable basis of a culture's most urgent imperative: the socialization of males. More than any other cultural invention, fatherhood guides men away from violence by fastening their behavior to a
fundamental social purpose. (Blankenhorn 1995, 25, 26, and 65)

It is essential to Blankenhorn's position to accept his view that
men are violent, self-centered, individualistic, and materialistic. Further, one must see fatherhood as necessarily highly gendered to
convince men that they possess unique abilities as fathers which
children need for successful development and to combat men's negative predispositions. Androgenous parenting means no essential,
unique role, and therefore the inability to persuade men that there
is a value to "right-doing," as well as the danger, according to
Blankenhorn, that society will write off fathers as useless and unnecessary. Not surprisingly, then, Blankenhorn not only decries patterns
of paternal abandonment, he also attacks paternal involvement
premised on the proposition that parenting is not gender defined. He
criticizes and demolishes "the New Father," the sensitive, caring,
involved father, because the New Father looks too much like a father
who has learned to mother. Blankenhorn argues that the children's
needs can only be met by mothers and fathers adopting gender-
specific roles. Furthermore, he argues, the notion of androgenous
parenting is nothing more than a selfish desire grounded in individualistic narcissism.

It is a denial of sexual complementarity and ultimately a denial of
generativity—particularly male generativity, which is, much more
than the female's, largely a social construction. Especially for men,
this particular promise of happiness is a cruel hoax. Like all forms of
narcissism, its final product is not fulfillment but emptiness. If fatherhood has anything to say to men, it is that human completion is not
a solo act. (Blankenhorn 1995, 123)

Blankenhorn's qualities of good fathering (the Good Family Man)
sound like the stereotype of the traditional father, only slightly
revised to accommodate companionate marriage and the nurturing
qualities of the New Father model. His claim that the essential
preconditions for fatherhood are "co-residency with children and a

parental alliance with the mother" is little more than a restatement of Parsons' discredited views (Blankenhorn 1995, 18).

Blankenhorn's acknowledgment of the primary role of mothers and the importance of the pairing bond of the couple to successful fathering nevertheless suggests the actual role of many fathers. Many fathers offer significant nurturing support to *mothers* as opposed to directly parenting children. Rather than unique, essential parents to their children, fathers are critical supports for mothers, who are the primary or sole caregivers. This pattern is a learned cultural role, not unique to fathers. Rather, it represents caregivers' need for support, the consequence of the essential care the caregivers give to children and the difficulty of providing that care.

This interconnected circle of caregiving is at the core of attachment theory. According to this theory, parental nurturing is critical to children at the early stages of life in order to provide a base from which a child may securely explore new challenges and skills. This base is seen as essential to healthy adulthood. Although most attachment theory research on infants and toddlers has focused on the *mother*-child bond, it is widely recognized that infants can bond as well to their fathers (or other adults), and that the infants can attach to multiple caregivers as well as to a single caregiver. Despite this potential for multiple, coequal attachment, the primary attachment theorist, John Bowlby, sees the role of the second parent not as a second caregiver to the child, but as a support structure for the primary caregiver. "If the job (of attachment) is to be well done and the child's principal caregiver is not to be too exhausted, the caregiver herself (or himself) needs a great deal of assistance. From whom that help comes will vary: very often it is the other parent; in many societies, including more often than is realized [in] our own, it comes from a grandmother" (Bowlby 1988, 2–3).

The strongest claim for a unique role for fathers, then, is that when fathers strongly support the mother in a full-time parenting role, their presence has significant, although indirect, benefits for children (Sigel et al. 1984, 55–56; Belsky 1990, 887). Two parents are better than one not because they are opposite sexes, but because one, ideally, provides economic and emotional support to the one who is parenting. According to this parenting model, a single or primary caregiver is dependent upon the economic and social support of a sole or primary wage earner. The primary caregiver must herself be cared for. This is the role of the second parent. One commentator calls this *doulia* from the concept of a *doula* (Kittay 1995).[6] A *doula* is one who renders service or care to another who cares for a dependent; *doulia* is the practice of cooperative, interrelational, interdependent care (Kittay 1995).

Two parents do not parent differently simply in style but also in form and function. Their parenting is qualitatively so different as to be almost entirely dissimilar other than in their parallel genetic or adoptive ties. One functions as a backup to the other, as a caregiver to the caregiver, not as an independent, coequal, and different parent. There is nothing in this model to prevent interchange of roles, or a multiplication of who performs the roles, nor is there anything that requires a marital couple as the sole basis for *doulia*.

The direct impact of fathers on their children, then, is "essentially redundant" (Crockett et al. 1993, 355). The support role does not require sexual intimacy nor heterosexuality as a precondition for its performance. As Bowlby points out, frequently grandmothers or other female kin or friends perform the support role. In addition, paid caregivers can perform the support role. Of course, it does not have to be so. The roles could be shared and changed, or entirely reconceived, and are not by their terms gendered.

While fathers can make a difference by supporting mothers or by playing the role of the primary or secondary caregiver to the child, this does not support the premise that fathering is inherently unique or that two parents are essential for adequate caregiving. The denial of an *inherent* essential or unique role for fathers should not be confused, however, with recognizing the *culturally* distinct roles of mothering and fathering. Mothering and fathering are differently conceived and lived. Those differences do not, however, translate into developmental requirements for children. To the contrary, traditional constructions of fathering at most align themselves with the *doulia* model, and at worst make fathers developmentally irrelevant by limiting fathers to an economic parenting role. Although both mothering and fathering are in flux, it is fathering that remains without a model to replace the traditional economic father.

Mothering is viewed as a unique, natural, caregiving relationship, biologically based but also somewhat mystical. Characteristics historically associated with positive mothering include sensitivity, warmth, love, acceptance, encouragement of exploration and expres-

sion, respect, encouragement of independence, and the use of reasoning and inductive reasoning in discipline (Crockett et al. 1993, 7).
These characteristics of mothering are associated with the role of
primary or sole nurturer.

This traditional picture of mothering persists, although mothers'
work-family role has undergone radical transformation. Across class
lines and including mothers of very young children, mothers engage
in both wage and nonwage work. This sharp reorientation of wom-
en's work roles has not been matched by an equivalent shift in
their family roles. Very little redistribution of household work and
childcare to men has occurred, creating a "second shift" of unwaged
work for women.

Concerns about work-family conflicts have focused not so much
on necessary changes in the workplace or family roles, but rather on
whether women can be good mothers if they are good wage workers.
Despite a concerted effort to link women's increasing employment
to negative child development effects, evidence indicates no such
link. Much current research points to the positive developmental
effects of good-quality childcare. Furthermore, children are influenced by external perceptions of their parents, and mothers are
perceived more positively, as more powerful and competent, when
they work outside the home (Cashion 1982, 78). This does not mean
that conflicts between work and family are not serious and do not
need to be addressed, but rather that work and family are not
incompatible, and more particularly that wage work and good mothering are not incompatible.

Because so much parenting is done by women, children do not
have significantly less contact with single-parent mothers who do
wage work than with other mothers who work (Sanik and Mauldin
1986, 56).[7] Socioeconomic factors have a strong impact on parenting
in single-mother households, far stronger than the absence of a
partner or the presence of a father surrogate (Bronstein et al. 1993,
274). Perhaps the strongest evidence of the quality of care given by
single mothers is the high proportion of gifted children in single-
mother households (Cashion 1982, 82; Adams et al. 1984, 139–40).

Despite the evidence that women's work and greater economic
independence is good for children as well as for their mothers, and
that single mothers are more like married mothers than not, mothers
continue to be held responsible for their children in a way that

fathers are not, and single mothers are blamed far more strongly than married mothers. One survey of major clinical psychological journals found that mothers were "blamed" for seventy-two kinds of psychopathology in their children, in sharp contrast to fathers, who are least likely to be seen as responsible for personality and behavior problems ("Feminist Psychology" 1992, 35).

Mothers also suffer the psychological burdens of parenting, burdens which are often hidden beneath romantic notions of children and mothering.[8] It is remarkable that the role strain pattern is so similar for both single-parent and partnered women. Single mothers nevertheless suffer additional stress, due to economic insufficiency, role strain, and social isolation. Single mothers are at high risk for depression, low self-esteem, a sense of incompetency, and helplessness. Never-married and lesbian mothers suffer additional social stressors and the legal risks of losing their children ("Feminist Psychology" 1992, 38).

While mothering in practice has remained largely constant despite radical change in the work-family context, fathering, on the other hand, continues to drift in a process of redefinition. Under Parsons's theories, fathers were agents of connection between families and the public sphere. Among psychoanalysts, theorists conceived of fathers as authority figures providing external rules and principles ("Feminist Psychology" 1992, 9; Adams et al. 1984, 19).[9] Alternatively, researchers measured fathers solely as economic providers.

Current views of fathering lack consensus on any new model. Commentators of all stripes recognize the issue although they disagree on proscriptions (Blankenhorn 1995). As parenting has moved toward an equality model, gender seems to be disappearing from the characteristics of good parenting. Yet the socialization and support for parenting remains primarily directed at women. Within married couples, parenting is commonly seen as the wife's domain. Husbands' secondary roles often extend to their parenting style. "Women invest more of their identity in parenting than do men. Men are usually much less involved than their wives in the daily care and supervision of the children, and they tend to see themselves as cast in a supporting role where their responsibility is to provide assistance to the primary parent, the mother" (Simons et al. 1990, 376). Both men and women are largely uneducated about parenting. They learn by doing. It is key to men's involved parenting that fathers do caregiving from the beginning, so that children do not see parenting as purely or dominantly a female responsibility and territory (Simons et al. 1990).

Studies also indicate women view parenting as a duty, whereas men view parenting as an option. Male socialization continues to emphasize qualities in conflict with good parenting, and parenting challenges men to adopt characteristics traditionally viewed as unmanly. Furthermore, the limitations of the workplace affect men's ability to change the parameters of their fathering. The combination of socialization and structural constraints on fathers' parenting role makes it seem "natural" that mothering and fathering are substantively different, gender specialized and differentiated, even while the ideology of equal parenting hides the inequality of parenting responsibility and care.

If there is no valid developmental claim of uniqueness, is there a valid claim that two-parent families create a healthier balance of power between parents and children? One legal commentator, Professor Ira Lupu, couches his support for the superiority of two-parent families in these terms: a two-parent system prevents the abuse of parental power. He analogizes this familial balance to constitutional separation of power as a check on governmental abuse of power (Lupu 1994). He states as a substantive premise that "children are best reared in regimes of adult equality, in which patriarchy and matriarchy are equally discouraged" (Lupu 1994, 1320).

The statement speaks volumes. It presumes that equality is possible and in fact exists in parenting. It assumes that in the absence of two parents there is an isolated single parent, that there can be no other family form that is equal to the presumed heterosexual two-parent family model of the presumption. It also assumes that patriarchy and matriarchy are simply differences in the gender of the head of the family, and that both patterns are hierarchical and reflect a similar power dynamic that is based on oppression of the less powerful.

Lupu sees the legitimate goal of the legal system as maximizing the number of caregivers of children, and sees two parents as the optimal number, regardless of gender or marital status. He presumes equality of the caregivers. He assumes that their function is to counter the inclination to foster self-referential behavior, and to monitor each other. This is to see the primary value of two parents not as multiplying and diversifying the care of the child, but as preventing abuses and controlling behavior. It makes the relationship between the caretakers preeminent over the child's relationships.

McLanahan and Sandefur similarly articulate the value of the two-parent family in terms of a system of checks and balances that insures parental responsibility and prevents abuse. "When two biological parents share the same household, they can monitor the children and maintain parental control. But just as important, the parents can also monitor one another and make sure the other parent is behaving in appropriate ways" (McLanahan and Sandefur 1994, 28).

One final developmental argument concerning the necessity of fathers is that two parents are necessary for healthy sex-role identification. The sex-role identification hypothesis is often connected to the Freudian assumption that a mother and father must be present for appropriate sex-typed identification and normal child development, with heterosexuality designated as "normal." Freudian and cognitive theories of child development hypothesize that children learn through modeling, particularly by identifying with the same sex-parent.

Recent research has undercut these theories by concluding that two heterosexual parents are not necessary for healthy cognitive, emotional, or sex-role development (Belchman 1982; Carlson 1987). As one researcher put it, "high quality mothering can compensate for loss of the father in the single-parent homes, whereas low-quality fathering can negatively influence children's development in intact homes" (Carlson 1987, 565). Children can learn sex-typed behavior, assuming that is desirable, from either the same-sex or an opposite-sex parent. Studies have found some fathers to be more concerned with sex-typed behavior. Hence, girls may learn feminine behavior from their fathers, based on their fathers' expectations, rather than modeling themselves after their mothers (78). Likewise, there is both theoretical and empirical support for the proposition that it is unnecessary for a father to be present for a boy to learn to be "masculine" (80). It is also important not to overemphasize the role of the family, or to view sex-role development as a one-time, fixed process; rather, it is a lifelong process affected by many variables (Ferree 1990, 868–70; Schultz 1990, 1816–17).

Sex typing is the means by which females and males develop

feminine and masculine behaviors, expectations, and life goals. As part of their development, individuals learn the expectations for their gender group. Sex-role stereotypes about desirable behaviors and personality have serious implications for women's and men's well-being ("Feminist Psychology" 1992, 42). Well-being is measured differently by mental health professionals for men and women; identification of sex-role functioning is therefore viewed as critical to individual self-perception.

The implications of sex typing for self-identity and self-esteem, within a context of highly unequal valuing of each sex, is an area that psychologists are continuing to explore. Some have suggested that a combination of masculine and feminine characteristics is most psychologically healthy, an androgyny model. Sex stereotyping research indicates, however, that adopting characteristics of the opposite sex may not be well received; violations of sex role standards are judged harshly (44). Other psychologists suggest a transcendent model is healthiest, whereby men and women will naturally learn (limited) gender roles, but will transcend them. A gender-free approach, on the other hand, would encourage children to reject gender stereotypes, rather than consider the adoption of stereotyped behavior as a normal "phase." Finally, under an empowerment model, individuals are presumed to be functioning in a patriarchal and sexist environment. The focus is personal power *within that environment.* The strategies include developing in girls the ability to avoid as women psychological disorders such as depression which are closely connected to aspects of traditional role modeling (47–50).

The family is a core institution that socializes children in sex typing.[10] It is through their families that children learn gender rules and roles. Traditional Western notions of family contain a "hidden curriculum," that implicitly and explicitly "informs women about who they are, what they may become, and how they should view themselves" (Snyder 1992, 60). In two-parent families the allocation of gender roles is extremely significant (60). Families teach by modeling, by what they *do,* by their reactions to what their children do, that reinforces gendered behavior (positive attention for sex-typed toys, reprimand for cross-sex play); by explicit instruction in gender roles and skills (who learns to cook, who learns sports); and the structure within which gender skills are tried, that is, dressing and dating (61–63).

The context of fathering, typified by unequal caretaking and economic dominance, suggests that a primary, albeit implicit, role for
fathers as parents is teaching gender roles that support patriarchy.
We have not established an alternative model of true shared parenting or how such parenting would function in the family and the
workplace. Nor have we clarified whether to accept or reject the
concept of gender roles. Families function in a context of gender
inequality that is both internal and external, affecting family dynamics in both obvious and subtle ways. Child development authorities and others presume the home is critical to the process of gender
role socialization, the locus for acquiring gender role, or at the very
least a strong influence on concepts of gender. Defenders of the
status quo may fear single-parent families because patriarchal patterns will not be taught. In the age of equality such reasoning is
both archaic and riddled with unjustified gender stereotypes unless
it is possible to rid it of its patriarchal presumptions.

What, then, is the role of fathers? The developmental perspective
suggests that they are important, but not essential, that their role is
not unique, but additive. Are fathers unnecessary? If fathers are
inessential and/or replaceable, fathers and husbands may fear that if
women are not kept dependent, they will not form relationships
with men or share children with men because they will no longer
be needed. However absurd this fear might be, fear of women's
independence with respect to reproduction and childbearing may
lie behind stigmatizing single-parent families. What may be most
troubling to many about single-parent families is that single mothers
establish support structures, as well as engage in relationships with
men, but control whether to establish a *legal* bond with a man or to
share parenting.

The fears generated about fathers can lead to Blankenhorn's asser-
tions of the threat to society as we know it. There is no doubt
fatherhood is in crisis. Blankenhorn is right that we should not write
fathers off. But the solution, from a developmental perspective, is
not to proclaim fathers' uniqueness. Rather, it is to acknowledge that
it is masculinity and intimacy that are challenged. For children need
continuity, commitment, and caring. How to culturally and socially
encourage that among men is the question. But it will not be accomplished by false assumptions of uniqueness.

While the developmental justification is unsubstantiated, the
mental health issues of single parents should not be ignored. Single

parents do suffer from depression and stress, but the source of the stress is, to a significant degree, tied to economic factors as well as related social issues of control and independence (Mednick 1987, 188; McLanahan and Booth 1989, 562).[11] Research indicates that poor women consider all options which allow them to retain control over their lives before turning to welfare (Mednick 1987, 189). Another source of anxiety for single mothers when they establish a family after a marriage or similar relationship with a man is managing the authority shift from fathers to mothers, and the impact of increased responsibilities and stress on familial well-being (187). Stress also has to be considered from a gender role perspective. "Autonomy, authority, and power are not congruent with traditional family roles for women, yet these characteristics have been cited as an important source of positive feelings for single mothers" (194). Social networks mediate some of the stress, but little research has been devoted to evaluating kin and other social and emotional support networks.

The developmental justification, therefore, is largely myth. There is no empirically based argument or developmental need for elevating the heterosexual, nuclear two-parent family, or denigrating the single-parent family. The consequences of poverty explain much of the negative behavior exhibited by children from single-parent families. As a proxy for poverty, father absence does provide a link to the problems faced by single-parent families, but it is *not the cause.* One cannot deny that single-parent families face psychological issues. Some of those issues are unique, some are no different from those of many two-parent families. The absence of a father as a father is not generally the cause. The developmental analysis exposes the fallacy of the presumed superiority and necessity of two parents, as well as the strong differences in expectations and roles of men and women as parents.

THE MORALITY JUSTIFICATION

Myth: Single Parents Are Sinful/Immoral

Stigmatizing single parents as immoral is less myth than belief. Unlike the other justifications for stigma, which purport to be based on "objective" harm, this justification is largely based purely on convictions. It cannot be challenged on the basis of actual realities, because the stigma is not attached to parenting or family function. Rather, it is stigma connected particularly to the sexual acts of adults which brought children into being. It is belief fundamentally grounded in religious doctrine that condemns sexuality and childbearing out of wedlock. It is also inextricably connected to preserving patriarchal privilege by protecting the designation of paternity as well as by preserving exclusive sexual access to married women.

The historic sanction for failure to adopt the patriarchal structure of marriage within which childbearing was permissible was quite powerful. Stigma was not limited to the adults who had committed the sinful acts; the moral opprobrium extended to children, labeled as bastards and scorned socially and legally. The illegitimate child at common law was labeled "the son of no one," without a legally recognized mother or father, without a surname (*Gubernat v. Deremer* 1995). Only in the nineteenth century did reformers partially remove this symbolic nonexistence by recognizing mother and child as a legal unit, so that the child would take the mother's surname. This made sense since the mother, but not the father, had an obligation to support the child (133).

Unwed mothers similarly were controlled by ostracizing them, as well as limiting their legal rights. Disreputable, immoral women included by definition those who violated the preferred norm of sexuality and children within marriage. Thus, unlike men, whose economic status determined their class, women derived their class from their sexuality and their relationship to men. Women who violated the preferred norm were seen as whores; those who conformed to it were madonnas. "Men take their place in the class hierarchy based on their occupations or on their father's social status. . . . For women, . . . class distinctions are based on their relationship—or absence of such—to a man who protects them, and on their sexual activities. The division of women into 'respectable women,' and 'disreputable women' has been the basic class division for women" (Lerner 1986).

The religious and social condemnation of "bad" women has been powerful. Biblical condemnation includes the Old Testament punishment of stoning a woman to death if she violated the code of sexuality and lost her virginity prior to marriage. The treatment of Hester Prynne in Nathaniel Hawthorne's novel of seventeenth-century New England, *The Scarlet Letter*, epitomizes the public humiliation and shaming of immoral women (Hawthorne 1850). Criminal laws surrounding pregnancy have reflected the religious judgment of single motherhood as sinful. This religious condemnation is also evident in the structure of divorce (prior to the advent of no-fault) which was designed to discourage and stigmatize divorce.

The strong moral condemnation of unwed motherhood lasted well into the 1960s. Some might argue that it has once again been revived with the recent advocacy of orphanages as a solution for the "failures" of mothers on welfare. Certainly one of the most powerful arguments for welfare reform was stemming the tide of teenage pregnancy and nonmarital parenthood.

Although society still condemns single parents for their perceived lack of morality, social norms surrounding parenthood have shifted dramatically in the recent past. Unwed motherhood is more acceptable, although mixed reactions persist. Unwed motherhood due to divorce has grown dramatically, fueled by a different view of marriage and intimate relationships that does not condemn the dissolution of what was intended as a lifelong relationship. At the same time, divorced mothers must exercise care to be "good" mothers, not sexually promiscuous mothers. Sue Miller's 1985 book, *The Good Mother*, critically explores this trend. In the book, the mother loses custody of her child when her ex-husband charges her and her lover with "sexual irregularities." In order to have even limited contact with her child, the mother's penance is that she leave her lover and renounce her sexuality.

Never-married mothers are subject to even more ambiguity of feeling. On the one hand, social consensus has shifted significantly. Unwed motherhood no longer translates into social isolation and ostracism, implemented by such means as suspension or expulsion of unwed mothers from school or the firing of teachers or other employees who are unwed mothers. Unwed mothers are not uncommon and their public presence is accepted. Today, most religious traditions, including some of the most traditional and patriarchal, support rather than ostracize single parents.

Courts have struck down policies excluding single parents from education and employment. Exclusionary policies have been successfully challenged using Fourteenth Amendment arguments based on procedural due process concerns about irrebuttable presumptions (dealing with immorality/unfitness); substantive due process arguments grounded in right to privacy cases (finding a right to bear a child and the right to decide not to marry from abortion and marriage cases); and substantive due process arguments based on respect for family integrity.

This shift in legal outcomes is somewhat contradicted by results in nonconstitutional litigation. In the absence of Fourteenth Amendment claims, justifications for firing single parents on the basis that their conduct is immoral and that they represent bad role models for students have been quite successful. Two particularly notable cases involved unwed African American women who were discharged from the YWCA and the Girls Club when they became pregnant, on the basis that they would be harmful role models for teenage girls (*Chambers v. Omaha Girls Club* 1987; *Harvey v. YWCA* 1982). The courts' acceptance of this moral justification, their refusal to evaluate closely the sex and race discrimination claims, and their capitulation to powerful negative stereotypes associated with single Black mothers figured prominently in these cases. It is difficult to imagine an employer refusing to hire a divorced single white parent on similar grounds or discharging an employee who divorced during the course of employment.

The sense of ambiguity created by greater acceptance but persistent stigma suggests a kind of secularization of the morality stigma. The rationale seems to have shifted from sinfulness to stupidity, from immorality to bad judgment, although the immorality factor has by no means disappeared. This is most evident with respect to teenage single mothers. Unwed parenthood is seen as a sign of immaturity and bad decision making rather than as a sign of unfitness.

We may be returning to moral condemnation of single parents. It is a complex moral question. Can we view single parenting simply as a matter of individual choice? Should we value particular family forms that seem to work better for children at the current time? The strongest moral claim, however, should be the care of children and strong support for their caregivers. As long as we structurally and functionally support a sole or primary caregiver model of parenting, and inegalitarian work structures, morality dictates support for primary caregivers as the best means to support children.

We justify punitive measures as deterrents. But they do not deter.

Existing legal structures, built on the theory of deterrence, have been monumentally unsuccessful in stemming the growth of single-parent families (even assuming that is a justifiable goal). So we punish only children. That certainly makes no moral sense. While it makes sense to foster responsible parenting by, for example, discouraging teenage pregnancy through education, counseling about reproductive choice, and the provision of genuine economic and employment opportunities, it does not make sense to punish the children of single parents. The rejection, then, of punitive morally based policies is not an appeal to libertarianism but rather an argument that the welfare of children should be paramount. It leaves plenty of room to exercise our moral commitments by insuring responsibility and care for children.

Teenagers appear to epitomize all of the worst negatives of single parenting. They are socially, economically, and developmentally "at risk." All of these negative attributes seem to justify a policy of deterrence, even of stigmatization, based on the belief that parenting at this age is bad both for the parents and for the children.

The number of teenagers who chose to bear and raise their children as single mothers increased 350 percent between 1960 and 1979 (Schamess 1990, 155). At the same time, the percentage of children born to single parents and placed for adoption dropped dramatically. Today 97 percent of women who carry a nonmarital pregnancy to term choose to raise the child themselves (Dickson 1991). The most serious problem facing teenage single parents is their disadvantage in the economic structure; they enter the workplace early, with few skills, and little or no experience. They begin parenting in poverty and are likely to remain in poverty.

The dominant view of teenage single parents is that by definition they are bad parents (Dickson 1991). It is important, however, to question what it is about teenagers that makes us so uncomfortable. It is not at all clear whether teenagers have short- or long-term problems, whether their deficiencies, to the extent they actually exist, are temporary or permanent. With social support, teenage mothers could be educated and employed. The consequences of parenting at a young age need not be disastrous or final for teenagers or for their children.

Furthermore, the stigma has been attached most strongly to teenage mothers, without addressing the role and needs of fathers. Interestingly, a significant proportion of the fathers are not teenagers;

according to a recent study, more than half of the fathers of children born to women aged fifteen to seventeen are age twenty or older. One-fifth of the fathers are more than six years older than the mothers ("Teen Pregnancy Study" 1995).

A punitive, rather than a supportive approach, makes sense only from a moral perspective. What is stunning is that morality justifies punishment for children, in the form of lack of resources and social support, as a moral solution to single parenting. More clearly, it is a punishment meant to "solve" the spiraling rate of teenage pregnancy. The best expertise on teenage pregnancy, however, does not identify punitive policies toward single-parent families as an effective solution or deterrent. Rather, better educational and job opportunities, coupled with sex education and self-esteem, are more effective in dealing with the issues that lie at the heart of teen pregnancy. In the face of that knowledge, policies designed to stigmatize children, by permanently punishing and disadvantaging their parents, are morally reprehensible for the state and society.

What remains, then, is a justification for stigma based on religious beliefs. Without regard to those beliefs, their religious basis makes them an unsound foundation for public policy. The religious norms are strongly intertwined with patriarchal family structures, and therefore these views are suspect as discriminatory. Historical religious condemnation of single parents has been singularly reserved for unwed motherhood, representing a sexual and moral double standard for women and men. In addition, secular morality judgments are often unsupported and counterproductive. With respect to teenagers, focusing on moral condemnation distracts us from confronting the causes of teenage pregnancy. More generally, focusing moral judgments on parents ignores and punishes their children. Punitive rather than progressive social and legal policy means that children must often endure a lifetime of poverty for what we view as their parents' mistakes.

IMPLICIT JUSTIFICATIONS: RACE AND GENDER STORIES

The economic and developmental justifications claim neutral, objective reasons that justify punitive policies toward single parents, as a necessary means to deter formation of families that are bad for children and bad for society. The morality justification appeals to belief, to an ethical or moral standard, as a basis for stigma. In addition to the lack of substance to these justifications, however, they also serve to hide, by their purported neutrality and objectivity on the one hand, and the claim of moral high ground on the other, implicit understandings about race and gender that justify stigmatizing single parents. These implicit race and gender justifications are central to the ongoing stigma attached to single parents.

The race story is that single parenthood is predictable, a mark of self-defeating, self-generated inferiority. Many commentators use the racialization[12] of unwed single parenthood to allot the highest level of social contempt to Black single mothers. The gender story is that women cannot raise children alone, and therefore their attempts to do so must be discouraged. Many view the failure to get married or stay married as antipatriarchal rebellion which must be harshly repressed.

Racial mythology is frequently tied to notions of difference and otherness. With respect to families, it is often linked to different patterns of family formation and structure. The dominant pattern for creating single-parent families differs by race; the most stigmatized single-parent families, never-married parents, are more common among African Americans, while divorced single-parent families are more common among whites.[13] Black children are far more likely to spend a longer period of time in a single-parent family during their childhood, and Black parents are less likely to remarry following divorce (Fine and Schwebel 1988).

The predominance of single-parent families (most created by lack of marriage, not divorce) among African Americans has been viewed in a number of ways. First, some argue it reflects the most advantageous family form for obtaining economic resources. The structure of public and private economic options provides support for this view. Second, some argue that it might be viewed as the consequence of the disempowerment of Black men or the limited choices imposed by poverty. Finally, some conceive of it as pathological, cultural suicide, something innate in the race. It is this last view that has prevailed (Moynihan 1988, 5–6).

The intersection of race and gender generates powerful stereotypes about Black women and is read as a challenge to white and male standards. "[Y]oung, single, sexually active, fertile, and nurturing Black women are being viewed ominously because they have the temerity to attempt to break out of the rigid economic, social, and political categories that a racist, sexist, and class-stratified society would impose upon them" (Austin 1989, 555). The goal, therefore, is to control Black women's perceived sexuality and fecundity; this goal presumes the existence of a dangerous culture that reproduces dysfunctional, matriarchal, single-parent families. By linking single-parent families to teenage pregnancy, in particular, policy makers label Black single parents as deviant.

Alternatively, Black families are criticized as matriarchal. But as one researcher has pointed out, this is a misguided portrait of matriarchy:

> Because of sexism and racism, the Black female-headed household is more likely than the white to be sorely deprived economically. While some writers mistakenly call the Western world a matriarchy, we see that at best it is a pseudomatriarchy. Women do not even have earning power equal to men—much less, greater earning power. (Adams et al. 1984, 61)

This is not to deny the lack of opportunities for Black men; rather, it is to notice and expose the lack of policies that support Black women.

The race narrative ignores problems facing single parents, especially problems related to public policy favoring private over public support, as well as structuring public support so as to discourage marital family. The economic support structure for single-parent families, to the extent it exists, relies heavily on transfers of income from one parent to another. The public support structure historically and to a significant extent currently, provides superior benefits to nonmarital families as compared to marital families. Moreover, policies favoring private support fail to utilize nontraditional family kin and friendship structures. "Policies that imply a nuclear-family structure would affect Black and white families differently simply because more Black families represent the extended-family form. . . . The extended family is essential, in part, to compensate for the impact of social policy failures on the Black community, specifically low AFDC payments and high unemployment" (Washington 1988, 93–101).[14] Thus welfare structures oddly encourage, but only in a marginalizing way, single-parent Black families. Poverty magnifies the inadequacies of AFDC for the Black community, which contains a disproportionate share of poor families.

The predominance of single-parent families among Black families makes the case not for racial self-destruction but for racial subordination. It reflects the unremitting attacks on Black families, and the ongoing disempowerment of Black men. Paradoxically, it also reflects resistance to white patriarchal norms (Austin 1989, 566). Whites and Blacks typically respond differently to single parenthood, both structurally and emotionally (Fine and Schwebel 1988, 3). Not only is the origin of single-parent status for Blacks less likely to be divorce, but virtually all divorce studies have been done with middle-class whites, so any generalization among races is questionable.

Available studies suggest Blacks may cope more successfully with single-parent status. This success may be tied to distinctive features of Black culture, particularly African traditions promoting the connectedness of the community, which translates into a broader kin and friendship network, multiple parenting, child-centered social structures, and flexibility in role definitions and performance (McKenry and Fine 1993; Hill 1971). One other consequence of this different cultural context may be a different concept of fatherhood. Fathers may remain more closely tied to their children both in nonmarital families as well as in postdivorce families (McLanahan and Sandefur 1994).

The challenges that face Black mothers are significant. These challenges are compounded by race, and these additional unnecessary hurdles must be acknowledged. The conditions under which many Black women mother are designed to defeat rather than support their families. The problems of women of lowest income are especially severe. But just as we must not romanticize Black mothers, and Black culture, neither should the strengths of that culture be ignored. In the face of powerful negative factors, many Black mothers have carved out an admirable model of parenting which is more fully explored in chapter 5. That model is hidden by racial stigma and myth.

Gender myths overlap and intertwine with racial stereotypes. The negative stigma attached to single parents is primarily directed at single mothers. For women, to be a single parent is to be a failure and an aberration. Woman as mother is one of our most powerful social categories; it wraps women in myth, mysticism, and awe. At the same time, the concept and reality of the single mother generates intense fear, anger, and a threat to men (Rich 1986). As Martha Fineman has observed, mothers without men are the patriarchy's

worst nightmare (Fineman 1991b). Protecting the patriarchy requires conceptualizing men as essential, economically and developmentally. Men's biological tie to children is the basis under this view
to claim rights or responsibilities designed to put men back into
the family picture, voluntarily or involuntarily, whether wanted or
requested by the single mother.

*It is striking, but often seen as unremarkable, that women domi-
nate single-parent families.* Women's dominance reflects women's
continuing role in caretaking, as well as the enduring power of
culture and ideology in reinforcing women's caretaking role. In another respect, the predominance of female-headed single-parent families highlights the definitional issues and the curious position of
men: there are just as many male single parents, but they are
virtually invisible because of the sharp distinction between their
parental role and single mothers' role. If single parenting is defined
by sole or primary caretaking, then the number of male single
parents is quite small; if parenting is defined solely by genetic
connection, then the number of male single parents is roughly
equivalent to the number of female single parents.

The disproportion between the number of female-headed versus
male-headed families in poverty is striking. Almost half of families
headed by women are poor, compared with less than 3 percent of
families headed by men (Funiciello 1990, 37). The average family
income for single-parent mothers (including child support) is less
than half that of single-parent fathers with custody (Bureau of
Census 1989). Gendered differentials between median incomes expose the inequalities women, particularly women with children, face
in the workplace and the lack of choices and options for reducing
that poverty.

It is frequently noted that one of the most common routes out of
poverty for lone mothers is marriage. Rather than triggering concern
about the economic dynamics of marriage and the gross inadequacies
and continuing discrimination of the wage labor market, or the
failure to redistribute private income or provide meaningful public
support, this pattern is cited as evidence that marriage should be
strongly supported as a deterrent to poverty. This is like saying that
women who cannot keep a man or who cannot find a new one cause
poverty.

The assumptions with respect to men are entirely different: it is simply presumed that most cannot parent adequately. Yet single fathers do as well at parenting as mothers when they act as primary or sole custodial parents (Bronstein 1993, 274). Father-custody families are currently the fastest growing family form (relative of course to a very small initial number). Fathers in these families have been little studied and were not included in data sources on child support until *1992* (Meyer and Garasky 1993). Early studies describe these fathers as white, middle-aged, relatively well educated, with good jobs and relatively high incomes. On the other hand, one 1988 study found those fathers more likely to have children were older, male, and Black. It distinguished between father-only families, where the father's income tended to be lower and who were less educated, compared to father/stepmother families, who had higher incomes, better educational levels, and more likely were white (Meyer and Garasky 1993).

In father-custody families the majority of fathers are unmarried, but a larger proportion than single mothers are remarried (41 percent versus 23 percent). The fathers are mostly divorced; 8 percent are widowers, 25 percent are never-married fathers, the rest are divorced fathers.

The children in single-father families tend to fall, in income, between single-mother and two-parent families. Fathers have far higher incomes as a group, almost twice that of mother-only families. The gap is greatest between never-married fathers and never-married mothers: the fathers' incomes are 2.3 times higher than never-married mothers' incomes. Nevertheless, a significant number live in poverty, 18 percent. Very few fathers receive child support, and the amounts indicate an unequal distribution—that is, less support is ordered—as compared to similarly situated women. The pattern of low incomes is present for custodial and noncustodial fathers.[15]

Despite the greater economic advantages of single-father families, the children in these families do not do substantially better, arguably defeating the father absence theorists but confirming the two-is-better-than-one theories. Or perhaps it simply confounds everything, because such a variety of explanations is possible. One study theorizes that women do better at delivering interpersonal skills and men do better at meeting economic needs, so you need both for kids.

Most male single parents are noncustodial, occasional parents, ranging from those who maintain regular visitation to those who have severed all except the legal links with their children. The number of never-married custodial fathers who actively nurture their children is even smaller and rarely studied. Single fathers remain unacknowledged, or viewed as odd or unusual. They are condemned only for the failure to perform as economic parents.

The pain of divorce for these fathers often translates into lack of connection. Children need regular and frequent visitation without conflict. According to one national survey, however, fathers averaged only two visits per month several years after divorce, and *almost half of the children had not seen their fathers in the past year.* The strength of the parenting relationship prior to divorce is not a strong factor in predicting postdivorce involvement by fathers; rather, the relationship with the ex-wife is most significant. The boundaries and configurations of the postdivorce family are muddled, and the role of the noncustodial parent is not at all clear. Factors that contributed to involved parenting in one study were satisfaction with parenting, perception of influencing child's life, and geographical proximity to children.

The pattern of father absence is quite strong: for children under age three, fathers are present for 70 percent of white children, for 59 percent of Hispanic children, and for 22 percent of Black children. The likelihood of father presence increases with the age of the mother at the child's birth. Father presence has the greatest impact for white children and children with older mothers. Interestingly, the greater occurrence of father absence among Black families makes father absence less problematic: there is less stigma and more compensatory social and economic support systems.

The practice of single parenthood is therefore remarkably different for mothers and fathers, mirroring the Parsonian divide in family roles. Overwhelmingly, mothers "do" caretaking and fathers "do" support. Mothers continue to do the unpaid work of childcare which has a negative impact on their economic position. Fathers remain primarily economic fathers, although historically and currently a significant number have avoided economic responsibility as well.

Despite or perhaps because of fathers' limited role, social scientists have given fathers who are strong nurturing parents supportive, even rave reviews; considerable attention from the legal system has been placed on nurturing fathers. Fathers have been found to be as competent at parenting as mothers, despite strong cultural models to the contrary (Warshak 1986, 199; Greif 1985, 77; Risman 1986, 101). Social scientists have applauded fathers' competence as extraordinary but also rare. As one researcher notes, "on the one hand, we assume the father is an extraordinary man. . . . On the other, we assume he needs our help" (Greif 1985). This sympathetic view of fathers with custody is in contrast with the view of noncustodial fathers, who are expected to accept the loss of their children, even if they technically retain the status of a joint parent.

> Although society furnishes models of conduct and defines the roles of married men, it does not do so for men that are divorced. . . . This sense of a 'social void' accounts for the findings. . . that divorced fathers claim that they have lost their identity and roots. Divorced fathers view their lives as lacking in structure, and are troubled by feelings of loss, guilt, anxiety and depression. (Guttman 1989, 248)

Fathers respond to the difficulty of single-parent status by giving up being a parent.

Finally, gender stories justifying stigma also reflect mainstream views on gay and lesbian parents. Homophobia overwhelms any preference for a two-parent family; courts often prefer a single parent to two parents of the same sex.[16] The law also tends to treat all homosexual parents as single parents by prohibiting marriage of same-sex couples and limiting, if allowing at all, the use of adoption to create a family.[17] The law's discouragement or prohibition of gay parenting flies in the face of studies showing no detrimental impact to children of their parents' homosexuality, and increased likelihood of coequal parenting in same-sex households (Gottman 1989, 186).[18]

Race and gender justifications operate differently from other justifications for stigmatizing single-parent families because they are more subtle and unarticulated, although often not far below the surface. They are no less powerful; to the contrary, it is these underlying stereotypes and assumptions that may operate most powerfully to create and perpetuate stigma.

Stigma based on these justifications is unfounded and unjustified. It is contradicted by the realities of the lives of single parents. The negative consequences falsely associated with the *form* of family are strongly linked to poverty, caused not by family form, but rather by a number of factors including the operation of the legal system. Law both incorporates and creates stigma. The structures of divorce and welfare assist in creating and perpetuating poverty among single-parent families. Ironically, strong legal ideologies of equality and choice justify and often hide harsh inequality and punishment.

Law affects single parents both by recognizing their family structure in ways that treat it as a distinctive status, and by the structural impact of the law in their lives. Single parents arguably are more affected by legal structures than two-parent marital families, because of the impact of the structure of divorce and the welfare system. Those two legal structures significantly impact their daily lives, especially their economic life, in a way that stigmatizes, devalues, subordinates, and ignores single-parent families. This has stark consequences for the children in these families.

In part II I explore how the law stigmatizes single parents by looking separately at divorced and never-married single parents.

PART II · LAW & SINGLE PARENTS

How does law stigmatize single parents? First, the mere presence and repetition of the justifications for stigma within a legal context cloak these justifications with the legitimacy and presumed objectivity of the law. The law as ideology reinforces and validates stigma. The law does this most clearly when single parents or their children are stigmatized as a matter of status. Naming nonmarital children illegitimate—unlawful—as well as maintaining a paternity structure designed to protect fathers rather than to connect children to their parents are examples of explicit stigmatization.

Second, the law incorporates the view of single-parent families as unworthy, or bad, as the premise for its denial or limitation of rights or benefits. One goal of the law becomes preventing or deterring formation of these "bad" families. The law's most potent weapon for prevention or deterrence of single-parent families is poverty. The law stigmatizes single parents most clearly in this respect in the operation of the welfare system.

Third, the legal rhetoric of equality and choice makes family

53

form the scapegoat for economic inequality and oppression. Legal guarantees of equality and protection of choice, if effective, point toward the individual as responsible for his or her circumstances. In other words, poverty is the result of individual choice and foregone opportunities. This rhetoric ignores structural problems which operate in a context of gender, race, and class inequality. The rhetoric of equality and choice also ignores the content and impact of legal structures coated with a veneer of objectivity and neutrality. In particular, the law ignores the limited choices for constructing work and family relationships. Those limited choices contribute to the creation of poverty and its associated ills. In this way, the law stigmatizes single parents by the structure and goals of both family and employment law.

Finally, the law fiercely supports the patriarchal nuclear family, even to the detriment of children. Existing legal structures of divorce and welfare which construct the lives of single-parent families harshly punish children raised within families which may deviate from the preferred norm. Stigma denies any positive model of single-parent families. The single-parent family is cast as a deviant social outcast or, at best, as a pathetic and needy supplicant.

CHAPTER 3

Divorced Single Parents

Law reflects and implements stigma by means of status and structure. By far, the more serious consequences for divorced single-
parent families flow from structural stigma as opposed to status.
Family law, employment law, and welfare law interact to impoverish
single parents. In doing so, they incorporate existing social stigma
and create new stigma. The law justifies stigma as necessary or
simply consequential, based on rationalizations that echo the myths
previously explored as justifications for stigma. Acting within a
context of inequality framed by gender and race, law uses the language and model of equality and choice to rationalize and obscure
the heavy sanction imposed on single parenting.

This interconnected structure operates upon a well-defined work
and family framework. It is essential to sketch that framework in
order to understand how it interacts with the legal regimes which
construct the lives of divorced single parents. In the sections of this
chapter which follow I map the context of work and family and then
examine the interconnection of family law, employment law, and

welfare as they affect the realities of single parents at divorce. In the final section I summarize this interconnection, focusing on mechanisms whereby the powerful ideologies of equality and choice of family law and employment law construct and justify stigmatizing single-parent families.

THE CONTEXT OF WORK AND FAMILY

Understanding the social construction of work and family is critical to evaluating the impact of legal structures on divorced single-parent families. The pattern of work and family responsibilities continues to be strongly gendered. Traditionally, the gender role allocation of work and family responsibilities dictated that fathers work in the wage workforce, while mothers care for children and the home. Even currently, so few women and men structure the allocation to the contrary that we continue to speak of such allocations as a "switch" and conceive of fathers and mothers in such situations as "unnatural," deviant, or acting out of necessity. But the traditional ideal has become a minority family pattern: less than 10 percent of families with children under age eighteen conform to the pattern of a single-male breadwinner and a female stay-at-home spouse (Dowd 1993). Most men with children are in the workforce, and most women are as well.

The strongest vestige of the traditional pattern continues only for very young children. Forty-five percent of mothers of children under age four are at home (National Research Council 1990). As their children grow older, most of these mothers will return to work rather than stay at home until their children reach the age of majority. Seventy-five percent of married women with children ages six to seventeen participate in the labor force, as do 78 percent of widowed, divorced or separated women, and 70 percent of single, never-married women (Bureau of Census 1994; National Research Council 1990).

The traditional pattern of women caring for children and the home *does* persist, however, despite women's participation in wage work. If someone stays home to do caretaking, most often it will be a mother. Whether or not they are doing wage work, women continue to do most of the household and caretaking work. Although

many men have conceptualized a broader role of fathering beyond the role of breadwinner and have expanded their family responsibilities, other men have not significantly expanded their household or child-care responsibilities. Mothers' and fathers' distinctive roles persist across class and race lines and are present throughout the work life of men and women, despite significant changes in women's work patterns. Women are far more likely to accommodate work to family, by their choice of job, by their choice of flexible hours, or by limiting their wage work to part-time work.

In evaluating work and family patterns, it is important not to limit the inquiry to the time spent on child care and household tasks. There is mental as well as physical energy involved in caretaking. The psychological aspect of this analysis is complex. First, it seems that men and women think more equally than they act; they are verbally committed to egalitarian ideals, but the allocation of family tasks to women is still phenomenally high. Second, while men have taken over some family work, especially the care of children, they have not taken over *responsibility*, in the sense of planning and thinking, short term and long term. That responsibility is left to women. Third, the patterns are strongly tied to gender, not to income differentials; the nonegalitarian pattern is found in households where women consistently contribute 40 percent of family income, across income levels. The pattern, then, is men providing assistance to women, not a pattern of primary caretaking by both spouses. It is usually women who "anticipate needs, remember schedules, and so forth" (Leslie 1991, 209). Men back up women, and that is not insignificant. Men's support of women, however, confirms the model of caretaking not as a coequal one, but rather as one of interrelated inequality. In the patriarchal model, the backup caretaker generally has the power and the money in the relationship.

The reconstruction of traditional gender roles also is evident by comparing the work-family responsibilities of women in dual-parent and single-parent families. When we compare dual-parent and single-parent families, what is striking is the similarity of work and family patterns. These patterns suggest that single-parent families are constructed within dual-parent families. In that respect, the strongly gendered pattern of single-parent families exposes the recreation of patriarchy amidst equality rhetoric.

Work demands on women are not distinguishable between married and single-parent households. Indeed, if anything, women spend less time working at home in a single-parent household, oreflecting a reduction in home-related responsibilities (Burden 1986, 40). Moreover, there are no significant differences in job-family management, role strain, or number of child problems (40).[1] Work in the household is still divided along gender lines, with women on average performing three times as many domestic tasks as men (Thompson and Walker 1989). Due to the allocation of sole or primary wage work to fathers in most households, most children in dual-parent households are essentially fatherless during most of their waking hours.[2]

The imbalance of work and family responsibilities powerfully affects both men and women. Because of actual or perceived family responsibilities, women do not have the same work opportunities as men. Employers' perceptions of women's family responsibilities are so strong that all women, regardless of whether or not they have children, are affected by the perceived impact of family responsibilities on their role as employees. Persistent sex discrimination is strongly connected to women's perceived family role.

The structure of work and family policy has done little to change this. To the limited extent that public policy has dealt with family, it has been built around pregnancy as disability, establishing the workplace as a neutral sphere where women confront the same terms as men. It is not a policy framed in terms of maximizing the protection of family life or collective social responsibility and valuing of children (Wright-Carozza 1993, 571–77). It is a structure and discourse that leaves children out of public spaces, and emphasizes the view of the worker as an individual (Wright-Carozza 1993).

Women's continuing economic disadvantage due to workplace discrimination translates into subordination within the family. Comparison of women within dual-parent and single-parent households reveals potential economic vulnerability and domination in the former. Recent research concludes that women can experience poverty *within* marriage and that single parenthood may in some instances be an improvement in women's living standard.

Women's poverty within marriage is simply less visible poverty. It is based on the combination of responsibility for unpaid domestic work plus low-paid market work, which results in economic dependency for women and the children for whom they are the primary caregivers. Thus, the shift from dual to single parenthood is often not a shift from well-being to poverty, but rather a shift from one kind of poverty to another. And for some women, single parenthood is "not only a different but a preferable kind of poverty" (Wright-Carozza 1993). In one study, over half of the women had been battered by their partners; becoming a single parent removed violence as part of the price of access to economic resources (Wright-Carozza 1993; Mahoney 1991). In contrast to the marital arrangement where husbands commonly *control* resources while wives commonly *manage* resources, single mothers have both control and management. Not only do they avoid marital fights over money, but they are able to make different choices in allocating scarce resources.

The poverty of single mothers is not caused by lone parenthood but rather has its roots in the sexual division of labor in the family and continuing sexual discrimination in the workplace. "For lone mothers their sex rather than their marital status is the real key to understanding why they are poor" (Millar 1989). The poverty of single mothers is particularly tied to the consequences of childcare, which also contribute dramatically to women's lack of economic independence within marriage. More critical than the direct costs of childcare are the indirect costs, including the impact of a break from the workforce or deviation from the standard forty-plus-hour work week. By one estimate, based on an eight-year break from employment for a mother with two children who returns to part-time employment, the mother would lose, over her lifetime, nearly half of what she would have earned had she remained childless (Millar 1989).[3] The impact of the existing work structure requires "understanding how paid employment has been constructed in industrial society as a gendered (male) form of work. . . . Women who enter conventionally male-defined careers do 'need a wife,' as the complaint goes, because the expectations built into the structure of the job and the workplace take such a full-time support system for granted" (Ferree 1990).

Placed in the social context of work and family, the single-parent family is created within the marital family which harbingers the common parenting patterns at divorce. In that sense, *every parent is a single parent, generally following a gendered parenting role*. Mothers' parenting is characterized by all or the vast majority of unwaged household work and caretaking, combined with wage work constrained by the real or imagined responsibilities of parenting. Fathers' parenting, on the other hand, is characterized by economic caretaking as the primary, although no longer the sole, responsibility, combined with minimal caretaking and household work. After divorce, most children will live solely or primarily with their mothers, and be cared for nearly exclusively by them. Fathers do little or no caretaking after divorce, and many abandon even minimal caretaking within several years of divorce. Furthermore, many fathers give up economic parenting as well at divorce or shortly thereafter. Despite continuous strengthening of the child support laws since 1975, the low percentage of payment has not dramatically changed.

In a dual-parent family we can believe parental choice explains gendered patterns and outcomes. In the single-parent family that facade is not present. Rather, the stark reality of the gendered structure of family and work is unmistakably evident. The consequences of "choices" made in dual-parent families distributing work and family responsibilities, most often along predictable gender lines, is economic devastation and emotional abandonment if the patriarchal tie is broken. Operating in a context of inequality, supported by the rhetoric of equality, family and employment law at divorce too often makes poverty the consequence of single parenting.

FAMILY LAW

At divorce, the single-parent structure that exists *within* marriage is reconstituted as a devalued family form. The structure of divorce law creates and perpetuates poverty as the price of creating single-parent families. The law also permits the abandonment of caretaking responsibilities, usually by fathers, allowing the surrender of all responsibility to one parent, usually mothers, who often take on *de jure* what has been *de facto* sole caretaking responsibility. The emergence of the typical single-parent family at divorce is entirely predictable, based on the context of work and family relationships during marriage and the way in which law structures families at divorce.

General Principles of Divorce Law

Certain identifiable principles, varying by degree in particular jurisdictions but consistent overall, inform the current divorce structure. Although the vast majority of divorce is resolved by agreement, in the form of settlement, those rules nevertheless affect the shape of settlement as well as our social vision of the form and function of the postdivorce family. Those principles consist of the following: that no party will be held at fault; that each party should leave the marriage with a roughly equal share of property created or acquired during the marriage by financial or other contributions; that neither party has a long-term financial obligation to the other party as a result of the marriage; that the parties will continue to share in the parenting and financial support of minor children; and that neither finances nor children will be allocated on other than gender-neutral principles (Czapanskiy 1991, 1989; Dolgin 1994; Estin 1993; Singer 1993; Starnes 1993).

These principles presume that marriage is a partnership among equals who share work and family responsibilities equitably and who have equal opportunities to structure their private lives, as well as to choose from an equal range of options in the wage workforce. Any variation from an equal (meaning similar) division of roles and responsibilities is understood as the product of choice.

With respect to postdivorce conditions, the principles presume that each spouse can function independently on the same terms as he or she did during the marriage, limited only by his or her individual effort and accomplishments in the labor market. A spouse with a shortfall of income can compensate by taking advantage of opportunities in the wage labor market. A spouse with a shortfall of time for domestic work can purchase childcare and housework services. A spouse with an excess of childcare responsibilities can rely on income provided pursuant to shared financial support of children to supplement income or finance care of children in order to do wage work, and can also rely on the other parent to provide childcare as part of shared parenting. This postdivorce model presumes that any interruption of wage work or modification of work behavior in response to family responsibilities during the marriage can be overcome by making different choices in labor market work after divorce. In other words, each partner resumes the position he or she had before the marriage, as modified by his or her responsibility for parenting children. Since parenting responsibility is shared, as it is presumed was done during the marriage, the burden of parenting is presumed to be equally distributed between two independent self-supporting adults.

The realities of divorced single-parent families are starkly at odds with these presumptions. The pattern of divorce is one of striking inequality, split along clear gender lines. Men and women continue to emerge from divorce at opposite economic poles: men's financial position improves, while women's sharply declines (Weitzman 1985). The labor market does not correct these inequalities; instead, the marked pattern of sex segregation and wage inequity frustrates women's attempts to equalize the economic imbalance of divorce, despite the divorce system's reliance on the ability of each parent to generate additional income if needed.

The caretaking patterns are equally gendered. Sole or primary custody is overwhelmingly granted to mothers (Weitzman and Dixon 1979; Mnookin et al. 1990). Most estimates still put mother custody at about 90 percent. The vast majority of custody is designated by agreement rather than by litigation. In contested custody cases, however, there is evidence that fathers are surprisingly successful (Polikoff 1982).

Many fathers without custody, however, abandon their relationships with their children, usually within two years of divorce (Czapanskiy 1989).

> Nonvisitation seems to occur in about fifty percent of the cases. . . .
> For about one-third of the children of divorce, it means that they will
> not see their noncustodial parent at all after the first year of separa-
> tion. Very few ever sleep at the home of the noncustodial parent or
> do daily activities with them. Instead, their contact is sporadic and pri-
> marily social. Fewer than one-fifth will have contact with the noncus-
> todial parent on a weekly basis. (Czapanskiy 1991, 1449)

According to another study, only one child in six saw his or her father weekly; another one in six saw his or her father less often than once a month but more often than once a year; and nearly half of the children had not seen their father in the previous twelve months (Furstenberg and Cherlin 1991). Ten years after divorce, according to the same study, only one in ten children had contact, while nearly two-thirds had no contact in the prior year (Furstenberg and Cherlin 1991). When fathers abandon their nurturing relationship, they also, usually, abandon economic support of their children (Pearson and Thoennes 1988). The level of paternal abandonment is high, and the lack of discussion about it disturbing.

Rather than supporting equality, the structure of divorce law seems designed to create stigma or at least to do nothing to prevent it. Current divorce rules create poverty by ignoring social roles created within marriage and barriers to opportunity and choice in the labor market. Under the guise of equality and choice, divorce law has recreated, or even worsened, the explicit gender hierarchy of earlier legal regimes. Single custodial parents, especially single mothers, are penalized for divorce by impoverishment. In turn, they are blamed for the consequences of poverty for their children. At the same time, until recently, the legal system has largely permitted noncustodial parents, mostly fathers, to escape financial responsibility without consequence, blame, or stigma.

The experience of single parenting for women and men after divorce is remarkably different, and that difference is accepted within the equality regime. Arguably, that very inequality is structured *by* the equality regime. Under the current legal regime, what is missing is the role of unwaged work in the family economy and the consequences of children's dependency. What also seems to be missing is a reconceptualization of work and family to reflect more accurately the consequences of an economy in which more than one income is essential for the support of most families. Finally, the legal regimes lack a vision of gender equality and nonsubordinating gender roles, and instead reveal the striking persistence of traditional, patriarchal gender roles despite the rhetoric of gender-neutral equality.

Economic/Financial

The financial consequences of divorce can be subdivided into alimony, property division, and child support. Alimony has shifted from a duty of support for life to a short-term transitional form of financial support. It is presumed that the labor market provides equal opportunity to both spouses; that both spouses likely will work during the marriage; and that any hiatus from the market can be overcome, or a shift from part-time to full-time work can be accomplished, without major difficulty or impact upon long range earning capacity. The ideal is autonomy and self reliance. Alimony is available only upon a showing of need, dependency, or incapacitation. Current inability to be self-supporting is cured by "rehabilitating" the dependent spouse into an independent wage earner. Care of children, even young children, is not usually a sufficient reason for even short-term alimony. As one commentator has pointed out, caregiving has simply disappeared from the rationalization for alimony; just as, arguably, it has become invisible throughout family law at divorce (Estin 1993).

Caregiving is only considered in a limited way. First, it may be a basis to permit temporary maintenance until the children reach a specified age, particularly to provide care to very young children. At least one study indicates, however, that temporary support provisions in reality are rarely used for this purpose (Estin 1993). Second, the caregiver may be compensated for the consequences of putting wage work opportunities on hold, but this is factored into property division, and is not a basis for alimony. A significant body of law supports providing compensation for this contribution or loss, depending upon one's perspective.

The shift in principles underlying alimony may be important in theory but not in practice because, just as before, alimony is rarely awarded. Property division and child support are the primary sources of private support between divorced parents. In these areas of divorce law, the principle of equality is strongly expressed. In property division, the principle of equitable distribution, with a presumption of equal contribution, by monetary or nonmonetary means, is the guiding principle. The goal is a one-time settlement of finances, a clean financial break. Although the concept of marital property has dramatically expanded (e.g., pensions, business and professional goodwill), that which is available to be divided is not, in most cases, a sufficient economic base on which to support a family. Most marital estates do not have much property to divide, and what property they do have is heavily mortgaged. A large proportion of displaced homemakers lose their house in the divorce process (Starnes 1993, 86). Furthermore, the presumed equality of contribution does not address the inequality of postdivorce consequences if one spouse, usually the woman, has foregone opportunities in the labor market which have lifelong consequences. It focuses, rather, on losses during the marriage, not on their postdivorce implications. The property division model presumes an ability to supplement marital property with employment. As a consequence, the dominant pattern is that women's income declines as their needs increase, while the reverse occurs for men. These patterns persist for years after divorce, especially if women do not remarry (Holden and Smock 1991; Weitzman 1981).

Between alimony and property division, therefore, most spouses receive little or no resources. Child support, then, is the primary financial consequence of divorce where minor children are involved. Divorce law conceives of child support as an entitlement which runs to the child, a conception that ignores the interdependence of the child with the primary or sole caretaker. The law of child support treats children as an independent economic unit. Although equality is the ideal, with each parent expected to support the child, courts calculate the amount of child support pro rata based on income, and consequently parental obligations are not likely to be equal given typical male and female wage-earning patterns. Support is calculated by adding the income of both parents, and then applying child support percentage, prorated for each parent's income. At upper-income levels the court has discretion how much above the guidelines to award (Ellman et al. 1991).

Support amounts are characteristically lower than actual expenses and lower than typical families of the same income level would spend on their children. The guidelines do not vary the percentage of income required to be devoted to children, yet studies show that as income rises, families spend more on children. Since this is not taken into account, the average percentage may therefore be considerably lower than resources expended predivorce. For example, for two children, 25 percent of income is appropriate according to the guidelines, while two-income middle-class families actually expend 40 percent of their income on their children.

Change in support is not usually automatic. Few parents can afford to return to court to seek a modification of the initial child support order. Payments commonly decrease as children age, and often end at age eighteen. Not surprisingly, there is a clear trend of downward economic and social mobility for children awarded support under the guidelines.

The level of support actually paid is very low. A common pattern is nonpayment, coexisting with the lack of regular contact with children (Ellman et al. 1991, 402–4). According to one study, "[m]odal per-child orders ... were approximately at the poverty standard and only about one-third of the estimated normal levels of expenditures on children within intact families. These shortfalls appear to be consistent with national estimates" (Pearson and Thoennes 1988, 328).[4] Federal efforts are focused on enforcement, not on amount; "the amount of money lost as a result of inadequate orders is five times as great as the amount of money lost as a result of the failure to collect ordered support" (Czapanskiy 1989).

Enforcement of support is a matter of individual responsibility, not state intervention, unless the household is on welfare. In many states support and visitation are uncoupled, so that failure to pay support does not result in denial of visitation. While courts recognize some nonmonetary contributions, caretaking by the primary or sole parent is ignored or underestimated in support calculations.

The divorce structure fails to provide sufficient economic resources to the typical single-parent family. By defining equality of parental responsibility in a narrow way which takes a snapshot of resources at one moment in time, current and future needs of the family are ignored. The consequences for children are disastrous. The typically drastic decline in income most immediately affects housing and education, which has both short- and long-term consequences. Education is the single most critical factor in children's future opportunities.[5]

Many believe that the labor market is the answer to the problem of impoverishment among single mothers. However, as more fully explored below, the labor market provides no assurance to women that it will operate any more fairly at divorce than it did during marriage. Regardless of one's parenting status, jobs that respect and support parenting responsibility, or that adequately support a family on a single income, are scarce or nonexistent. Furthermore, to the extent that mothers work full-time or attend school full-time in order to improve their competitiveness in the workforce, the workforce solution poses the risk of losing custody. As described in chapter 2, some courts have sanctioned single parents' choices to work full-time or attend school by using such choices as justification for an award of custody to the other parent.

Parenting/Custody

Just as the economic principles allocate resources unequally, the divorce structure distributes actual caregiving and other responsibilities on a highly unequal basis. Moreover, the inequality is as strongly gender-differentiated as the economic consequences of divorce. Despite gender-neutral rules and a preference in most jurisdictions for joint custody, most women continue to provide primary or sole nurturing for their children after divorce (Maccoby and Mnookin 1992; Furstenberg and Cherlin 1991). Although men have increased their share of parenting, the overall pattern has not changed significantly. Furthermore, the theoretical predisposition for joint custody has resulted in lower levels of child support under that custody framework, even if actual custody becomes entirely or predominantly vested in the mother (Fitzgerald 1994, 60).

Although most divorced children have two parents, socially and legally we do not demand equal caretaking responsibility by both parents. This highly unequal caretaking pattern has traditionally included acceptance of fathers abandoning the role of economic as well as nurturing parent. Although as a matter of social policy we continue to renew the effort to enforce economic responsibility for children, we continue to allow withdrawal from the nurturing role. Law arguably did not create the pattern of one parent as the sole or primary caretaker, but law quietly accepts voluntary surrender of parenting without consequence or rebuke. The law assumes that shared legal custody and gender-neutral custody rules will solve the problem of unequal parenting. Nevertheless, equal parenting remains an illusion for most male single parents. Many men have not seized their opportunity to parent during or after their marriage. Emphasis on and expansion of fathers' rights has not resulted in significantly greater paternal nurturing of children. Perhaps this is nowhere more clearly symbolized than in the fact that "fathering" has not shifted in meaning to mean "nurturing" or "caretaking" in the same sense that connotation applies to "mothering." Rather, "fathering" continues to mean sexual reproduction, not parenting.

Socially, the common phenomenon of the uninvolved divorced father is widely accepted. This may simply reflect the social acceptance of maternal caregiving. Data on the impact of fathering postdivorce may also, ironically, reinforce father absence. Increased contact by fathers postdivorce does not translate into better outcomes for children (Furstenberg and Cherlin 1991; McLanahan and Sandefur 1994). In part, researchers suggest, this is because the nature and quality of postdivorce fathering is characteristically minimal, more like a visitor or a relative than a parent. In part, it is because fathering in marital families similarly is mother-centered and fathers' role is minimal (Furstenberg and Cherlin 1991).

Family law arguably is not the primary culprit, then, in wide-

spread father abandonment. Admittedly, some courts, out of mis-
placed gender stereotyping, deny custody or visitation to deserving
fathers, or fail to enforce fathers' rights of access to their children.
Some evidence suggests that the legal system continues to favor
mothers in terms of custody outcomes. One study indicates that
mothers simply assert their preferences more strongly regarding
custody in the legal system (Maccoby and Mnookin 1992). But other
research indicates the contrary pattern of men's significant success
when seeking custody, suggesting that family law strongly supports
father's rights to parent if and when those rights are asserted (Krause
1990; Ellman et al. 1991; Greif 1985, 6–7). Furthermore, as noted
earlier, the norm of some form of shared or joint custody is widespread. If voluntary abandonment of relationships with children,
not legal denial of such relationships, determines most caretaking
patterns, then family law appears, to a great extent, to protect maintenance of father-child relationships if and when fathers elect to
continue parenting.

The failure of family law with respect to fathers is not that it has
failed to increase fathers' rights, but rather that it does not require
that fathers fulfill their nurturing responsibilities nor does it impose
consequences for the failure to do so. Any version of custody short
of joint physical custody presumes less than equal paternal involvement. On the other hand, an imposed structure of joint physical
custody defies existing caretaking patterns, and both joint legal and
joint physical custody can too easily perpetuate patterns of dominance and control rather than mutual sharing of care (Fineman
1991a). In addition, if the right to custody exists without a corresponding duty or responsibility of caretaking, and is coupled with a
gendered pattern of marital household and childcare responsibility,
then custodial rights may be twisted into a weapon to deny support,
rather than to protect fathers' relationships with their children.
Indeed, many fathers have used their custody rights as bargaining
chips in order to reduce their economic obligations. The power im-
balances between men and women at divorce have long been documented, yet we have done little in the equality structure to deal
with it.

In addition, most custody structures do not impose penalties on
fathers who fail to fulfill even limited nurturing responsibilities.
Custody arrangements which permit fathers to abandon nurturing

responsibilities without economic or other compensation for the lack of caretaking leaves fathers free to be "take it or leave it" parents.

The law has, to a great extent, moved in the direction of acknowledging the equal ability of men and women to raise children, at least in theory. The legal structure need not abandon this position, but it need not stigmatize those families, currently the majority, in which parenting responsibilities are unequally divided. Indeed, it is ironic that the law permits many fathers to be parents in little more than name (or genes) only, while condemning single-parent families for, among other things, the absence of a father. Instead of seeing the single-parent family as inherently dysfunctional, the law should recognize the prevalence and importance of single-parent families. Critical to that recognition is an understanding of the actual division of caregiving during marriage and after divorce, as well as understanding the scope of children's needs and dependency, and the nature of caregiving and household work. This is not to say that men's parenting is not important, but rather that single-parent parenting has been the most common pattern of parenting within marriage as well as after divorce.

The vast gulf between family law's theory of equality and the reality of unequal caregiving is ignored by placing blame on single-parent families. Single parents are blamed for the phenomena of financial impoverishment and the breakdown of parent-child relationships, focusing attention away from the structure of family law and its impact upon a highly unequal familial structure. To the extent inequity is recognized at all, it is viewed as a product of choice, capable of change by new choices. The ability to change especially presumes the availability of opportunity in the workplace, reinforcing the focus away from the equality and choice issues within family law. Expecting single parents to resolve their financial difficulties in the workforce, where structural constraints and shortcomings confound their ability to succeed, simply creates further blame of single-parent families. Shifting expectation to the workplace not only moves attention away from dealing with dependency and unwaged work, but also shifts evaluation of single-parent families toward an arena where choice again can be blamed for individualized problems.

EMPLOYMENT LAW

Expectations about the labor market pervade divorce law. The economic structure of divorce presumes the ability of single parents to be self-supporting and the ability of single parents to support the children of the marriage on one salary. The divorce structure also presumes that parents have remained in the wage labor market during the marriage or that the market permits withdrawal from the market or accommodates children's needs, as well as enabling parents to resume full-time wage work. To the extent that divorce presumptions fail to achieve shared child support and parenting, family law also presumes that the labor market is flexible enough to permit time to parent or the ability to generate income to buy parenting or household services.

Family law's presumptions concerning the workplace are grounded in the expectation that equality of treatment and opportunity is insured by the nondiscrimination principle of employment law. Some view the increased presence of women in the workforce, particularly women with children, as proof of nondiscrimination. In addition, gendered patterns of workforce participation, income, opportunity, and job distribution are viewed as the product of "choice," not discrimination.

Actual conditions of the workplace contradict these presumptions. First, a substantial proportion of jobs do not provide sufficient income on which to support a family, thereby challenging the notion that any person can support a family on a single income. Second, although both parents work outside the home in many dual-parent families, patterns of labor participation by women are strikingly different, reflecting women's disproportionate childcare responsibilities. As a result, women's presence in the workforce does not guarantee her the same income as most men. Finally, the labor market takes an inflexible and punitive stance toward even short-term withdrawal from the workplace, as well as toward part-time work.

Overall, the labor market has shifted only slightly to accommodate demands to reconfigure the balance between working and parenting. The Family and Medical Leave Act of 1993 entitles covered employees to take twelve weeks of unpaid leave upon the birth or adoption of a child, *or* for the serious illness of an immediate family member, *or* for the employee's own illness.[6] Only an estimated half of the workforce, however, is covered by the act. Employees who do not fall within the statute's coverage, unless they are covered by state family leave act provisions (also unpaid), risk losing their job simply for caring for their children (Dowd 1993).

Providing regular childcare for workers' children continues to be a daunting task. Both the quantity and quality of childcare remain inadequate, and the need for childcare and the inadequacies of the current system are most pressing for those with least income. While parental leave, flexible work schedules, leave for illness or other childcare purposes, health insurance, and other important benefits are available in some workplaces, they are all too infrequent in others. The employment law structure remains primarily oriented to the male breadwinner rather than to the caretaking parent, male or female.

Labor market policies and legal structures concerning parenting operate upon a context of strong and persistent gender differentials. Women do not have the same opportunity structure as men. As one recent study demonstrated, very little differential exists in the employment pattern of women with or without children; both were found to be significantly disadvantaged as compared to men (Dowd 1993). Furthermore, the absence of children does not translate into equality of opportunity. Women do not have the same choices, they do not make the same incomes even within the same opportunity structures, and they do not advance within labor market hierarchies at the same rate or to the same heights as men. Marriage and children exacerbate these differences, but as already noted, the absence of both marriage and children does not eliminate the inequality.

To a significant degree, gender differentials in the workplace are accepted by the equality principle of antidiscrimination law (Dowd 1989a). Although equality is the purported goal of employment law, employment law fails to reach significant gender inequality. In part, this narrow reach is a product of the limitations of the equality structure of discrimination law, which focuses primarily on barriers and discrimination based on biological sex. The impact of the law has been far more ambiguous and equivocal in attacking the cultural construction of sex and its impact on the workplace. For example, although courts have clearly established that sexual harassment is a form of discrimination, courts and employers frequently trivialize and ignore sexual harassment, blame the victim, or view harassment as an issue of workplace culture unreachable by law. Gender stereotyping, which figures prominently in hiring, promotion, evaluation, as well as other aspects of employment, has been struck down by courts when it is blatant and facial, but appears less reachable when it is the basis for unconscious gender discrimination. In addition, courts regard gender segregation, which continues to restrict employment opportunities, as largely beyond the reach of equality guarantees, seeing it as a product of choice rather than of legally sanctioned employment policies. Generally, higher-paying, higher status jobs are structured, one way or another, to accommodate men more readily than woman. The structuring of such jobs for employees without significant caretaking responsibilities is not discrimination within the meaning of Title VII. As a result, women and men face different choices: men can be ideal workers and fulfill family obligations; women cannot (Schultz 1990, 1756; Williams 1989, 834–35). In short, employment law appears to permit inequality because, as with family law (and perhaps in conjunction with family law), the rhetoric of equality and choice acts as a barrier or limit rather than as a floor of rights or a weapon to insure real opportunity by affirmative restructuring.

Equality does not guarantee any particular workplace structure; rather, it only insures equal opportunity or access to that structure. The absence of structures that would enhance equal opportunity cannot be reached under existing discrimination law. Nor have litigators been successful in challenging existing structures as gendered, that is, as male-defined or male-oriented. The employment structure continues to be viewed as objective and neutral.

Single mothers are harmed by the limitations of discrimination law and its inability or unwillingness to dismantle barriers connected with sex stereotyping, sex segregation, and sexual harassment. Structural barriers which make it difficult or impossible to combine work and family are perhaps the greatest barriers to equality of opportunity which single mothers face.

Due to the absence of any meaningful acknowledgment of family responsibilities and their distribution within families, and of the needs of children, equality and choice are illusions in a labor market that remains largely hostile to parenting. Employment law does include structures such as unemployment compensation that attempt to preserve the economic contribution of the primary breadwinner and protect the economic contributions of dual or secondary breadwinners. Beyond unemployment compensation, employment structures fail to acknowledge explicitly the role of family. Family work is hidden, even invisible, and not even recognized as "work" at all because it is not waged. The continued refusal of the law to accord any recognition to unwaged family and childcare work presents a significant problem for all families, but again is exacerbated for single-parent families, because, by definition, there are fewer parents in the household to do the work, but much of the work remains. While the labor market's hostility toward parenting disadvantages all who parent, it disadvantages women disproportionately. That disadvantage is exacerbated still more for single mothers who, as noted above, disproportionately assume most parenting responsibilities in single-parent families.

The lack of support for parenting also effectively prevents more involved and extensive parenting by men who wish to be more than an economic parent. Employment law has failed to support structural changes and work-culture reorientation necessary to support all parenting, but has particularly failed to change and support a child-centered caregiving model for fathers, a model that would benefit all parents. Current law does not support reconstituting fathers' traditional gender role from that of a purely economic father.

The public/private dichotomy underlying employment law, which undercuts all families, further undermines single-parent families. From the perspective of the workplace, family is private, an expected support for the workplace but clearly a secondary priority for workers, for whom work must come first. Moreover, viewed from the perspective of employment law, the rhetoric of family equality supported by family law means that choices made with respect to family which impact work are freely made, voluntary choices. As a result, to the extent that such choices impact one's employment, they are attributable to the employee. The structures of the workplace are viewed as neutral, and the opportunity structure as governed by real equality.

One might argue that the equality structures in work and family law are merely aspirational. The persistence of inequality is not a sign of the inadequacy of the structures, but is only a challenge to create better means to the end. One could also argue that we must pay the price of getting to equality by suffering with inequality. If we ameliorate existing inequalities we may simply replicate them. But what we seem to be doing is perpetuating inequality with the ideology of equality. The position of single-parent families makes that clear.

How is it that the operation of family and employment law, which largely creates and perpetuates the poverty of single-parent families, escapes scrutiny? As the previous discussion of employment law suggests, the powerful intersection of ideologies of equality as articulated in family and employment law serves to deflect analysis and rationalizes stigma. Before analyzing how these ideologies work together, however, it is necessary to examine one final piece of the legal structure that impacts single parents at divorce: the welfare structure. Instead of providing meaningful temporary or long-term support, the welfare structure serves to penalize those who use its benefits. As with family and work law, the operation of the equality principle and the "choice" principle as applied to the welfare system masks and justifies the stigmatizing of single-parent families.

WELFARE

Although the complexities of welfare merit close analysis, this discussion is limited to welfare's place among the legal structures facing divorced single parents. Divorced single parents, constituting nearly half of those going on welfare, are the largest group of entrants on AFDC.[7] This statistic confirms the utter failure of family law to insure a decent family support structure after marriage and the perpetuation of inequality during marriage. It also clearly demonstrates that the paid workplace provides no alternative relief, as such a high proportion of divorced women cannot find work sufficient to support their families.

Because the situation of many divorced women is not temporary, nor can it be cured (or past harm recouped) for substantial numbers of women in the foreseeable future, long-term welfare is a necessity for many divorced single parents. The direction of current time-limited welfare reform proposals, in contrast, casts welfare as temporary transitional assistance and labels any ongoing needs as individual dysfunction. Reform proposals appear to be in consensus in one respect: all proposals ignore actual conditions for many single mothers after divorce in favor of continued stigmatization of those on welfare.

The dual equality structures of family and employment law increase stigmatization of able-bodied women on welfare, more so than at any point in the history of the welfare program. Because of equality, it is argued, women have and make choices: choices about family, choices regarding work, and choices concerning the construction of the work-family relationships. Furthermore, under equality, most women do wage work as well as raise families, including women with young children. It is therefore reasonable, according to this view, to require all women to perform wage work; women who do not, regardless of any factor, are unworthy.

The welfare structure implicitly accepts the highly gendered structure of work and family and the value of the patriarchal family. Welfare benefits provide only the most begrudging support of the single-parent family but clearly not enough to insure a solid opportunity for support or survival. Welfare benefits do not supply a sufficient support framework for most single-parent families to maintain income levels above poverty, and therefore condemn these families to the consequences of poverty. Nevertheless, welfare provides a superior framework to the wage work available to many women with children and therefore encourages many single-parent families to remain on welfare as the lesser of two evils (Kamerman and Kahn 1988, 155–56). The main reason few welfare mothers work is that it is hard to earn one's way off of welfare, without higher wages and benefits than low-skilled people typically earn.

Legislators' unwillingness to provide adequate support may be tied to fear that to do so would encourage the creation of single-parent families, despite the fact that virtually no evidence supports the view that welfare creates single-parent families. Welfare permits choice only to the same extent that wage work does; it gives women some independence and economic means, however flawed, to leave marriage. Moreover, as Professor Martha Fineman has argued, much of the reason for the failure to increase benefits lies in patriarchal views of the superiority of the nuclear family. Fineman argues the discourse around welfare identifies motherhood without a man as the "problem," and the forced return of the man, in the form of enforced economic support, as the "solution." Single motherhood, then, is viewed as a practice of resistance to patriarchy, particularly in a world where motherhood is by "choice" (Fineman 1991b). Resistance justifies poor treatment.

More than ever, "welfare" is a dirty word, perhaps a dirtier word than "single parent." Many policy makers stigmatize welfare in order, in their view, to prevent laziness. In doing so, poverty is presumed to be an individual failing rather than a structural problem. The welfare structure and ethos feed into an explanation for poverty of individual responsibility and dysfunction that lie at the core of the stigma attached to single-parent families. Parallels between the stigma attached to the poor and single parents, and connecting factors of gender and race, seem not merely coincidental.

CONCLUSION: LAW, STIGMA, EQUALITY, AND CHOICE

Amid ongoing inequalities in both families and work, law takes equality as its goal but utterly fails to provide the structures to insure equality or to support dependent children and those who care for them. When a marriage dissolves, family law revives the myth of equality of opportunity in work and connects it to the family law goals of gender neutrality, gender equality, and self-sufficiency. Law no longer permits the dependency of women and ignores the dependency of children. But divorce exposes the hidden construction of impoverished single parenting within the marital family, the consequence of the combined equality regimes of family and work law. Family law equality justifies conceptualizing employment patterns and family responsibilities as private. Employment law equality justifies conceiving of workforce positions and income as matters of choice. Both family and employment law equality rhetoric support a punitive welfare policy.

The law ignores much of the context of inequality as well as the consequences of legal structures. The law is an active creator of stigma in this sense, as much so as in its role in structuring the postdivorce family. As is clear from equality analysis, the law ignores unequal gender roles and the perpetuation of a highly gendered work-family structure. The law lacks a real concept of ungendered or shared parenting. It refuses to consider structural change in the

workplace and lacks flexible notions of work and family combinations. The law relies on individual responsibility and self-sufficiency,
despite the practical impossibility of self- or familial sufficiency on
the sole earnings of many jobs. Law also perpetuates the concept of
the sole economic provider, even though most families must rely on
two incomes. The law continues to pull more adults out of the
family and into the labor market, supported by equality rhetoric that
expects adults to both work and parent, but provides little support to
insure that children are nurtured.

In addition, the law ignores dependency. Previous legal models of
family presumed dependency; the current equality model rests on a
presumption of independence.[8] We ignore dependency created within
marriage by walling it off as private. In the welfare structure, we
ignore both the care of dependent children and women's economic
dependence by insisting that poor women work outside the home
without providing adequate childcare and failing to insure them jobs
that provide sufficient economic support for the family. Finally, by
ignoring gender roles and dependency, it is easy for law to under-
value or disregard entirely unwaged work.

The rhetoric of the law is that you exercise your liberty and
freedom to make choices. Choices are equal, in family and work, that
is, they are equally available. Once you make your choices, where
opportunities are equal, if your choice is a "bad" one, its your fault,
not a structural problem. If we are responsible and make good
choices, we succeed. If not, society has justification for stigma, as a
necessary negative punishment since you were so stupid or perverse
as to ignore positive incentives.

CHAPTER 4

Nonmarital Single-
Parent Families

Socially and legally there has been a sharp distinction between children of divorce and children born out of wedlock, and between parents whose marriage has failed and parents who have never married. The children and parents in nonmarital single-parent families are the most heavily stigmatized single-parent families. While illegitimate children may no longer be called bastards, the condemnation of their parents has not ended.

The danger is that this distinction between types of single parents and their children will be used to separate and isolate nonmarital single-parent families from divorced single parents. Just as widows are honored and legally supported distinct from most single parents, divorced single parents might separate themselves, or allow themselves to be separated, as deserving single parents entitled to public support. Dividing single parents between divorced and nonmarital single parents also marks a color line between groups of single parents. Nonmarital single parenting is more typical of nonwhites than of whites.

On the other hand, the sense that nonmarital single-parent families can be attacked without challenge means that they can be used as the target to denounce all single parents. To the extent, then, that single parents are viewed as an undifferentiated category, culturally and legally, the perceived negative characteristics and moral faults of single parents who never marry are ascribed to all single parents.

The law's treatment of nonmarital single parents incorporates both of these approaches. Historically, and to some extent currently, the law has treated these families distinctively by attaching great significance to illegitimacy, explicitly stigmatizing the children in these families on the basis of that legal status. More recently, however, those status distinctions have been minimized in favor of a model which, in theory, treats children and parental obligations as generally indistinguishable for nonmarital as well as divorced single parents.

To the extent the law eliminates the status approach and treats nonmarital children the same as marital children, nonmarital single-parent families are subject to the interconnected structures of family law, employment law, and welfare law which shape the lives of divorced single-parent families. The core insight about those structures was that single parenthood is constructed within marriage, as a combination of the work and family structure plus the equality paradigms of employment and family law. The realities of inequality both in the family and the market mutually reinforce each other. Behind the shield of equality language they construct very different experiences of parenting for mothers and fathers. Those differences are evident at divorce, and construct both the different experience of single parenting for mothers and fathers, as well as the dominance of primary or sole parenting as the parenting model.

The same dynamic operates for unmarried single parents. Because it is not hidden within marriage, however, the consequences are even harsher. The same core problems exist of work and family, and highly gender-differentiated patterns of parenting. These problems are exacerbated (or, more clearly exposed) because there is no cushion of marriage within which dependency work can be done, albeit at significant cost if the marriage ends. Rather, the problems of balancing work and family, gender and race discrimination, and limited economic opportunities exist from the outset. They are made more difficult still because they are viewed as just consequences for the immoral or stupid choice of bearing children outside of marriage.

Despite these similarities, in other significant respects unmarried single parents operate within a quite different legal framework from divorced single parents. The parameters of nonmarital single parenthood are not created within marriage, in relation to another parent and in combination with work and family roles. Rather, their single parenthood is defined at its inception by their status as unmarried parents. Functionally they are most similar to widows: the absence of fathers for economic and psychological support to the mother or as caretaker to the child or children, means that the father may as well be dead. But instead of being honored and supported as are widows, nonmarital mothers are more heavily stigmatized than any other group of single parents.

The choices for unmarried mothers are limited. At the point of pregnancy or childbirth, and in the absence of adoption, the choices for the mother, if she is not self-supporting or cannot meet all child-related expenses, are establishing paternity in order to get child support, or seeking welfare, which also may require seeking paternity or assigning paternity rights as a precondition to obtaining benefits. Unmarried mothers face the same discriminatory employment structure as divorced single mothers, that is, the generally lower income that most women earn as compared to men.

For unmarried fathers, the choices are acknowledging paternity or, at present, abandoning the child with the likelihood of little legal consequence for doing so. As a practical matter, paternity is unlikely to be established, and all legal obligations flow from paternity. Unlike divorce, where the legal system has the power to impose financial and other obligations as a condition or consequence of dissolution of the marriage, with unmarried parents the law treats fathers as if they do not exist, almost as if the child was the product of immaculate conception, until a legal father voluntarily comes forward or is established by private, or usually state, action.

The single most critical statistic about nonmarital single-parent families is that paternity is established for only 30 percent of nonmarital children. Paternity is a critical precondition to several legal entitlements. The high rate of unestablished paternity means that a disproportionate number of nonmarital children are denied minimal support. For children, this means that they are granted equality with marital children in name only. The structure for unwed parents operates under the guise of gender neutrality and purported equality. The purported equality here is that between married and unmarried parents, and between mothers and fathers. The realities, however, are as distant from theory here as are the realities of postdivorce families, although they operate in a different fashion.

The most common economic pattern for nonmarital single parents is that the mother generates a low income, the father provides no economic or other support, and the welfare system provides below-poverty-line benefits to the family. Compared to divorced single-parent families, the nonmarital single parent is more likely to remain unmarried, the children are more likely to remain within a single-parent household for a long period, and the likelihood of family poverty is greater. Fathers are less likely than divorced fathers to provide support and unlikely to provide any nurturing.

The legal system makes it easier to have an abortion or place a child for adoption than to parent as a single parent. If an unmarried mother decides to parent, the legal structure paradoxically in some cases *discourages* marriage where the prospective spouse lacks significant employment opportunities, because marriage may disentitle one to even meager AFDC benefits. This result especially impacts women and men of color who are disproportionately disadvantaged in the wage labor market. If an unmarried father decides to parent, the legal structure discourages or outright prevents parenting outside of marriage.

THE CONTEXT: NONMARITAL SINGLE PARENTS

General Characteristics

The increase in nonmarital families over the past twenty years has been striking. According to a 1989 report, 4.7 million or 30 percent of children lived with a never-married parent (Saluter 1989).[1] Childbearing among never-married women is at record levels. The rate of nonmarital childbearing is higher for Blacks than for whites, but increases in the rate of nonmarital childbearing have been greater and faster for white women.

To some extent, of course, not all of those counted as nonmarital single-parent families in fact conform to that family form; not all of these nonmarital single parents are parenting alone. Some unmarried couples, not cohabitating, marry soon after the birth of their children, or will eventually marry. An estimated 90 percent of people will marry during their lifetime, and of those who divorce, about 70 percent will remarry (Saluter 1989, 11). Other unmarried parents are cohabiting heterosexual couples, although they are counted as single parents. Three in ten cohabiting couples have children in their household (8). About 60 percent of cohabiting couples eventually marry. When cohabitants do not marry, the average duration of their relationship is eighteen months (9). Finally, those gay and lesbian couples prohibited from marrying but counted as unmarried single parents despite long-term committed relationships, are hidden within the count of nonmarital single parents.

Although single-parent families in general tend to be poor, nonmarital families are the single-parent group most likely to be poor and receiving public support. The differences in income between nonmarital families and divorced families are significant. In 1990, median family income for never-married mothers with children under the age of eighteen was $8,337, compared to $15,762 for divorced mothers with children under the age of eighteen (Bersharov 1992). Black mothers' median income in 1990 was 32 percent less than white mothers' income; divorced Black mothers earned 20 percent less than divorced white mothers. These economic circumstances translate into higher welfare usage. Just over three-quarters of unmarried adolescent mothers were likely to be on welfare within five years of the birth of their first child. Forty percent of nonmarital mothers receive welfare for ten years or more, compared to 14 percent of divorced mothers (Bersharov 1992). Welfare usage is connected to unmarried mothers' much lower rate of obtaining child support and the paltry amount received if support is ordered: only 20 percent receive child support, and the annual payment is about half of the average received by divorced mothers. All of this reflects a difference in the dynamic of poverty, but arguably it is only a more severe version of the problems of divorced single parents in general.

Severe economic constraints also affect the configuration of the household. Currently 21 percent of single parents live in extended families, versus 2 percent for two-parent families. Nonmarital single parents are more likely to live in extended families than divorced single parents. Three-quarters of single parents who live in extended families live with relatives, usually parents, the remainder with boyfriends or other nonrelatives. If given the choice, most families would opt to create their own household of parent and children (Vogejda 1992).

Never-married mothers are on average ten years younger than divorced mothers. Two-thirds of these mothers are between fifteen and twenty-four years old. Lack of education also characterizes this group (Besharov 1992). Thirty-nine percent of never-married mothers do not have a high school education. Finally, only half of these mothers are in the labor force (Lino 1994).

Teenagers

Teenagers are the focus for a great deal of the concern about nonmarital single parents (Rhode 1993). Twenty percent of female adolescents bear a child. Teenage parents are nearly evenly split between marital and nonmarital families. At the birth of their children, 42 percent of teenage mothers are married to the father, and an additional 20 to 24 percent marry the father within a year of giving birth. Only about 5 percent of teenage mothers place their babies for adoption. Approximately two-thirds of all births by teenage women are to eighteen- and nineteen-year-olds, while only 2 percent are to teenagers younger than fifteen.

Teenagers generally do not choose to become pregnant, although once pregnant they may choose to become mothers. Of all teenage mothers, 79 percent of young Black women and 84 percent of young white women did not intend to become pregnant (Thomas 1994, 83–84). Early motherhood has serious negative consequences for young women. It is especially likely to affect their educational level, which directly affects their present and future economic status.

Children in households headed by teenage single parents are likely to be poor. Four out of every five children with teenage mothers are poor. This compares to a poverty rate of 20 percent for all children, already an alarmingly high figure.

Women who become teenage single parents are more likely to be women of color. This is connected to a higher rate of teenage sexual activity, less use of contraception and abortion, and a lower rate of marriage (Rhode 1993). By age eighteen, 7 percent of white women, 14 percent of Hispanic women, and 26 percent of Black women have given birth, despite a 40 percent abortion rate for all pregnancies to women fifteen to nineteen years of age. Teenage motherhood is also more common among women from a low socioeconomic status, with low educational achievement, poor employment prospects, and relatively high rates of welfare dependence.

What is particularly important to remember about teenage single parents is that most of them are nearly in their twenties and so might best be thought of as young mothers rather than as teenage mothers; that they constitute only a small proportion of the single-parent population; and that the most obvious solution for their economic problems is education to insure better employment opportunities and self-sufficiency. Their disadvantages are correctable; they can be temporary instead of permanent. Separating the politics surrounding prevention of teen pregnancy from support of teen parents and their children accounts for the persistent difficulty in following that course.

Black Families

In analyzing the situation of unwed mothers, in addition to paying attention to teenagers it is critical to pay attention to race. Within the African American community, where single-parent families are the dominant family form, nonmarital families are the most common type of single-parent family.[2] In 1993, nearly 60 percent of Black children resided with a never-married mother, more than three times the percentage for white children. Since 1970, the proportion of Black children living with only one parent has doubled, increasing from one-third to two-thirds. The proportion of single-parent families among whites rose even more quickly during the same time period, 141 percent, as compared to an 82 percent increase for Blacks (although the increase among Blacks was from a higher initial base figure).

The increase in the number of nonmarital births among Black women is connected to an increase in the age at which Black women marry and the shorter time period they remain married, not to overall increases in the birth rate among Black women (Taylor 1990, 1001). Among Blacks in general, especially among young Blacks, marriage rates are declining, although sexual activity is high among teenagers (Taylor et al. 1990, 1003).

The dominance of single-parent families headed by women is connected to the labor force position of Black women compared to that of Black men. Thirty-four percent of Black mothers work full-time, but the majority, nearly 60 percent, are unemployed or not in the labor force (Saluter 1989). In March 1993, there were more Black women than Black men in the civilian labor force (Bennett 1995). Occupationally, a higher proportion of Black women than Black men are employed in jobs likely to bring in higher incomes, that is, managerial and professional specialty jobs. The wage gender gap between Black women and Black men is narrower than between white women and white men, with Black women earning about 75 percent of the income of Black men. This is a reflection not of less gender discrimination, but of the pervasiveness of race discrimination. The occupational pattern of Black men is strikingly different from that of white men, in terms of the proportion of Black men in the workforce, their unemployment rate, and their occupational distribution. Not surprisingly, the per capita income of the Black population is only 59 percent of that of the white population.

About half of all Black families maintained by women and about 30 percent maintained by men were poor in 1993. For female-headed families with children under age six, median income was $8,690; for households with children aged six to seventeen, $12,460. The corresponding figures for white women were almost double, $11,980 and $21,320 (Bennett 1995).

Since child support is tied to the father's income level, rather than a living standard, the average child support awarded to a Black mother is half that received by white mothers, reflecting the disadvantaged economic status of Black men. According to a 1987 report, only 36 percent of the eligible Black mothers had child support orders; of those, 73 percent received payments. White women had an award rate of 69 percent, but the degree of actual payment of support was similar to that of Black mothers.

The poverty of Black single-parent families is not dramatically different from the presence of poverty in two-parent Black families.

Divorced Black women more often than white women come from poor households; the change in family structure therefore has little impact on poverty in the household (Claude 1986, 21).[3] This is caused in large part by the labor market position of Black men, which is substantially different from that of white men. Black male participation in the workforce has declined substantially since the 1970s, and investments in education and job experience are not rewarded as highly as for white males (22). In the Black community, the feminization of poverty is matched by masculine poverty. There is a widespread problem of economic marginalization of both women and men (Brewer 1988, 334). Over half of Black female-headed families are in poverty, as compared to 15 percent of male-headed families (Taylor et al. 1990, 1005).

The strong stigma attached to Black single mothers connects to a long history of devaluing Black families as well as Black motherhood (Roberts, D. 1991, 1994; Austin 1989). Black feminist scholars in particular have been sensitive to this harsh stigma.[4] Dorothy Roberts gives three examples: the historical removal of children from their mothers during slavery; the disproportionate removal of Black children from their families for abuse and neglect; and the sterilization abuse of Black women. The treatment of Black single mothers should be added to the list. The negative popular images include sexual licentiousness, careless and incompetent mothering, dominating matriarchs, and lazy welfare mothers who refuse to work and "breed" babies in order to increase the size of their benefit check (Roberts, D. 1991, 1437). As Roberts points out, Black women have deviated from traditional female roles and for that deviation they have been strongly condemned. When a woman defies both race and gender proscriptions, she is blamed for being *too* strong. Her strength is not the rock of her family, but rather is viewed as the dangerous hazard on which the family is destroyed. This also plays into the devaluation of Black children as inferior due to the harm inflicted by matriarchy, justifying programs which punish and deter childbearing by incompetent Black mothers (Roberts 1994, 878).

It is interesting to contrast the value attached to Black women's reproductive capacity during slavery with the effort today to cut off the reproduction of Black children who are viewed as an economic drag on society (Burnham 1987, 198–99; Harris, C. 1993). The ultimate discipline for slave women was the threat of separation, from husbands and children (Burnham 1987, 201–2). The stubborn persistence of family outside the law is a testament to resistance and the strength of intimate bonds. The law viewed family as racially limited, a difference expressed in Jim Crow and perpetuated beyond Jim Crow in the treatment of different family forms today (225).

Cheryl Harris argues that the law values whiteness, and sees race as a form of valuable property which confers the right to exclude. The same right to exclude is arguably at stake in control over legal definitions of family (Harris, C. 1993). She also argues that the value of whiteness, expressly addressed in the dismantling of segregation, has been perpetuated through the refusal to deal with the consequences of segregation, thus incorporating racial privilege within supposed neutral principles (Harris, C. 1993).[5] She cites as evidence of the value of whiteness a survey by Andrew Hacker where white students were asked to set the amount they would seek if they were changed from white to black. The answer, on average, was $50 million, an implicit recognition of the value, in terms of relative advantage, of whiteness.

Single parents have been a significant family form for over a century in the African American community. There is a history of strong mothers who have raised children in their own household or as part of an extended household, as well as a history of continuing oppression of Black fathers by whites (Jones 1985). Mothers have parented successfully despite the dominant culture's overwhelmingly negative views of their mothering and their families. They have been enabled and empowered by their communities and their culture, and that model provides extraordinary insight and lessons for policy making for all single-parent families. The strengths of some single-parent families should not detract from the real problems faced by many Black mothers, and we must be careful not to recreate the stereotype of the invincible matriarch. Whether those strengths can be replicated in other cultural contexts is also unknown. But neither should we continue to ignore patterns of success despite a very hostile social structure.

We might think about single-parent families differently were we thinking about them as the dominant family form, and nonmarital single parents as the dominant form of single parenting. Imagine if we were to accord to the nonmarital single-parent family the legal support given to the married traditional nuclear family. Before envisioning that, it is important to explore the existing legal structure. The legal structure for nonmarital single parents to some extent overlaps that facing divorced single parents, and therefore shares the inadequacies of that legal framework. But because establishment of paternity triggers the availability of that framework, paternity law has critical importance for nonmarital single parents. The more severe economic crisis of nonmarital single parents also makes them more dependent on the welfare structure, and therefore that structure requires reexamination.

NONMARITAL FAMILIES AND THE LAW

The law wants nonmarital families to fail.[6] Historically, that was explicit. The older model was that nonmarital children had no legal connections, rights, or entitlements from their father unless legitimated; the child was legally solely the mother's child, a clearly disadvantaged status in an explicitly patriarchal structure; and the child was shamed for the acts of the parents, labeled a bastard for life even if later legitimated. The contemporary model of the nonmarital family is based on constitutional condemnation of differentiation between marital and nonmarital children, and child support statutes requiring support of children regardless of the parents' marital status. It is a model of parental gender equality which views mothers and fathers as substantially equal in rights and responsibilities.

But the older model persists. The equality model is a sham: gender neutrality is undercut by the difficulty of identifying fathers and the perpetuation of mothers' poverty by inadequate child support and welfare structures. So the current framework is not a model of equality, but rather of a stigmatized mother-child family, justifying the harshest economic consequences. Father absence is not decried because father presence is not expected. Illegitimacy may be a more invisible badge, but the realities of differential treatment between marital and nonmarital children maintain the stamp of inferiority.

The striking similarity in the legal and social science discourse about the "problem" with both never-married and divorced single-parent families, as Professor Martha Fineman has pointed out, is the identification of the problem as the absence of a man in the family.

The focus of legal reforms, she argues, has been to reimpose the patriarchal family, by custodial reforms in divorce and by requiring establishment of paternity for never-married women to qualify for welfare (Fineman 1991b, 281; Fineman 1991a, 1983).

For never-married mothers, however, neither in theory nor in reality is there much of an effort to truly bring the father in. Paternity is indeed the critical legal structure, because it theoretically entitles children to equivalent support to children conceived within marriage. But paternity is designed to protect fathers against mothers, to provide only limited, economic rights for children, without a vision of paternal caretaking.

Legitimation

The current legal and social policy structure replicates the history of blatant stigma attached to illegitimate children and their parents. Ancient custom dictated that an unwed pregnant woman be stoned to death, killing her unborn child as well. In Roman society, and at early common law, women were allowed to give birth, but the children were marked for life as being outside of recognized kinship bonds. Children born out of wedlock were viewed as being children of no one: filius nullius, the son of no one, or filius populi, the son of the people. Daughters were irrelevant, since they were presumed eventually to take the name of their husband. Within this expressly patriarchal system, it was the name of the father which was critical, since the father's name determined inheritance rights. Legitimation was a purely paternal right. The mother could not legitimate her child or even give the child her name. Instead, the child's name was gained by the child's reputation in the community. The child had no legal mother or father, and no legal rights.

In the sixteenth century, English common law was modified to add a criminal cause of action to permit punishment of the mother and father of an out-of-wedlock child, and either or both parents could be required to support the child. In the nineteenth century, English and American law shifted to decriminalize the status of unwed mothers and to require them to support their children. Interestingly, English law initially forbade mothers from suing putative fathers for support. The law was eventually amended to permit mothers to seek support.

Mother and child, therefore, were made the legal family unit, by granting legal custody of the child to the mother, and imposing an obligation of care for the child. This maternal preference was, according to one legal historian, based on the ability to identify the mother, and the presumption, like the tender years presumption, that a mother would be a better parent. It was completed symbolically with the mother's right to use her surname to name the child. Under this regime, the putative father was not part of the legal picture whatsoever.

Courts continue to label children born out of wedlock as illegitimate (Stier 1992). Although illegitimate children are no longer disadvantaged to the extent historically permitted, they continue to have less rights than legitimate children, and the very persistence of the status, with its pejorative connotation, expresses strong stigma toward these children. That bias is apparent in adoption, where transferring a child from a disfavored single mother to a favored two-parent marital family is the paradigm. Because the process of adoption involves the reissuance of the birth certificate, removing the name(s) of the birthparent(s) and inserting the names of the adoptive parents, this permits the stigma of illegitimacy literally to be erased. Similarly, the negative connotation of "single parent" is apparent in paternity determinations, where the legal process presumes the stereotype of the unwilling, irresponsible unwed father.

The very concept and meaning of legitimacy embody a blatant example of stigma intertwined with gender hierarchy. Legitimacy is father-controlled and father-related. Status is through the father, epitomized by the father's gift of his name to his children. Also deeply embedded in this concept is the view of children as property, property which can be "claimed" or ignored. Children's rights to support are limited to the nature of their legally recognized relationship to their father, a relationship defined purely biologically.

Legitimation has a different impact depending upon whether the father is married or unmarried, at least with respect to inheritance. Legitimation of a child by a married father, where the child is borne by a woman not married to the father, entitles the child to equivalent inheritance rights to other children, but the child does not have any status with respect to property of the wife of her father. Given the irrelevance of inherited property to the support of most children in single-parent families, the focus of legitimation on access to property at death is largely meaningless (or perhaps only interesting for its symbolic statement).

The reform of this structure has been quite recent. Under the guise of gender neutrality and elimination of historic discrimination against illegitimate children, in some states the formal legal structure has eliminated distinctions between marital and nonmarital children, between fathers and mothers, and between married and unmarried parents. The reform moves toward treating nonmarital children the same as divorced children and making all single parents fit the divorce model.

Theoretically, this represents a radical shift in status and treatment of these children. As a practical matter, however, the enormous gulf between the treatment of marital and nonmarital children persists. Partly this may be because the presumptions of similarity are insupportable. The structure of nonmarital relationships is quite different from that of divorce, and most notably the rate of male rejection of responsibility for their children is strikingly high for nonmarital parents. Second, the hurdles to acknowledging paternity and therefore being an economic parent are quite high. Third, expectations of more than economic parenthood are quite low. The presumption of mother custody and father absence is more explicit.

The pattern of deeper deprivation is repeated with child support. While the overall picture for child support is abysmal, it is even worse for women with nonmarital children. In 1989, women who had been previously married were *three times* more likely to have a support order than women who had never married, 72 percent versus 24 percent (Bureau of the Census 1992). The amount of the average award is low, but it is even lower for nonmarital women. In 1989 the average annual support payment was just under $3,000; for nonmarital mothers, it was $1,888 (Bureau of Census 1992).

One final perhaps obvious difference between non-marital and divorced single parents is that there is no property division, however meager, that might provide even short-term financial support for the caregiving parent. The identified problems of property division at divorce, the unfairness and inadequacy of a one-time financial settlement and minimal ongoing support, are magnified for nonmarital families. Obviously, any effort to replicate the divorced single-parent family can only achieve what the limits of the divorce framework permit, which I have demonstrated is itself inadequate for the vast majority of single parents. Parity or equality with marital families is then only an equal opportunity to be a little less poor, but no guarantee of real support. Finally, with respect to custody and visitation, anecdotal evidence suggests an even more pronounced extreme of the divorce pattern of paternal noninvolvement.

Paternity

Paternity law is a glaring example of a place where the law discourages fathering, perpetuates second-class status for nonmarital children, and devalues mothers. The rate of paternity establishment for nonmarital children has remained steady at approximately 30 percent of all nonmarital births (Wattenberg 1993, 214). The rates by state range from a high of 67 percent in Michigan to a low of 14 percent in Louisiana and 20 percent in New York (Wattenberg 1993, 215). *Over two-thirds of nonmarital children have no legally recognized father.* That is a stunning figure. For those children, they are formally acknowledged to have only one parent who provides all psychological, social, and economic support.

The majority of unwed mothers must operate both legally and socially without a father in the picture. For these single-parent families, the analogy to widows seems very clear. It is particularly the case if one defines the family from the perspective of the child or children, and their needs.

Although the protection of fathers' rights has increased, there has been an amazing continuation of the common law tradition that an unmarried putative father owes no legal duty to his child and in effect is a "stranger" to the child. The fathers' rights cases, for example, all focus on the nature of the father's rights when the child is born out of wedlock, particularly in cases of adoption. They require that the father seize the opportunity of parenting afforded by the biological tie, in order to claim rights which may conflict with those of the mother or of other third parties. These cases see the biological connection as presenting an opportunity, one that is presumed to be present. The biological connection entitles the father to develop a parent-child relationship, regardless of his relationship to the mother. This case law also sees the father's decision as a choice, not as a responsibility. At least one scholar has suggested that the father's opportunity is really seen in terms of the mother, not in terms of the child; the opportunity is to pursue marriage or a committed relationship with the mother, thereby replicating the traditional two-parent family (Dolgin 1994). The opportunity also is defined in relation to other men: the "biological connection . . . offers the natural father an opportunity that no other male possesses" (*Lehr v. Robinson* 1983, 262).

Unmarried putative fathers are treated differently from married putative fathers. Married fathers are presumed to be the father of children born to their wives during marriage, and the U.S. Supreme Court has upheld that presumption by focusing on the marital relationship, not on the child's perspective nor the mother's perspective. In *Michael H. v. Gerald D.* (1989), a single father sought to maintain his relationship with his biological child, born as the result of a love affair with a married woman. Although cast within the framework of evidentiary rules and presumptions, the case seemed to rest on seeing the issue as the opposition between the single father and the marriage, or the threat to the marriage by an ongoing relationship with the child by the biological father. The stigmatized single father, further morally reprehensible because of his interference with the marital relationship, had no chance to recast his request as one to expand and enrich the relationships of the child against this view of his presence as a detriment to the marriage, and therefore to the child.

The process of establishing paternity is not inherently difficult, given genetic testing which can exclude a man not the father in more than 99 percent of cases, for a cost ranging from a low of $150 to a high of $500–$600.[7] More accurate DNA testing ranges from $550 to $870. If a deposition is required, it can usually be completed for $200; if an expert is needed to testify at trial, the cost is usually $1,200 per day plus expenses.[8]

Paternity can be established voluntarily or involuntarily. The father can acknowledge paternity in most states by a statement filed under oath with the court or the vital statistics bureau. A father claiming paternity based on a biological connection is a "putative father." Under the uniform paternity act, and many state laws, an unmarried father may also become a "presumed" father by "receiving the child into his home and hold[ing] out the child as his natural child" (Uniform Parentage Act 1973).

Paternity establishment is time-consuming and the rate of establishment remains stubbornly low. One study identified the quasi-criminal or criminal nature of some proceedings, triggering height-ened procedural and evidentiary standards which slow the process (Williams and Williams 1989).[9] In some jurisdictions, where several hearings may precede a jury trial, it may take as long as nine months for each of up to four hearings, and another year before the case goes to trial (3). Even with respect to voluntary acknowledgement, many existing procedures are cumbersome and invasive.

The disincentives to establishing paternity lie both with these structural barriers and limited commitment of public funds. The state brings most paternity actions, and the state contracts for most paternity testing. Even with a legal structure which facilitates and streamlines the establishment of paternity, if public resources are not committed to this goal, then the rate will remain low. One sampling of the states in the late 1980s indicated a range of paternity establishment from under 2 percent to 50 percent (Williams and Williams 1989).

Anyone other than the child must file a paternity action within three years of the birth of the child, under the uniform act; the child has a longer statute of limitations which expires three years after the child reaches majority. That timing is interesting: it limits the number of claims significantly. The likelihood that a child would have the knowledge or resources to pursue a claim seems very low, while at the same time this greatly limits the actions which can be taken on their behalf by adults. It suggests that the mother is allowed a choice of whether to pursue paternity. That would be consistent with the statutory framework of some states which requires the mother's consent to allow the action to go forward. That framework appears to be common in the majority of jurisdictions, which do not follow the Uniform Parentage Act.

Paternity establishment should be in the process of transition to more streamlined processes under the requirements of the Omnibus Budget Reconciliation Act of 1993 (OBRA), which requires states to establish simple civil processes for *voluntary* establishment of paternity, to be available at the time of birth and after birth, in and out of the hospital (*42 U.S.C. 666 et seq*). The programs are to be in place by January 1995. The voluntary acknowledgment can be treated by the states as conclusive or as a rebuttable presumption. Court action will nevertheless still be required to establish paternity.

Involuntary/contested paternity processes are also governed by OBRA 93. The statute requires the states to legislate that genetic testing demonstrating a high probability that a man is the father will establish a conclusive or rebuttable presumption of paternity. Alternatively, the statute requires enactment of a process to establish paternity by default after service and notice of default.

Involuntary paternity proceedings can be initiated by the mother or by the state. The mother may use a private lawyer to establish paternity and obtain a support order. In the alternative, she can request the state child-support enforcement agency for assistance. The state can collect a fee and costs for benefits which it obtains. States have the option of setting up a program so that support is paid to the state and distributed, rather than creating a state role reserved solely for back payments.

If the mother has filed for AFDC benefits, she is *required* to assign payment rights to the state under Section IV-D of the Social Security Act. The state then theoretically establishes paternity and enforces support, which, after the first $50 paid, is then deducted from AFDC. The model is that AFDC provides necessary family support only until child support can be established and replaces welfare as the long-term economic solution for single-parent families.

The reality, however, is that the advent of the child support/ AFDC model has not resulted in a significant increase in paternity determinations or in the payment of support. According to one report, nearly two-thirds of welfare benefit claimants in a six-month period had valid reasons for not cooperating in the search for the father; of those alleging good cause, nearly two-thirds claimed a threat of physical harm either to the child or to themselves as the reason (*Social Security Bulletin* 1983, 7). The low rate of AFDC paternity determinations appears to be happening for several reasons. First, the mothers legitimately fear the consequences of naming the father and either lie or withhold information. Second, even where information is provided, there is little incentive to pursue the fathers because of their perceived inability to pay, and the lack of incentives in the structure which reward the establishment of paternity separate from its consequences for economic support. Third, given the limitations of welfare benefits, mothers may do better not to lead the bureaucracy to the father, if the father will continue informally to provide support; the mother can then combine under-the-table contributions from the father with meager welfare benefits. This may be a reasonable quid pro quo for fathers who fear the long-term consequences of a legal support order.

A recent study of two large Arizona counties indicated that 70 percent of paternity cases were brought under the AFDC process. The process is slow; less than 6 percent of the cases opened during 1988 and 1989 had established paternity by 1991. Where paternity had been established, 87 percent of the fathers were employed, compared with 62 percent of putative fathers. The study also indicated that 36 percent of the fathers whose paternity was not adjudicated were in prison.

The steps necessary to establish paternity are especially interesting in light of what we know about the relationship between the parents at the time of birth. According to one survey of 334 unwed parents, most of the children were not conceived in casual encounters (Wattenberg 1993, 10). Half the fathers lived with the mother before the birth of the child, and one-quarter of the fathers were still cohabiting with the mother when the child was one year or less. Approximately two thirds of the fathers were present at the births of their children. According to another researcher, nearly 85 percent of fathers who do not marry the mothers of their children continue their relationship with the mother during the pregnancy, but this drops to 64 percent two years after the birth, and to 55 percent three years after the birth (Williams and Williams 1989).

These patterns are significant because some states have established voluntary paternity procedures in hospitals, with a success rate as high as 40 percent voluntary acknowledgment of paternity before the child and mother were discharged. In one program studied there was a significant race differential between those putative fathers provided with a declaration of parentage form: 62 percent of white fathers were presented with the form, but only 41 percent of Black fathers (Wattenberg 1993, 226).[10] In the same study, only about 15 percent of the men stated that they disavowed fatherhood, so a high proportion of fathers acknowledged their fatherhood privately to the mother, even if not legally. A very high rate of the fathers in the study saw their children to some extent after their birth: 84 percent of Black fathers, and 78 percent of white fathers. This connection with their children raises fascinating questions about how the connection is viewed and the distinctive characteristics of male and female nonmarital single parenting.

The legal establishment of paternity entitles the child to a range of economic support. In addition to child support, the child has the right to other benefits which derive from the father, including social security payments, veteran's benefits, worker's compensation, and health benefits. The establishment of paternity may also provide access to family medical history. Finally, paternity can provide rights to custody and visitation, or, in the alternative, can confer the right to voluntarily surrender parental rights in an adoption.

The establishment of paternity is also a prerequisite to rights of custody or visitation. Under the Uniform Parentage Act, there is a list of factors to be taken into consideration to determine whether and to what extent a social/psychological relationship should be permitted. The relationship is not presumed; under the Uniform Act, the father's paternity does not entitle him to a relationship in the same manner that marriage is presumed to entitle him to establish or preserve some noneconomic relationship. In order to be entitled to visitation, a putative father must take some steps to acknowledge the child by developing an emotional relationship or providing financial support. It seems clear that visitation and custody are not encouraged, but there are very little empirical data to confirm or challenge the anecdotal evidence.

The paternity structure, and its concept of fathering, is a strong disincentive to alternative family forms. Preserving or creating the opportunity (right?) for a relationship is sacrificed due to lack of marriage. Another way to think of this is that the mother should not be subject to the same constraints or required to be part of the same legally constructed "family" when the father was not willing to establish a marital relationship. But that sacrifices the child's potential gain of another adult relationship in order to preserve the independence and choices of adults.

This structure makes it very difficult to support a single-parent family qua single-parent family. Instead, the consequence of the failure to form a "real" family is to discount and discourage relationships, economic or otherwise, to support this family form.

If the benefits for widows were available to nonmarital single parents, those benefits would be roughly double the benefits currently paid on welfare. Social security benefits include both a benefit to the surviving caretaker parent and a separate benefit to the children, adjusted according to the number of children. The basic formula under social security is that the surviving spouse of a fully insured worker caring for a child under sixteen may collect 75 percent of the amount the worker would have received had he or she retired. The spouse's benefits are only paid until the youngest child reaches age sixteen, although the child's benefits continue until the age of eighteen or nineteen. The caretaker is not then eligible for further benefits until age sixty, at which time he or she can receive 100 percent of the benefits which would have been due to the deceased worker had that worker lived to the age of retirement (O'Connell 1993). The downside to this system is that the eligibility requirements for benefits may disproportionately impact young single parents, and the differentials in the amount of the benefits which are based on the income of the deceased worker.[11]

Welfare

Because the paternity rate is so low, access to the child support or widow support structures is denied for the majority of nonmarital single parents. Their most critical legal support structure is the structure of welfare. The situation and treatment of nonmarital mothers on welfare demonstrates the severe consequences deemed justified by rationalizations based on stigma. The complexities of welfare merit close analysis here, because welfare is the most powerful legal structure in the lives of nonmarital single parents.

Welfare reform particularly targets nonmarital single parents, although its provisions will equally impact divorced single parents. The underlying analysis of the bill is that marriage, or rather lack of marriage, is the cause of poverty. In addition, poverty programs support the failure to marry and continue the cycle. Welfare, then, encourages the creation of single-parent families, and that creates more poverty. The solution, then, is to diminish welfare support and encourage marriage as the solution to poverty. In order to accomplish those goals, the proposed legislation does several things. It eliminates entitlement to support and shifts funding to bloc grants, with the amount of the grants fixed and capped, thereby refusing to provide support according to need, and to provide support at all for some in need. Depending upon the bill, the legislation discourages or denies benefits to teenagers, mothers who have additional children while on welfare, children whose paternity is not established, and those who have collected benefits for a certain period of time (House Report 4 1995).[12]

What puts women on welfare and keeps them there is women's low pay for women's work, and lack of care and security for their children. In order to qualify for welfare, there must not simply be a gap between income and expenses, but rather significant poverty. The eligibility requirements stipulate the depletion of resources which might be helpful in increasing employment opportunities, particularly the availability of transportation. In addition, payments of child support and even more so, income from employment, are highly taxed, arguably penalized, by the existing structure of the welfare system.

For example, in Florida as of mid-1995 the claimant's total assets could not exceed $1,000, plus a car valued at less than $1,500. Earnings on average could not exceed $570 per month. Every dollar of income from wage work is deducted from the benefit amount. The benefit amount, however, is quite low; for example, in Florida the maximum AFDC grant for a family of three is $303 per month (Committee on Ways and Means 1993).

Welfare on average covers only slightly over *half* of income needs, requiring most welfare mothers to work off the books in order to survive (Meucci 1992, 65). In 1992 Christopher Jencks estimated that in the absence of noncash benefits, single mothers need $15,000 per year to pay for essentials (Jencks 1992). This need is far more than what one can obtain on AFDC. Few of the women on welfare can earn that much if they leave AFDC; it is more realistic to expect them to earn $10,000 to $11,000, Jencks estimated, still leaving an annual gap of $4,000 to $5,000. The gap might be closed by payment of child support, but fathers typically do not make a large income and under then-current guidelines, might only be ordered to pay an average child support payment of $2,000 annually. For nonmarital single parents, there may be no child support in the absence of established paternity. Even with child support, the mother will need an additional $2,000 to $3,000 per year of public support (Jencks 1992). More support is needed if the mother cannot find work, cannot find full-time work, or is not paid child support. The impact of welfare reform will be to remove the net entirely and subject poor women to free-fall. Jencks has estimated that a two-year time limit would cut the number of recipients by 70 percent.

Most welfare recipients do wage work, many of them off the books, to deal with the gap between welfare benefits and family needs. Single parents in general have a high rate of labor force participation. *Those most likely to leave welfare when they begin wage work are nonmarital single mothers.* Divorced mothers are more likely to combine work and welfare. At any point in time, about one-third of welfare mothers are working; over time, about one-half have some labor market contact; work is the dominant means out of welfare. Investments in education have greater value than investments in work experience in mothers' ability to get off of welfare. Raising a family on welfare does not destroy the work ethic: a high proportion (81 percent) of the daughters of women who are "highly dependent" on welfare, that is, on welfare for more than seven years, do *not* live off the welfare rolls (Bray 1992, 5).

The presumptions of the welfare system, that single parents are lazy or that after a temporary transition they could find work sufficient to support their family, are simply unsupported. The ability to place responsibility for maldistribution of resources on single parents is possible only by believing in the justifications for stigma.

It is also important to note that the welfare system, according to the studies, has little or nothing to do with the rate of marriage (McLanahan and Sandefur 1994; Furstenberg and Cherlin 1991). Welfare benefits may enable divorced mothers to move out of their parents' house, or lessen the pressure to remarry. The system does impose a penalty on marriage in the sense that marriage may legally connect the welfare recipient and another adult, and their resulting combined income may exceed the allowed limit. Not marrying may preserve the ability to pool more resources.

The failure to marry may, however, simply reflect the decline of marital prospects, and a greater likelihood of working your way off welfare. Poor single moms are not good marriage prospects themselves, and in addition find it difficult to connect with men who can contribute economically and otherwise to the family (Harris, K. 1993, 322).

Just as there is little or no impact of welfare on the rate of marriage, there is little or no impact on the rate of childbirth (Handler 1994). Yet the myth that it affects both is widespread. Our policy of justifying punitive policy toward these single parents in particular is simply not borne out by the facts; that is, people do not have children to get benefits, so the existing structure does not foster the creation of single-parent families, and better support of single-parent families should not be resisted on those grounds.

It should be emphasized that the attack on women's dependence on welfare does not extend to women's dependence generally. The pathological label attached to poor women on welfare is not attached to poor women dependent on a husband within marriage. To the contrary, the welfare reform rhetoric clearly views dependence on a spouse (marriage) as healthy; it is dependence on the state that is not (Murray 1995).

In addition to the inadequacies of wage work, the welfare structure increasingly takes less and less account of dependency work. Single mothers are expected to work, despite the fact that the workplace structure does not accommodate parenting and despite the significant costs of even low-quality childcare. Non-welfare-dependent mothers are not engaged in full-time work. About one-third of married mothers work full-time full-year; of those who work, only 23 percent have children under three. So if welfare moms are permitted to do what marital moms do, that would allow significant parental presence of the mother as a primary parent (Segal 1992, 32). Some research also indicates that when mothers work, children are more likely to gain the model of work, which supports the value of part-time or flexible work, versus full-time mothering, as a positive role model for children (33). All of this would support a part-time work option, with benefits to provide additional support.

As Martha Minow asks, does it make sense to provide childcare for the youngest children, or would it make more sense for the mother to take care of the child at home? Even more important, is the vision one of temporary dependency, with the goal of economic self-sufficiency? Is there a valued place for caretakers of children (Minow 1994)?

The economic consequences of nonmarital parenting would seem to lead in the direction of marriage; the rapid rise in nonmarital parenting (plus the rise in divorce) suggests a revolutionary change, I think, or resistance, despite the strong condemnation and disincentives to the contrary. The position of nonmarital single mothers also exposes the gendered causes of women's impoverishment, and its difference from men's impoverishment, as well as distinctions between patterns of poverty by race and gender when looking at the Black community. A realistic ability to be self-supporting would have to deal with the context of work in the lives of the women on welfare. Current structures particularly fail most to help women with the lowest incomes (Parker 1994).

It is apparent that a single income is insufficient in most instances to combine with parenting. So the challenge is to maximize economic resources while admitting that for many single parents, wage-connected resources will be insufficient; to maximize child support resources, with a government guarantee of support if paternity cannot be established or if the father is unable to pay; and to introduce a means-based child allowance, as well as housing or some form of housing allowance. If two parents in one household can generate enough income to raise children, or in some cases one male parent can generate enough income, but a female parent cannot, then in my view the immediate goal has to be redistribution plus subsidy, while a more long-term goal would be a radical change in the workplace to insure a "family wage" by which every parent could unilaterally support a family, and reconfiguring the balance of work and family to one of family (first) and work (second). The economic disadvantage of minority men cannot be ignored in the process, and must be factored in here.

In the current harsh political climate, reform of the welfare structure must combat the propositions that first, we need not take care of all children; and second, that poverty is not so bad. But perhaps most significantly, we have to argue that single-parent families should be supported as families of value and worth. Critical to that enterprise is demonstrating not only that stigma has no basis and only does harm, but also that single-parent families have unique characteristics, positive attributes which can contribute to all families.

CHAPTER 5

Single Parents as Positive Role Models

One of my strongest, and most surprising, memories from the first year of my daughter's life was the number of times that people would say, "Oh, how can you do it by yourself?" but then return to say, "Ah, how lucky you are to be doing it alone." These utterly opposite responses used to stun me. But then it began to make sense. What made me so "lucky," in their eyes, was that by parenting alone I could parent without negotiation, consultation, or conflict with a partner. I have help and support, but the parenting of my children is done largely on my terms. But my sense was and is that this was not the meaning of their comments. Rather, it was that the benefit of parenting alone is that you are not torn between your children and your intimate partner, nor are you trying to maintain your relationship with your partner at a time when it feels that all of your attention must or should go to your children.

I often get a different set of responses from other single parents.

The idea that one might chose, in the sense and manner that I chose, to be a single parent, was stupefying to some. But the other response which I often got was emotional solidarity: sympathy for what is difficult about single parenting, and affirmation that this is very satisfying and unique parenting. You are a pioneer, seemed to be the message. It's hard being out there, but incredibly satisfying and wonderful too.

Despite the fact that single-parent families operate within an environment which expects to see them fail and despite their undeniable problems, we can nevertheless discern a remarkable story of success within these families, and we can identify distinctive patterns of parenting and family dynamics. The successes of single-parent families suggest not only the value of this family form but also its distinctiveness. The strength of single-parent families is surely the strongest rationale to remove stigma and provide support, by the legal structure and other structures as well. The affirmative lessons such families teach have something to teach other families, and may inform legal structures which affect families of all forms. The families who have the most to teach are arguably those who have faced and overcome the greatest obstacles, those led by African American women. In this chapter I outline the findings about Black single parents first, followed by a summary of the research on single-parent families in general.

BLACK SINGLE MOTHERS AND THEIR FAMILIES

In three-quarters of families headed by Black women, the women are identified as the head of the family; in the remaining quarter, the mother lives within another family as a subfamily (Malson 1986, 6). Two economic patterns are prevalent for Black mothers: AFDC-dependent households, and households dependent on wages and salaries. Overall, the majority of Black women maintaining households are in the paid workforce, with higher participation for women with children under the ages of eighteen. Black women's earnings are lower than white women's earnings, however, because Black women are usually younger, less experienced, less educated, and have more dependent children than white women (6).[1]

The range of economic resources and household configurations is mirrored in one study which identifies two typical Black mothers. One is an older, middle-class woman capable of supporting herself and three or four children, living in her own or a rented home in a Black or integrated neighborhood. The other paradigm is a younger, working-class woman managing to support the same size family with public assistance and work, often off the books, living in a rental apartment in a transitional neighborhood (Peters 1981).

Young Black mothers operate within a fundamentally different framework than young white mothers. It is young white mothers who are usually devastated by single parenthood, at least in part because they lack strong self-image and community support.[2] Despite the greater economic challenges faced by most Black single mothers, Black mothers are often a model of independence, satisfaction, and strength. As a group, they are frequently characterized by a mothering style of strength without dominance or abuse of power. That this has occurred in the context of race and gender oppression, coupled with strong criticism of Black families, is a testament to their culture (especially the socialization of Black girls and women, and positive role models of mothering), community support, and social structures (especially extended family structures).

As a group, Black women are self-reliant and self-confident. They see themselves as autonomous and independent (Peters 1986, 169).[3] One study of Black mothers described their perspective on family life as one of "heartiness, strength and resiliency . . . struggling and not dependent, . . . proactive and not reactive, . . . involved on a daily basis in trying to solve the problems" (Malson 1986, 1). A number of studies document the better emotional adjustment of Black women than white women to single parenthood (McKenry and Fine 1993). Black mothers have higher self-esteem and "inner directedness" than white mothers. The parenting practices of both racial groups are quite similar, so the difference is not tied to parenting differences, but rather to Black mothers' expectations of themselves and their children, and to the realization of those expectations (Jacobsen and Binger 1991). Black mothers have higher expectations of their children being independent, having higher emotional self-control, and doing what parents ask. Black mothers perceive themselves as successfully exercising authority and achieving high expectations. Their self-perception also correlates with less traditionally sex-typed expectations and behaviors (McKenry and Fine 1993, 61). One study hypothesized that Black mothers may have a higher sense of self-esteem because of the support of their families and lack of stigma surrounding single parents in the Black community. "Children tend to be valued regardless of their parentage and their personal achievements" (107). Nonmarital children usually develop normally, particularly when they are supported by the structure of an extended family (Hill 1971). Another factor may be a culture that is committed to well-paid work for women and egalitarian relationships between husband and wife, but also recognizes the likelihood that women may spend some of their time as single parents (Peters 1986).

The success of contemporary Black mothers despite enormous odds is grounded in a paradoxical history of deprivation and extraordinary survival. Historian Jacqueline Jones (1985) has eloquently captured this ironic interplay in the historical record. On the one hand, there were, and are, legally enforced structures which have prevented marital, two-parent family formation: separation of Black family groups during slavery, underemployment and unemployment of Black men, and the nature of available wage work for Black women. Intertwined with this history of disruption of Black families, however, is a coexisting history of strong nuclear and extended family structures with distinctive characteristics as compared to dominant cultural models. Thus, Black families characteristically demonstrate greater flexibility in gender roles, rely upon extended family and community support systems, and have strong work and religious orientations. Key characteristics focused on by Black culture include collectivism, cooperation, obligation, sharing, and reciprocity.

Families headed by Black women exhibit an alternative family structure, not a deviant family structure, which draws upon this value structure, as well as upon social and historical traditions (Malson 1986, 2–4). African Americans are twice as likely to live in an extended family structure, with grandmothers most commonly part of that structure (Ford et al. 1991, 72). Among Blacks the extended family is a more common family form among all marital groups than among whites (44 percent vs 11 percent), and whites are more likely to live significant distances from closest kin (26 percent vs 16 percent) (Hogan et al. 1990). Support for single parenting in the

Black community arises from this structure, and includes help with childcare and household tasks, as welll as money.[4]

The extended family structure is not, however, a cure-all. The support provided by family and community is not enough to lift the Black mother out of poverty, reflecting the limitations of noneconomic support. For example, arranging for adequate childcare has been more difficult for Black single mothers, only one-quarter of whom have adequate care, compared to the most advantaged, married white mothers, two-thirds of whom have adequate care. Blacks more often than whites use unpaid care, and more often use kin, but the assistance of extended family cannot totally close the gap. According to one 1990 study, living in an extended family had no impact on the wage work behavior of divorced white mothers, but did increase the likelihood of work by both Black and white nonmarital mothers. Extended family also helped ease the burden of preschool-aged children for Black mothers (Rexroat 1990). In another study in role strain, although religious support and extended kin support were important, the factor that most affected the sense of role strain, especially parental role strain, was the presence of a supportive partner (Lewis 1989).

Just as Black mothers often demonstrate stronger self-esteem and an alternative model of mothering, in one respect Black fathers also demonstrate a positive model of fathering which extends the concept of fathering beyond the economic father. Although rarely studied, Black fathers demonstrate a record of involvement with their children (Taylor et al. 1990, 996). Their involvement is without regard to legal status; some of the most involved fathers have not legally claimed paternity, often tied to fear of thereby disqualifying or reducing welfare benefits to the mother. In instances where fathers cannot economically provide support, their involvement includes services or in-kind contributions. Black men often embody a model of noneconomic fathering that demonstrates the maintenance of nurturing without formal legal ties.

One must be careful not to romanticize or essentialize the strengths of Black women, or the nurturing and care by Black men. Strength and care out of adversity can easily become an argument for a "benefits of poverty" argument. In addition, one has to be careful that the support structure for single parents within the Black community not be misread as *creating* the preconditions for single parenting. Perhaps what most strongly refutes this view is research demonstrating the strong persistence of the two-parent nuclear marital family as an ideal amongst all single mothers. Support for single-parent families does not create single-parent families; what creates single-parent families are choices voluntarily or involuntarily made. I do not mean to suggest that creation of a single-parent family is a bad thing or to be avoided; I simply mean to emphasize that support of single-parent families is critical.

What Black families and community structures have to teach is the positive result of providing support for all children, regardless of family form. From a child's perspective, this is the core of what children need—love and acceptance, coupled with high expectations. Such structures also suggest social versus individual responsibility are valued and understood differently.

The patterns of Black mothers demonstrate the ability of women to manage multiple roles and do it well. The long history of doing so enriches our ability to draw from this experience to provide role models for white women, especially because Black women have functioned, survived, and succeeded despite layers of stigma and deviance associated with their families. If matriarchy is simply replacing patriarchy with a female face, then this is not matriarchy. The experience of Black mothers suggests doing away with the notion of a family "head" who uses power to control and dominate, and instead sees parents as functioning in a much more egalitarian, cooperative, and communal way.

The experience of Black families also demonstrates that the consequence of the dominance of single-parent families, predominantly headed by women, is not the rejection of men or the devaluing of men. The cause of the degradation of Black men is not Black women but rather racism, which is determined to keep Black men in their place. The economic patterns starkly indicate that economic resources will not come from Black men. Support must not be at their expense, but clearly additional economic support is needed.

GENERAL CHARACTERISTICS OF SINGLE-PARENT FAMILIES

Just as research on Black mothers has disputed stereotypes about Black families, more recent research on single-parent families has been fueled by curiosity about what those families reveal about family dynamics, rather than a presumption of pathological dysfunction. Many studies confirm that single-parent families are not inherently bad; when analysis takes into account economic variables and social stress, the outcomes with respect to parenting and child development are virtually indistinguishable between two-parent and single-parent families (Free 1991; Vosler and Proctor 1991; Amato and Keith 1991; Watts and Watts 1991; Turner et al. 1991; Olson and Haynes 1993).

Other research has begun to evaluate whether there are any affirmative differences between single-parent and two-parent families. What is beginning to emerge is a portrait of the dynamics of single-parent families that exposes some significant differences in family dynamics. What is particularly noticeable is the presence of a less hierarchical family dynamic, greater gender equality, and evidence of greater independence and self-esteem. The pattern evident in the families of Black mothers is replicated to a significant degree for single parents as a whole, even though white single mothers lack the comparable cultural and social support provided by the Black community and experience single parenthood as a more negative and stressful status.

Less Hierarchy, More Autonomy

Single-parent families are far less hierarchical, and far more cooperative and communal, than most two-parent marital families (Cashion 1982, 80; Hamner and Turner 1985, 172). This may reflect the needs of parents for children's assistance, and/or the consequences of mothering without a father present (or fathering without a mother present). But regardless of cause, the shift in family dynamics is remarkable and provides a model of family that operates on different assumptions and may have different outcomes. The dynamic contributes both to the independence of children and their sense of interconnection. The danger that lurks here, in the opinion of some experts, is single parents treating children as peers and imposing too much responsibility which children are emotionally unprepared to assume. The dynamic in these families certainly challenges the assumption that hierarchy is essential for achieving developmental goals.

Children in single-mother families are given more responsibility, and demonstrate higher self-esteem and aspirations than children from two-parent families (Barber and Eccles 1992, 114). Where increased responsibility is encouraged within a strong, supportive family environment, this often is very positive for children. Greater autonomy does not correspond to disengaged parenting (Kissman 1991, 25–27). One reviewer of family interaction research has suggested children may get more undivided attention in single-parent families (Mednick 1987, 197).

A Different Gender Dynamic

Single-parent families also generate a different gender dynamic, one which is more supportive of egalitarian sex roles and undermines traditional gender roles (Belchman 1982, 185; Cashion 1982, 80, 83; Adams et al. 1984, 137–40; Russell and Ellis 1991; Measell 1992). Single mothers perform multiple roles, and most significantly, in the role of family breadwinner combined with family headship, strongly challenge conventional gender roles. For both boys and girls, this has tremendous significance. Older commentators seem to suggest that this is one of the reasons single-parent families are justifiably stigmatized. In their view the girls in such families, in particular, will be "unsuitable" for marriage, because they will adopt a sex role which conflicts with traditional marriage. If marriage can only accommodate traditional assumptions about gender roles, then that conclusion may be supportable. On the other hand, this outcome also suggests that it may be the children of single-parent families who will most strongly push the lingering traditional paradigms out of the center of marriage, and continue the process of constructing true equality within marriage. Or, they may move toward some other structure that supports gender equality, celebrates gender difference, and insures gender freedom. It is interesting to speculate on what a nonpatriarchal model would be; the farthest that single parents can take us, perhaps, is to a nondominated single parent, but not to coparenting—the closest we have to that is some gay and lesbian parenting models.

Unconventional families challenge gender roles and influence gender typing both by what they say and by what they do (Weisner et al. 1994, 23). One study of children raised in single-mother families after divorce confirms that in families where mothers do full-time work outside the home, adolescents separate gender roles less at home, and all work is more perceived as equally open to women and men (Barber and Eccles 1992, 115–18). When the analysis controls for income, there was also evidence that school performance and job expectations were high; that is, when mothers do not have to worry about income, then their expectations for their children are similar to those of two-parent families (120–21). In sum, the advantages are that children may develop "a greater sense of personal responsibility and self-esteem, and girls and boys may develop less gender-role stereotyped occupational aspirations and family values, which could lead to their increased success in the labor market" (122). The impact is particularly strong on daughters, who may shift or reorient goals, and not make occupational sacrifices because of the consequences should their marriages end in divorce. Thus, economic independence is strongly reinforced, which affects occupational choices (115; Measell 1992).

Just as growing up in a single-parent family affects children, being a single parent affects the parenting behaviors of adults (Mott 1994, 99; Heath and Cavanaugh 1993). There is strong evidence of differential parenting by mothers and fathers, with mothers more egalitarian and fathers more traditional in their gender role orientations and teachings. While mothers in general may have stronger influence than fathers in two-parent families, their role is stronger in single-parent families. On the other hand, a countervailing factor is that single mothers tend to be less educated, a factor strongly associated with more traditional gender role orientation. The stronger egalitarian orientation of mothers suggests a greater egalitarianism in gender role teaching associated with greater father absence, a disturbing conclusion (Russell and Ellis 1991, 6).

The findings of one study on the impact of differential parenting or of different family structure on the sex role behavior of boys and girls are quite fascinating, suggesting a striking differential in behavior (Hilton and Haldeman 1991, 114). The children who were least sex-segregated in the household tasks they performed were daughters of single parents; but the sons of single parents were *more* sex-segregated in household tasks than the sons in two-parent households. The perception of married and single-parent mothers was that the quality of work done was about the same, although in single-parent homes the children on average spent nineteen minutes more per day on household work than did children in two-parent families (Barber and Eccles 1992). Whether mothers worked had a sex-differentiated impact: according to one study, when mothers work full-time, this correlated with higher self-esteem and goals for their daughters, as compared to the sons and daughters of unemployed single mothers (Allessandri 1992, 429).

Single-parent families are a developing, imperfect model of the families which women choose to make, rather than the families which women are often forced to live with, or unconsciously fall into. The choice of single parenthood, despite the economic consequences and strong social stigma, can be interpreted as a profound revolution in the family and a strong rejection of marriage. It is not, I think, a rejection of men. Rather, it is a rejection of patriarchy, of a system in which men are in control. Many, if not most, single mothers have men in their lives, as lovers and/or friends. The choice of single parenting is not a choice to exclude men.

Similarly, for men it is not a rejection of women. It is, rather, a rejection of the traditional male role as dictated by patriarchy, a role largely limited to economic fathering. For men, single parenting seems even more strongly to be a recasting of fatherhood. It is single-parent fathers, I would argue, who have contributed perhaps more than most other groups of fathers, to opening a dialogue in order to explore a different conception of fatherhood. What is fascinating about this process is how the legal system, by its rules and structures, pushes that dialogue and exploration toward confrontation, adversarial conflict, and woman-blaming. Instead of supporting a different notion of fathering, the legal system pushes in the direction of an either-or battle for children conceived of as parental property. The emergence of a different notion of fathering has been in spite of, not because of, the legal system.

The new fathering exemplified by single parents is a radically different model from traditional fatherhood, whether within the marital family, at divorce, or as an unwed father. Single fathers teach that men can parent as well as women *despite*, not because of, their socialization and the structure of wage work. This begs the question of what fathering might look like with different socialization and radically altered wage work structures. Perhaps the sons of single fathers and mothers will show us. Nevertheless, the model of single fathers, with sole or primary custody or as involved noncustodial parents, is a model for all men to use as they begin to challenge ingrained assumptions about fathers. Their success suggests a model for two-parent families. Their interrelationships with women suggest that an interesting comparison could be made with mother's relationships with men.

Support Networks

Single-parent families also provide models of support networks, familial and nonfamilial, which are essential to parenting. Necessity is the mother of invention. The necessity of support for caregiving and nurturing work is an inescapable fact for all parents. The single parents who function well commonly have good support networks. The strongest model is African American single-parent families, who have strong extended family patterns, stronger than in white communities. Based both on necessity and cultural traditions, in this model the child is the child of a larger community, not simply the responsibility of the parent or parents in the household. Furthermore, the structure of the child's household or immediate family is irrelevant to the child's value or the community's responsibility for the child's well-being. Extended family includes kin and nonkin, connected by ties of blood and affection. This social, communal model of parenting stands in sharp contrast to the individualistic model which pervades dominant culture and the legal structure. To the contrary, it suggests the importance of social support for all parents, regardless of their number or location or the form of family, because of the very nature of caregiving work. It also suggests an answer to the dilemma often posed by those who reject support of single parents because that support might encourage the formation of single-parent families. The answer is: *but what about the children?* The focus of the extended family model is the welfare of the children and the welfare of the group. The children come first. One can only wonder what legal structures might look like if this were part of the underlying model of family, work, and welfare law.

The model of single-parent families is of caretakers within a support structure—whether kin, friends, or paid care. The extended family is simply one form of a support structure. It has its downside in the impact of group dynamics which may prevent or deter individual advancement and thus cause the individual to leave the group

(Stack 1974). But that dynamic is a dynamic of poverty, not simply a dynamic of extended family. The extended family model suggests that the role of the husband as *doulia* can, in the single-parent family, be replaced by the presence of a strong support network. I should be quick to add, this is not simply a replacement. It is different, and not every piece can be replaced. The dynamic between partners, and between parents and children, and each with the other, is a complex and dynamic one, and constantly changing.

The traditional, and I would argue, the persistent caretaking model even within more egalitarian families is the model of a primary caretaker supported by a secondary caretaker who focuses more on the caretaker than on the children. Thus, classically, the husband is a backup to the wife who parents the children; this seems to be modified in the egalitarian model to mean an expansion of childcare help and, to a much lesser extent, some housework help. Often the support comes from paid caregivers filling the gap. The support structure as backup is also the dominant structure of single-parent families, although the form of that support structure is much more diffused than the marital model. Support for the single parent comes from extended family or friends, or from intimate partners who may or may not cohabit with the parent. The single-parent model provides an alternative that can be easily supported and which would benefit all families. We do not have a well-developed egalitarian caretaker model inside or outside of marriage. Single-parent families also illustrate the value of nonparental figures and the benefit of a model which supports maximizing the presence of loving adults in the lives of children.

The importance of support networks and the use of support networks is to a far greater degree a distinctive practice of single-parent families (Duffy 1993, 57; Kissman 1991; Olson et al. 1994; Marks and McLanahan 1993, 481). "The additional adults in these extended single-parent households may fulfill the same support and control functions carried out by many fathers in two-parent families" (Stolba and Amato 1993, 544).[5] All caregivers need a support structure; single-parent families may tend to more strongly recognize this, but they also show the way toward a different caregiving structure. Within their example is the answer to the developmental justification, which requires a daddy or another adult in the child's household.

CONCLUSION

Talking about the positive aspects of single-parent families is very threatening. It is apparent that even in countries with the best of policies toward single-parent families, there is concern that these families not be *too* well supported, because to do so would challenge the social, cultural, political, and ideological position of the heterosexual marital family. It is important to think through the implications of supporting single-parent families. From the successes and positive aspects of these families, what might we predict about them if they were supported? First, economic support would mean that they could structure their lives without poverty dictating their choices or the opportunities of their children. Second, social support would mean that the children and parents would not be stigmatized. This should go a long way toward undercutting the negative consequences of single-parent families for children. But would that be a good thing? Do we want such families to be supported?

Imagine a world in which one could choose whether to parent with a partner or not; where the sex of the partner would be irrelevant if one chose to parent with a partner; where whether one married or not was irrelevant. Imagine a world in which being a single parent was unremarkable because all parents were sufficiently supported economically and socially. Imagine a world in which the special challenges of single parenting would be addressed, and the value of single parenting acknowledged. What, then, do we imagine people would choose to do in such a world? The answer, it seems, lies in our assumptions about why people choose partners and commitment, and why some of those relationships fail; it also lies in our expectations and understanding of parenting, and whether our understanding differs when one parents outside of marriage and in spite of the lack of or breakdown of an intimate relationship. If our fear is that people would not parent together, then we have to ask why. The answer, I suspect, lies in our disquiet and trepidation about the ability of marriage to reconstruct itself. It also arises out of our awareness of the pressure to return to traditional, known, "safe" gender roles to resolve ever-deepening work-family conflict and the crisis of care for dependents.

Fear is the wrong response. It contradicts virtually everything we know about single-parent families, and particularly what we know from the positive attributes and teachings from these families. The lesson is the power of diversity, and the attraction of connection. The goal should be developing pluralistic approaches which value the richness of families, including the broad array of single-parent families. We should trust the choices of adults as most beneficial for them and their children. Anything else is paternalistic and undermined by the reality that the stigma against single parenthood is unjustified.

PART III · LAW REFORM

CHAPTER 6

Policies for
Single-Parent Families

When I have asked for recognition as a single parent, as a basis for understanding the demands on my time or my economic needs, I often fear that the response will be "well, you chose to do this." My choice somehow disentitles me to support, whereas presumably one who became a single parent involuntarily through divorce or death would be more entitled to support for this unforeseen and unwanted status. Alternatively, I have sometimes been told, "Well, we don't do that for married couples, so why should we do it for you?" I should not ask for special treatment, I am told; it is presumed that I want to be treated like all other families.

Many of the problems and quandaries of single parents are in fact similar to those faced by all families. Nevertheless, they certainly are exacerbated, especially if, as in most cases, there are no resources to substitute for the income or backup parenting of a spouse or partner. Some of the problems of single-parent families are distinctive, however, and require thinking about the particular situation of single parents. The needs of single parents require the use of both approaches in constructing policy.

These are not auspicious times to draft a policy of support for single-parent families, indeed for any family. The watchwords of current public policy about family are personal responsibility and family values. They translate into ideological support for traditional families and condemnation of unwed mothers (and by extension, all single parents). Current policy also emphasizes private support, maximizing resources for those with greater resources, and minimizing public economic support of any families, and particularly disfavored families.

I have no illusions that any of the recommendations I set forth here are likely to be followed in the present political climate. My hope is that they might be heard. At best, the ideological war can be waged; the discourse can shift. The potential for resources to shift is much less likely in the short term. Even if single-parent families were positively viewed and assisted, support for public resource redistribution is low. Furthermore, we provide very little support for families of any form or function, as is evidenced by the high and increasing rate of children in poverty. Nevertheless, it is critical, I believe, to imagine and envision what a different policy would look like, and what implications it would have for families and children.

Devising policy requires a clear sense of where we are as well as where we want to go, short term and long term. We must begin, then by assessing the lessons of the current context. What does it tell us about ongoing dynamics? Where does it tell us to direct our attention? In the first part of this chapter I extrapolate from the current context lessons that should guide policy. I begin with the fundamental premise that single-parent families deserve not only the elimination of stigma, but also affirmative support. Second, policy must pay attention to gender, race, and class differences. Third, children's perspectives and needs should be heard and valued. Fourth, we must value all single parents, whether divorced, unmarried, widowed, or separated; whether teenagers or adults; whether fathers or mothers.

In the second half of this chapter, I suggest more concrete policy goals with these premises in mind. I recommend a system of economic support which most closely adopts for all single parents the model of Social Security benefits for widows and widowers. Second, I call for support of caregiving work, both by empowering sole or primary caregivers and by providing necessary support, economic and social, for primary caregivers regardless of family form. Third, I advocate restructuring of the workplace for all parents to the extent that we expect parents to engage in wage work. Finally, I recommend replacing welfare with universal family support. These specific recommendations are grounded in the perspective that single-parent families must be specifically addressed by policy, that is, they have particular, unique needs, but that their interests are best served within universal entitlements rather than by policies solely directed to single-parent families.

LESSONS FROM WHERE WE ARE NOW

Affirmative Support of Single Parents

Perhaps the quintessential policy issue concerning single-parent families is whether to affirmatively support them. This issue must be resolved before anything else follows, since it will inform every policy decision. Current policy is a policy of active discouragement, stigma, and deterrence. It focuses primarily on economic sanctions. These economic policies are intended as disincentives to the creation of single-parent families, save for the small minority of single parents with the economic resources to overcome the negative paradigm. The most recent policy to reflect this view is time-limited welfare.

Economic discouragement has been largely unsuccessful. The formation of single-parent families has continued and increased, despite the harsh economic consequences for most parents of this form of family. These patterns sharply challenge those who argue that economics drives decision making, particularly in the family arena. The consequence of this negative policy has been not to limit the formation of single-parent families, but rather to hurt those whose conduct is not at issue—the children.

What we can learn from this phenomenon are two things. First, people create families of particular configurations largely in response to factors other than economics. The state may make it harder or easier, but the decisions are often intended and emotional, or unintended and not logically thought through. The state has enormous impact, however, on the ongoing existence of particular family forms and the organization of family, particularly the distribution of work and family responsibilities. The record of the current negative policy clearly demonstrates that. Punitive economic policies powerfully impact the lives of children in single-parent families, limiting their opportunities and life choices as well as affecting their daily lives.

Second, demographic patterns suggest that single parenting is here to stay. That single parenting is on the rise despite economic disincentives suggests that the strong positive attributes of single-parent families need to be understood. If family form means a difference in parenting and family, but not a distinction between "good" and "bad" families, then it is time to understand the benefits of single parenting as a choice of family. What we know about single-parent families suggests a very different family dynamic as well as very successful parenting. We also know that success is not a matter of form, and that problems are associated with the external context, not family structure.

The failure of a deterrence policy is not, of course, a strong argument for a policy of support. Indeed, current policy seems to take the view that the answer is to increase deterrence by more harsh consequences. The failure of a negative policy does, however, tell us that single parenting is, in many instances, seen as a better alternative than a two-parent marital family, *despite its significant disadvantages.*

A policy of support could conceivably be articulated as either a policy of neutrality or as a policy of affirmative support. Under a *neutrality or tolerance model,* the negative, stigmatizing policy approach would be dismantled. As I argue at greater length in the next chapter, there are strong legal arguments for state neutrality toward family form based on principles of privacy, freedom, and pluralism. Neutrality is a policy which honors individual choices.

In practice, given the context in which single-parent families operate, neutrality would be simply a less negative form of state policy, one of ignoring the issues unique to single parents or exacerbated for single parents, rather than the current policy of active, negative public policy with the goal of deterring or undermining such a family form. Even were we to abolish all legal preferences for

marital families, the context in which all families operate disproportionately hurts single-parent families. Most significantly, the problems of balancing work and family are exacerbated beyond the double shift of women doing wage work for a two-parent family, and
the problems of race discrimination are magnified. A neutrality
policy would at best represent a tolerance policy. The consequence of
eliminating negative structures would be a begrudging tolerance of
single parents: if you can be as good as two-parent families, or reach
some minimum standard of acceptable family behavior or function,
then your family will not be actively punished or sanctioned because
of its form.

A *policy of affirmative support* would go beyond dismantling
existing negative policy structures and actively support single-parent
families. It would recognize single-parent families as a viable and
valued family form. The premises for such affirmative support are
simple. First, single-parent families should be supported as a family
form because that structure works. Second, and interrelated with the
first, a policy of affirmative support is one that values children. It
simply should not matter what form of family a child is in; that
family should be supported, because of the critical role that family
plays in the child's development. Third, supporting single-parent
families supports private choices while insuring social support.
Fourth, supporting single parents values the families of all ethnic,
racial, and gender configurations, insuring the most basic and fundamental of opportunity structures.

Support for this exercise of freedom and choice is inextricably
intertwined with gender and race equality. The gender explanation
for the creation of single-parent families, when viewed from the
perspective of single mothers, is the choice to parent alone outside of
the power dynamics conventionally present in two-parent heterosexual relationships. It also means that parenting as partners may begin
from a different threshold than when it is assumed that two parents
are essential. Single parenting, then, is a challenge to gender partnerships. It is a challenge both because it is read as a rejection of
partnership with a man, and/or because it is read as supporting a
different configuration of paired parenting. If women do not need
men in order to parent, then those partnerships must be created and
sustained by some other dynamic. That thesis should be, I believe,
tremendously liberating. But I recognize that for some it may well

be very threatening because it changes often unacknowledged patterns within adult relationships.

The gender perspective when seen from the viewpoint of single fathers is somewhat different, but similarly liberating. From the perspective of single fathers, parenting alone rejects economic parenting and embraces mothering as a model for parenting. Whether explicit or not, this adoption of a female model, combined with its implicit critique of capitalist labor market structures, challenges conventional gender and social hierarchies. If all fathers parented like those single fathers who parent like mothers, it would force radical change in the wage labor market. The adoption of a female model would value what has been both romanticized and trivialized as women's work. It would also require rejection of the current model of fathering, a model tied to economic breadwinner and disassociation from children.

When race is considered with gender, what is apparent is that the choice of single parenthood by African American women also includes a rejection of dual parenting where conventional gender roles are reversed, that is, where the man cannot contribute to family income, or cannot contribute a nearly equal or superior economic share. This is reflected in the disproportionate share of nonmarital families in the African American community. This is not unique to the African American community; the same dynamic operates across race lines. But it is more common in the African American community, where maleness does not mean economic privilege and power generally available to white men. For Black men, the intersection of race and gender is not a mixed blessing of benefit and burden, or a double benefit as for white males, but a double burden that makes the choice of single parenting most often an involuntary choice dictated by circumstances.

The support of single-parent families is grounded on principles of freedom and choice that are essential to the equality of children. Supporting single-parent families will help break down the inequalities of two-parent families. What we know about single-parent families demonstrates their ability to function in that critical role for children. The problems which single-parent families face are not problems of their making, and solutions to their problems are largely beyond individual capabilities, as they relate to structural inequities which require massive change, not simply better individual decision making. An investment in and support of functioning families more than pays off in social benefits, beyond their intrinsic worth, simply because children deserve them.

Support will not necessarily mean encouragement. Even if comprehensive and sufficient policies of support were implemented, it would not mean the end of two-parent families nor accelerated growth of single-parent families. First, decisions about the structure of family simply are not decisions which law controls. The fine line between support and encouragement exists elsewhere within our system. Providing health care support does not encourage illness; providing disability support does not encourage permanent injury.

Yet another reason support of single-parent families will not encourage the formation of single-parent families is that the two-parent marital family ideal is too strongly entrenched to be overcome by family support mechanisms. The strength of the cultural preference is seen in the reconstruction of two-parent families in the gay and lesbian community, and in heterosexual cohabitation. Extended families do not reject the two-parent model, but rather enfold it within a multiple parent structure. Cultural and religious preference as well as personal desire for meaningful intimacy all support the perpetuation of the two-parent family as the ideal. As one student of mine put it, certainly single parenting would not be anyone's first choice. Of course not. This is so because of the powerful cultural support of marriage and the understanding that parenting alone is not easy, regardless of the level of economic support.

Finally, of course, we must remind ourselves that what we have now is a single-parent system of childrearing within many if not most ostensibly two-parent families. Arguably what we mean by support is to acknowledge and support in many other family forms what is already there within two-parent families. By supporting single parents we support their presence in nonpatriarchal family forms, outside of marriage.

Gender, Race, and Class Perspectives

We must pay careful attention to race, gender, and class in devising policies to support single-parent families. I put race deliberately first because it has the greatest significance. The racial composition of single-parent families in relation to the population at large, the predominance of Blacks in poor single-parent families, the pattern of reserving the harshest results for nonmarital families most common in communities of color, all suggests that race is a critical factor which must not be ignored in understanding and devising strategy for single-parent families. Moreover, the context in which single-parent families operate is constructed by race. The causes and origins of the problems faced by single-parent families mirror the broader racial divide; solutions can either challenge that divide or be undermined and ultimately fail when they are swallowed up by that ever-widening chasm.

Black families must be at the core of constructing policy. Within that focus the distinct patterns of Black women and Black men must be addressed. The single greatest danger in supporting single-parent families is to further minimize and oppress Black men. Policies which might be enacted from the perspective of white men will not work for Black men as long as their economic status continues to stagnate and further decline. Surely there is a way both to support Black women *and* empower Black men. The success of Black women, despite race, gender, and class adversity, should be studied and analyzed as an extraordinary parenting model. Finally, the class differences among African Americans can lead us to distinguish the need for a policy to address not only the temporarily poor, or the consistently near poor, but also the always poor.

Like race, gender is at the heart of current policies toward single-parent families. Its presence is just as confounding, as the law has only reluctantly helped women; it has never totally embraced or supported women. Patriarchy sees itself pitted against matriarchy. Although challenged by equality, patriarchy has nevertheless reconstructed itself to hide inequality and justify the maintenance of women's connection to men within families. We cannot and should not hide the dominance of mothers in single parenting by insisting upon gender neutrality. Mothering must be validated and recognized as sufficient parenting, not as deficient parenting; and mothering alone must be validated as a legitimate family form.

Gender suggests cross-race and cross-class connections between women. The ties between divorced and never-married women are clear to many, but equally clear is the potential to divide women against themselves, between the worthy and the unworthy. Furthermore, the parallels between dual-parent/marital women and single parents are also strong. Implicit race and class appeals can be used to keep women divided, but just as importantly, a coalition of women, even if well intentioned, can ignore or silence race, or operate from an implicit white middle-class perspective.

A gender perspective does not mean further rendering fathers invisible, but rather acknowledging that the needs of single fathers and single mothers are different. The very strongly gendered nature of single parenting reflects the strongly gendered pattern of parenting in general, a reality that we continue to ignore in dual-parent families but which is inescapable in single-parent families. Women's strongest needs are for financial support and for recognition of the nature and value of dependency/caretaking work. Men's strongest needs are for social and structural support for caretaking and a changed understanding of fathering. That understanding must emulate mothering rather than traditional notions of fathering; that is, less tied to biology and economics and more tied to nurturing.

Third, attention to class means that policies must realistically reflect the needs of single-parent families. While many single-parent families are poor, the distinctions between them are significant, particularly the sources of poverty, whether it is temporary or long term, and the opportunity structure in order to become self-supporting. Analyses of poverty must take gender and race into account, and elimination of poverty must be a key goal of policies for single-parent families.

Working from Children's Needs

The other critical perspective to bear in mind is the perspective of children. We must examine and refine our sense of children's needs. To fulfill the promise of equality requires real commitment to the reality of equal opportunity, not simply formal opportunity. Such an analysis will expose the nature of dependency and nurturing work. It is absolutely critical that we begin to think about the place of children and their care within current structures. Thinking from the perspective of children means you cannot disconnect children from their parents. So we must stop punishing parents.

It will also refine our sense of what children need over the life course, instead of thinking statically. The needs of infants are different from the needs of teenagers; the needs of urban children are different from the needs of rural children. Policy for single-parent families should incorporate the flexibility and difference that would be informed by attention to different children's needs.

To take the perspective of children is to question why they should not be viewed as a social responsibility and a social benefit. The basis for doing so might be purely pragmatic. Society's economic and social stability and growth depends upon the strength of future generations. A more compelling reason is that the care of children is a fundamental ethical responsibility. Social responsibility for children arguably underlies our strong support of two-parent families. We implicitly recognize the inability of family alone to nurture children without social support. We provide significant subsidies to two-parent families, yet even with those supports, they are struggling. Stronger collective, communal support for all families regardless of form should be our model.

Valuing All Single Parents

Finally, support of single parents should mean support for *all* single parents. Any change in policy must take account of the complexity of single-parent families, honoring their differences, rather than seeing them as fitting a single paradigm. The context within which divorced, nonmarital, and widowed single parents operate is significantly different, as are the circumstances of teenagers as compared to older single parents, parents of older versus younger children, and mothers compared to fathers. The place of single parenting as compared to other family forms is qualitatively and quantitatively different in various race and ethnic communities. While many single parents are economically disadvantaged, not all are, and of those who are poor, there are differences in their poverty, ranging from temporary to permanent. The dominant pattern of economic disadvantage is a strong connecting link among most single parents, and particularly among most mothers.

It is tempting to understand the nature of the problem as a gender issue. Indeed, the treatment of single mothers crosses race and class lines, suggesting a crucial core explanation for stigma as well as an opportunity for alliances among women. The connections must be exposed to defeat attempts to separate single parents from each other, particularly any effort to segregate out nonmarital single mothers or those receiving welfare. But I believe it is also essential to clearly articulate the differences among single parents. The very attempt to identify distinctions between types of single parents exposes the importance of race and class differences. Extending greater support to divorced single parents, for example, disproportionately benefits white women and their children. Focusing exclusively on gender ignores the role of race in the stigmatizing of single parents, when single-parent families are the dominant family form among African Americans. Building connections exclusively among women again renders invisible single-parent fathers, including the significant differences between the issues confronting Black and white fathers.

Our models need to begin from the least economically advantaged single parents and work toward the most advantaged. If we can grapple with the problems of those families in greatest economic need, then we can more easily revise policy for those with lesser needs. An economic floor is essential to building any constructive policy. Our models must begin, then, with nonmarital families, the permanently poor, and nonwhite communities.

The policy analysis must include both immediate and long-term strategies. Certainly the present political climate does not favor public benefits for families. Even if the political climate were more favorable, the policies might need to be gradual rather than an immediate, massive overhaul. I will identify several strategies after setting out key policy needs.

ELEMENTS OF CHANGED POLICY TOWARD SINGLE-PARENT FAMILIES

So where does all this lead? The answers seem both easy and difficult, simple and complex. The easy part is what single-parent families need. The overall goals would be insuring economic support and the elimination of stigma. Additional goals of policy are economic independence and support for caregiving and caretaking of dependents. The areas of legal reform include divorce, welfare, labor law, and paternity laws. We must consider short-term and long-term answers.

Economic Support

The first priority is economic support. The specifics are not difficult to identify: (1) income sufficient to support a reasonable lifestyle, similar to the concept of a guaranteed minimum income, generated by wage work and/or family benefits, with the combination of wage work and benefits changing to reflect different balances of work and family over the life cycle; (2) decent housing and education (for parents who need it, as well as for children, including afterschool and summerschool programs); (3) high-quality childcare when needed; (4) development and encouragement for support structures; (5) health care; (6) wage replacement for necessary periods of parental leave due to short- or long-term illness of the parent or the child (sick leave for the parent or the child, paid and job-protected).

For all that follows, economic support must be seen as a precondition, although not a sufficiency, for equality. While eliminating or reducing poverty does not guarantee equality, it is a critical first step.

We also need to break the connection between economic support and other rights (of parents or the state). Nonpayment of child support has been connected by many researchers with declining visitation: if I don't get to see my children or do not play a significant role nurturing my children, so the reasoning goes, then why should I pay for them (or, why should I pay money to their mother, who cannot be trusted to devote those resources to the children)? Under current family law, child support and custody or visitation are technically separate. Failure to pay support does not affect the right of access; failure of nurture does not increase the obligation of support. But in practice the two are commonly viewed as intertwined rights and responsibilities.

Economic support should be separated from parental rights. One should not be the quid pro quo for the other; that simply replicates patriarchal family structure. The break in connection is justified at the very least due to the potential for domestic violence. The separation of economic support from other responsibilities or rights also would undermine the conception of children as property, and economic support as buying rights in property.

I recognize that this view is controversial, and in particular that it seems to disagree with some advocates of father's rights. Is it practical to expect that children will be economically supported by absent fathers without better support for liberal visitation and joint custody? Is it fair to impose economic responsibilities without guaranteeing nurturing rights? Let me be clear that while I am a critic of traditional notions of fatherhood and appalled at the overall patterns of paternal uninvolvement or limited involvement in both single- and two-parent families, I do not advocate sanctions against fathers or imposing nurturing responsibilities, or simply disregarding fathers. Rather, I deem it critical both to the welfare of children and the future of fatherhood that we provide adequate economic support for children without recreating the model of the economic father.

What structure would best facilitate this and how would it work? We should look for models at those areas that society recognizes trigger public obligation but not public rights. The public education system is one example; military service is another. Any of the spending items in the federal budget paid for with taxes also fits the model.

Economic support could be provided according to several possible scenarios. In the short run, those scenarios would reform existing support systems which nevertheless would maintain distinctions between single-parent families rather than supporting them under a single system of family support. In the long run, economic support should be provided under an undifferentiated family support system, with universal benefits supplemented where necessary with additional need-based benefits.

A moderate reform proposal would include economic support provided through modifications in the child support and widow's benefit systems. First, full enforcement of child support, with payment through a central system administered by the state or federal government, and the government insuring support if there is inability or unwillingness to pay. Under this system, the caretaker parent would apply to the government for the benefit, and then the government would seek payment from the noncaretaking parent. Included within this system would be generous support, including retraining, for men unable to pay despite their best efforts. The government system would also subsidize those parents who cannot pay the full amount. The amount of the support would be set at a level sufficient to insure a reasonable level of income and would not be subject to negotiation.

Nonmarital single parents would benefit from reforms to the

child support structure only if paternity is established and if the structure is further modified to guarantee equalization of the amount of support to that received by children of divorced parents. For the majority of children of nonmarital single parents, for whom paternity has not been established, however, the benefits currently paid to widows should be paid to these parents as well. Such a reform is based on the similarity between these mothers and widows and widowers, and their level of financial need. What would fairly equalize the benefits with those afforded to divorced women would be to insure for divorced women a reasonable level of child support guaranteed by the state.

Alternatively, the system set up for widows could be expanded to include all single parents whenever the man is functionally dead, that is, where paternity has not been established or there is persistent nonpayment of child support. Support for children should not vary based on the connection between the father and the mother, or the failure of the father to be a part of the child's life. A single benefit ought to be paid, while the money for the fund could come from various sources. One can even conceive of a tax fund, paid from general tax revenues. Or, the system could be based on a family support model, such as the Swedish system. This model would support all families, regardless of origin or form, with an entitlement universally available to all families, supplemented by needs-based support for housing, childcare, and income that would be focused on the needs of the child within the circumstances of the family.

I will first discuss the short-term policies based on the child support structure/divorce structure; then incorporation of nonmarital single parents in the widow structure; then the longer-term solution of integrating all single parents into a single-family support structure, including a description of the Swedish model.

CHILD SUPPORT AND PROPERTY DIVISION   The most immediate pragmatic change necessary for divorced single-parent families is to restructure divorce and educate judges in order to prevent the creation of poverty for children. Many critics of the existing divorce structure have argued for a more equitable distribution of resources (Estin 1993). The one-time, clean break model of resource distribution is seriously flawed, as well as the formulas or principles for resource division. It is also necessary to reconceptualize child support more broadly to capture the actual expenses of childrearing, rather than simply the "necessaries" (Fitzgerald 1994). A more equitable system also points toward the importance of family policy insuring sufficient economic support to shore up inadequate resources divided between two households.

The long-term question is what we envision as the relationship between work and family or the appropriate range of relationships. In the setting of divorce, given the interrelationship of the marital and postmarital family and the construction of single parenthood within the marital family and at divorce, our vision must encompass both our understanding of the marital relationship as well as the boundaries of divorce. In particular, we must decide whether it is desirable or imaginable for children to function with more than one parent as a nurturing, caretaking parent during their minority, and particularly at younger ages when children are most dependent. We must also decide whether, if we permit parents to choose the level of their involvement in nurturing and caretaking, we are committed to removing gender as a determinant of who does full-scale parenting. Furthermore, if we permit variability in parenting, will we define legal responsibility and social support differently for different kinds of parents? We might envision parenting as varying not only as to number and quality of parenting but also as to potential parenting configurations over the developmental years of children, and as including biological or adoptive parents, single parents, stepparents, and extended family or friends who serve as parents.

If we want to leave parenting arrangements to choice and allow for the greatest variety of configurations and combinations, max-imizing freedom, flexibility, pluralism, and difference, then we must focus on making choice equally available and on supporting equally the consequences of choices once made. The substance of work/family relationships as well as gender and race factors must be vigilantly scrutinized. Neither gender nor race should determine the range or nature of the choices available to an individual. If certain choices are deemed better for children, then we must construct our economic system to support those choices for all children, not simply for those lucky enough to be born into economically advantaged families. The economic structure must insure both that good choices for children are supported and that parents are not penalized for parenting.

In the short term, we must end the association for children between divorce and poverty. This goal suggests hastening implementation of federal child support machinery. More importantly it points toward the necessity of amending current law to make child support, whether by parents or the state, automatic, as well as calculating into child support children's need for quality unwaged caretaking. Welfare payments to single parents and divorce law must calculate the cost of caretaking in all its complexity, including expenses, psychological and emotional costs, foregone work and other opportunities, in order to account for both the temporary and the permanent costs of parenting where one person does the primary parenting. Such a recognition would entail creation of a family support mechanism radically different from the current welfare system.

Family law must recognize actual conditions within which single parents operate and factor these conditions into the structure of the family as well as the economic support of the family. Divorce law must face the realities of wage work. It must account for the overwhelming sex discrimination women experience in the workplace which is exacerbated by the consequences of parental responsibilities. If men are to have an equal opportunity to parent, divorce law must support men's demonstrated parenting in the face of workplace resistance or nonsupport. Family law may also push greater work law equality as a necessary precondition to equality in personal and family relationships. Family law is a powerful perspective from which to point to the inequities that persist in waged work which threaten and undermine individual freedom in our most intimate relationships, as well as the ability to raise a new generation with a realistic expectation of equal opportunity not governed or dictated by gender or race.

EXPANDING SOCIAL SECURITY BENEFITS In the short run, at least, nonmarital families should be treated like widowed single-parent families. If paternity is not acknowledged or established, then it is functionally equivalent to the death of the father, as there is no father from whom support can be legally obtained. If paternity is established, then support should be obtained and custody/visitation permitted to the same extent as for divorced single parents, modified by consideration of the relationship between the unmarried parents and between each parent and the child. The father's choice is responsible birth control, plus marriage in the event of accidental or unintended pregnancy if that is acceptable to the mother. If not acceptable, the father may still be a father both economically and emotionally, by voluntary acknowledgment of paternity and payment of child support with entitlement to custody or visitation. The father is entitled to seek sole or primary custody, although unwed fathers currently rarely do so. If the father does not want to emotionally parent the child, he would still be required to provide financial support. Under current law, if the mother does not want to parent with the father, she usually cannot block access.

The mother's choices are to marry and be entitled to the rights and privileges of marriage, or, if the father acknowledges the child, she would be entitled to the same support as other divorced women. If she does not marry, she should be entitled to a state benefit equivalent to that paid to widows. The state can require the father's economic contribution. If the father is not present, the family should not suffer for his lack of presence; rather, the state should treat the family in the same manner as it treats a family upon the death of a parent.

Is this a disincentive to marriage? It makes marriage a choice rather than an economic necessity. It assures the parent that she will have sufficient economic support to raise children. The evidence suggests that removing economic considerations will likely have little impact on marriage. Every available study indicates that welfare is not a disincentive to marriage, nor is it an incentive to have children. While economics can affect marriage decisions, the fundamental decisions to marry and to have children are emotional and social (or simply sexual), not economic. The social incentives and support for marriage remain very strong. The practical challenges of parenting similarly are a strong incentive to parenting as a couple.

Is this a disincentive to parent? Parenting, like marriage, cannot be forced. The only part of parenting that can be mandated is the payment of economic support. Every other part of parenting can merely be supported, but cannot be required. It seems that the structure of the law should require economic contribution, mandate a living standard of support, and then provide every encouragement to psychological/social parenting. The only exception to this would be a harmful relationship with the primary or sole psychological parent.

How would this work? Under the Social Security system, a surviving widow with dependent children, which includes all children under age eighteen, is entitled to benefits for the children as well as benefits for herself as the children's caretaker (Sugarman 1993).[1] She may earn up to more than $600 per month before losing any caretaker benefits (Sugarman 1995). If she earns more than $600 per month, she loses $1 of benefits for every $2 that she earns until the benefits phase out entirely. There is no reduction in the children's benefits based on the income or the marital status of the surviving parent. The amount of the benefit is uniform in the sense that it does not vary state to state, and is based on the income of the deceased or disabled parent. In order to be covered, the deceased parent must have paid into the system for six of the last thirteen quarters. The average family benefit for a widowed caretaker and two children was over $1,300 per month as of December 1994 (McCormick 1995). The benefit amount replaces a larger proportion of the low-wage worker's salary than of the high-income earner's salary, but since payments are related to wages, the benefit amount varies according to the wages of the earner.

In order to make such a system work for nonmarital single mothers (or the smaller proportion of single fathers), either paternity would have to be established or a fictional father would have to be created. In addition, even if paternity were established, some fathers would not have an account on which benefits could be drawn. In either the case of the fictional father or the actual father without qualifying income, the state would stand behind the benefit, much as the state would stand in the shoes of the father if child support could not be paid. The amount of the benefit would be the system's minimum or some calculation of the average benefit.

One of the features that is most attractive about the widows' system is that it provides a decent level of income that can be combined with part-time work. The downside to this combination is the current consequences of part-time work, unless workplace structures and their consequences are reformed. Part-time workers generally have less benefits, such as health insurance and pension contributions; earn less; have less upward mobility; and less job security. There are less jobs available in which part-time work can be done as compared to full-time work. The long-term consequences of part-time work, even for only a portion of an individual's employment, can be a marginalization and a devaluation of the worker.

Even with these caveats, the combination of family support and wage work permitted by social security, instead of the wage work permitted in conjunction with welfare, allows for, and values, nurturing of children. I do not mean to overly valorize the system of benefits for widows. But I do want to emphasize that this benefit structure permits a healthy combination of work and family. If that seems to tip the balance in favor of single-parent families, it is only because similar support for dependency is needed for all families. Single-parent families are a good place to start.[2]

It seems clearer, viewed from the nonmarital single parent perspective, that it is essential to separate economic and noneconomic parenting. All parents who conceive and bring into this world a child should be obligated to provide support for the child. It simply should be a responsibility to the child. Furthermore, in order to emphasize that economic support of children is not a responsibility to the other parent, payment should be made into a central fund, which would distribute the funds to the custodial parent. Both parents would be obligated to provide economic support, with credit given to the person providing caretaking. The state would step in for anyone unable to pay.

Here as with divorced single parents, the clear goal is the facilitation of choice as well as the support of nurture. Sufficient economic support insures meaningful choice and allows for the valuing of diverse family forms. It supports children in families, rather than limiting support to families of a particular form or style or composition. The goal is to maximize the involvement of both parents (or more), while insuring sufficient support if there is only one or primarily one parent.

None of these benefits should be class-based, but rather should be sufficient for the family to live at a modest level and to insure economic opportunity for the children. That might best be accomplished by not limiting economic support to income supplements, but also including housing, childcare, and educational opportunity. That is, instead of providing monetary support, support in kind or in services could be provided. Housing is the single largest expense for single parents. Housing assistance that insures a safe and healthy environment for children with access to good-quality educational opportunity would make a critical difference to families. Similarly, access to good-quality childcare, including afterschool care, would have significant impact on parents and children. Income support maximizes choice and minimizes bureaucratic interference; support in kind is more problematic, but could have greater qualitative impact and more significantly change the context of single parents' lives and the opportunity structure for their children.

The more difficult question is the level of economic support which should be provided. At a minimum, families ought to be able to live free of poverty. We must carefully define what that level is, given the common consensus that our official definition of poverty is inadequate. The model that is particularly useful in this respect is Sweden. The poverty rate for Swedish children is 5 percent, compared to the U.S. rate of 20 percent. The Swedish level of support for single-parent families should be our floor or point of orientation; we should consider whether it should be our ceiling as well.

Dependency Work

Economic support for single-parent families has another integral piece: the place of caregiving or dependency work. Should economic support remain tied to a paradigm that requires women to work a double shift of wage work and unwaged work? Should the system be structured in a way that continues to allocate the vast majority of dependency work to women? Should dependency work continue to be connected to short- and long-term disadvantage, so that women do it at their peril while also being socialized to do the work that brings them so much economic peril? This is an issue which has divided women by providing only limited support to some women (widows) to care for their dependents, although increasingly all women are expected to do wage work full-time in addition to unwaged household and childcare work.

The question of a model or goals, and the role of law, is unclear. I believe that the goal should be to maximize the nurturing of children by as many loving adults as possible. Clearly a parent-child relationship cannot be required and should not be imposed. Where one parent does not want to parent, the system should support alternative support structures rather than force parental involvement. Most single parents operate within some support framework, and the structure could be arranged to support alternative networks, like kin or family or childcare, or all of those in combination.

Valuing dependency work requires universal entitlement. Care for dependents is an inescapable need that cannot be ignored. The content of dependency work can vary considerably and therefore any policy must be responsive to maximizing different family configurations while insuring that dependency work is valued.

Another piece that is tricky here, however, is how to value dependency work without romanticizing it and creating a new gender cage. Or, how to find the right balance by which children will benefit from their parents' wage work by the role model it presents for them, while also insuring that children have the undivided attention and presence of their parents.

The divorce model of single parenting in both structure and operation is a single-parent model. It perpetuates the single-parent roles set up in marriage, with the nurturing parent, usually the mother, as the primary or sole parent, and the economic parent, usually the father, as a far secondary parent. The descriptive language of the legal structure is that there is joint legal custody with a primary residential parent with whom the child or children reside and a noncustodial parent with liberal visitation. Under this model, the reconstituted family after divorce is a hierarchical model that oddly mirrors the dominant parenting pattern, that is, the presumption that it is primarily one parent who does the work of parenting.[3] *That model is a model of parental inequality.* The model does not contemplate two coequal nurturers, but rather a dominant parent and a secondary parent, viewed in terms of nurturing. Under the guise of joint legal custody, it is labeled as a gender neutral, egalitarian structure, but it is neither gender neutral nor egalitarian in structure or in operation. It is gender neutral only to the extent that either parent could be placed in either role. In reality, women primarily continue to fulfill the caretaker role, either because they were the sole or primary caretaker during marriage, or due to judicial presumptions at divorce. It is egalitarian in theory only with respect to parental decision making, not with respect to nurturing, because it presumes the primary custodial parent is the dominant nurturer.

The nonmarital model of single parenting splits into two possibilities. First, with acknowledged paternity or involuntarily established paternity, the parties can replicate the divorce model. That is, they can create an unequal parenting relationship either where there has been no prior parenting relationship or to replace shared parenting within a cohabiting or non-cohabiting intimate relationship. This points to another distinction between divorced and nonmarital parents: while they may have cohabitated and/or coparented, there is less likelihood of this, and therefore no parenting history from which to judge what might be the best allocation of parental responsibilities. In the alternative, in the absence of the establishment of paternity, the other model is a mother-child model.

The policy issue here is whether to encourage the formation of two-parent families, that is, to maximize paternal involvement, or to set up a model that honors the mother-child model even in cases of acknowledged paternity. Under that model, custody and control would remain with the mother, including the determination of what kind of relationship with the father would be in the best interests of the child. What is difficult here is the goal of maximizing the nurturing of children by as many parents and other caretakers/friends/family as possible, versus resolving differences and conflicts between the parents which affect the child. Is hierarchy (meaning one primary or controlling parent) necessary? Can you have an equality model of parenting only if it is voluntary? Or is the child entitled to have that model imposed even if the parents cannot get along with each other?

Given the realities of the lives of nonmarital children, it makes the most sense to support the caregiving of the sole or primary parent, and allow that parent the ability to control the relationship with other caregivers. Questions arise around what to do when the adults do not get along with each other, or when a decision needs to be made; and whether the role of adults should be that of equals, or of recognizing the primary parent as the first among equals (and requiring the designation of a primary parent). What of the instance where one parent, usually the father, wants a relationship with the child while the other, usually the mother, does not want to allow him to have a relationship? Should the model be coequal parenting, or something like the divorce model, with a dominant and secondary parent?

One answer seems to be to support those who want to nurture to the fullest extent possible, and if conflicts arise between parents, then require the parents to work out the conflict in the best interests of the child. You could divorce your spouse as spouse but not as parent; the parent's relationship with the child would be protected. With nonmarital parents, it would require the opportunity to develop as a parent once the demonstration of willingness and ability had been made, despite the absence of prior parenting.

In the alternative, the model would be one where the custodial parent's determination of the child's best interests would presumptively be determinative. This custodial parent veto could range from the most minute and unimportant details of parenting to whether to permit a relationship with the other parent at all. Implicit in this model is the importance of a primary parent whose decision making cannot be challenged except in instances of abuse and neglect.

Under one model, both parents have rights and access to the child and their relationship with the child is protected; in situations of conflict they must resolve their conflicts or the child is forced to live with the conflict. If the machinery for resolving conflict is expensive, time-consuming, biased, or in any other way faulty, it may have perverse effects. Under the other model, the child's relationship with the primary parent is protected. The nonprimary parent is forced to negotiate rather than entitled to assert rights. To the protests of this parent the response is that he or she can avoid this situation by constructing a healthy relationship, within or outside of marriage, within or outside of intimacy, with the custodial parent.

Wage Work

Virtually every model of support for single-parent families presumes that all parents will work. In the short run it is fair to presume that single parents will likely work full-time, although in the long run the goal should be part-time work for parents of, at least, young children.

The challenge for work law is generating significant workplace change to support families. If women are to have their economic status improve through the workplace, wage equity, wage sufficiency, and job opportunity must be priorities. Even under existing discrimination concepts, it would not be a revolutionary concept to make sex segregation in the workplace a primary target of discrimination law. On the other hand, if men are to have an opportunity to parent, and/or if we determine that two involved parents are more desirable than one, this would require more radical structural changes. We need to shift the current paradigm of the adverse consequences of parenting on labor market position to perhaps considering active parenting as a preferred employment status like veteran's status (Strauss 1989).

The demise of the presumption that a single wage-earner can support a family requires revolutionary change. Equally revolutionary and challenging is restructuring the wage labor market to recognize and support the consequences of dependent caretaking and imagining a different relationship between caretaking and wage work. If wage work could insure equality of opportunity and support for dependent caretaking, then work law would be a powerful impetus to dramatically increase gender equality within marriage, while also supporting single parenting as an alternative family form.

At least some of the issues which must be resolved are whether the model or expectation is full-time or part-time work; and whether it is presumed that parenting might involve an extended period of time out of the workforce or working at a less-than-full-time level. These questions are interrelated with the presumptions about caregiving and the level of support for nurture of the caregiver.

Universal Family Support

Removing stigma from single-parent families would entail a role for public-sector family support far different from our current conception of welfare. Initially, reconstruction of public-sector support for families requires long-term support to supplement the inequities permitted by family and work law that currently operate to the disadvantage of children and women. In order to overcome inequities in the existing structure, single parents need adequate economic support to become self-sufficient (by education and/or training which can insure employment at a sufficient wage with essential benefits), or must be supported with earnings to supplement their efforts to achieve self-sufficiency under the existing structure. The challenge is to shift the paradigm of public support of families and elevate the unmet needs of children in a political climate that vigorously blames, stigmatizes, and penalizes (or separates) children of single-parent families.

A policy for teenage single parents seems straightforward; the disadvantages of teenage single parenting need not be permanent. Those disadvantages are tied to age, which precludes or makes difficult acquiring sufficient education and/or experience in order to become self-supporting or reasonably supporting even with public assistance. The most obvious cure is education geared toward insuring qualification for jobs sufficient to support the family. This would require temporary economic support to permit attending school. A policy to encourage delayed childbearing, and thereby less teenage parenting of any form, is particularly dependent on sex education, availability of birth control, and strong educational and employment opportunities for young women.

The existing welfare structure is premised upon principles that undermine single-parent families. The long-term solution is to shift toward a universal family support structure complemented by needs-based supports. Alternatively, needs-based policies could be implemented as a prelude to universal supports, on the rationale that those families most in need of support would be assisted first. If that rationale and policy goal were fully carried out, support based on need would mean shifting support from two-parent, middle- and upper-class families in order to fully support families with the greatest economic needs.

There are many family support models which might be used to construct an affirmative family support system, rather than a punitive one. Because Sweden is widely viewed as having the most expansive, although admittedly costly, family support policy, it is a good model to examine and work from, as a long-term model for support of families.

First, we need to consider the context (Rosenthal 1994). In Sweden, single-parent families account for 20 percent of families with children. This is connected to a long-established cultural pattern of cohabitation before marriage, plus a high divorce rate. Teenage parents are virtually unknown, a phenomenon that should be carefully studied. The unemployment rate is 2 percent. Although there have been concerted efforts to bring women into the economy, the wage labor market is highly sex segregated and part-time workers are nearly all women. Women who work full-time earn 78 percent of men's wages, but because so many women work part-time, women on average earn only 37 percent of the total yearly wages of men.

The Swedish public benefit structure has several components, some universal, some means tested (Dowd 1989b; Bradley 1990). The universal benefits are child allowances and state-supported child support payments, called advance maintenance allowances. The child allowances are provided to all families with children younger than nineteen, and constitute 5 percent of the average wage (Bradley 1990). Both married and unmarried parents must provide support for their children. Under the advance payment system, the state pays the caretaking parent, and then the state seeks reimbursement from the parent owing support based on a percentage of minimum income, usually 40 percent of the base (Bradley 1990). Swedish policy also follows a policy of individual taxation which presumes self-support. Parental leave and government-supported childcare complete the benefit picture. Combining the child allowance and advance maintenance payment, this is equivalent to about $445 per month, which is equivalent to about 60 percent of the base amount, or 30 percent of average earned income (Bradley 1990).

The means-tested benefits include social assistance, which must provide a reasonable level of living. The average length of time on this assistance is four and a half months, making it truly transitional assistance, usually connected with the loss of a job, or other temporary situations. The number of single- parent families using social assistance grew 50 percent between 1980 and 1984. Sweden also has a housing subsidy. There is no evidence that these policies have undermined the work ethic.

With all of these benefits combined, single mothers receive 64 percent of median family income; their income rises to 67 percent of the median with half-time work at minimum wage. In contrast, families in the United States with no earned income receive only 27 percent of the median, and with half-time work at minimum wage receive 39 percent of the median.

Comparatively, single mothers in the United States are in a substantially poorer position than their counterparts in other industrialized countries (Garfinkel et al. 1993). The main reason is means-tested versus universal support policies. Non-means-tested policies allow all single mothers to work somewhat less, but do not reduce income as a consequence, as do means tested policies. The availability of childcare, according to one pair of researchers, "dwarfed the sum of all other public benefits for children" in Sweden and similarly in France (180).[4]

Not all analysts of Sweden applaud this model. David Poponoe is critical of the impact of welfare state policies on two-parent families (Popenoe 1988). Although much of Swedish policy was designed to support families, Popenoe argues that it has had the opposite effect. At the same time, he does not style himself a critic of the Swedish welfare state; to the contrary, he acknowledges the benefits of the structure for most families:

> Though in some ways it may look like a battle between the welfare state and the family, with the welfare state usually winning, I am not at all certain that in many respects, even if the family is the loser, Swedes in general do not come out the winner. I am at this point only suggesting ways in which the very existence of the welfare state compromises the institution of the family, and not making any kind of political, much less moral, judgment of the outcome. (Popenoe 1988, 238)

The ways in which Popenoe identifies family decline as a result of the welfare state include education and health care, as well as child and elder care. He characterizes shrinking family responsibility as decline. He also identifies economic equality as undermining family interdependency. Finally, he sees state concerns with efficiency as counter to the inherent inefficiencies of families.

We should not read too much into Popenoe's comments; instead, at most, his research is a caution for clarity in our goals and for consideration of alternative means. What is needed, then, is a commitment to universal family support as well as quality childcare and housing. The economic base must be universal, a tax-based funding rather than employer-based funding. This is inextricably intertwined with a recognition of social responsibility and social benefit of families and children, all families and all children.

The policy goals for single-parent families can be summarized simply as eliminating stigma and insuring support for all children, regardless of family form. Economic needs are primary, and a precondition for other goals. Short-term reforms can alleviate the most glaring needs, but significant, serious, and radical change is unavoidable if we mean to make a difference for children.

CHAPTER 7

Legal Strategies

What single parents need is an end to stigma, and support for their children. This requires ideological change as well as concrete economic and social support. Existing structures do harm to single-parent families by stigmatizing and undermining these families. Existing structures do harm mostly by what they *fail* to do; it is the *absence* of support, not its presence and negative consequences, that results in so much harm.

Law has the potential to play a role in reorienting policy toward single-parent families, and in the process transform itself from an agent of oppression to a guarantor of empowerment and equality. Law can be a tool to challenge existing structures as harmful to single-parent families. Law could provide powerful principles to frame and justify affirmative support for single-parent families.

A constitutional basis for ideological and practical support for single-parent families requires reexamining principles of pluralism, freedom, and social responsibility. What I sketch here is how one might reconceive constitutional doctrine to ideologically support single-parent families, and to enshrine that value so strongly that policies which stigmatize would be constitutionally invalid. Such a principle would not be inconsistent with continuing to favor a particular family form, but would not permit harm to other forms performing the functions of family. A more radical perspective would be to challenge the legitimacy of allowing the state to elevate any particular family form, particularly to the extent it has gender, race and class implications.

Based on existing principles and doctrine, it is difficult to be anything other than pessimistic about the law's role in changing policy in the United States toward single-parent families. Constitutional doctrine, at best, might provide the basis for inclusion of single-parent families within the scope of protected family forms. Although entirely absent from the explicit language of the Constitution, the protection and valuing of family is a venerated constitutional principle, recognized as an implicit touchstone of our political and social structure. The core of this concept of family is the traditional two-parent nuclear marital family. Other family forms have been recognized, but subordinated to that preferred ideal. The Supreme Court has valued the critical role of extended family, as well as the contributions of foster families. The Court's support of the rights of unwed, single-parent fathers also arguably implicitly recognizes the structure of single-parent families. The explicit inclusion of single-parent families, therefore, would not be as an equal, but rather as a tolerated alternative to the preferred marital two-parent heterosexual nuclear family.

Rather than permitting the elevation of one kind of family to justify stigma of all others, it could be argued that recognition of a social unit as a family, of whatever form, justifies constitutional protection and heightened constitutional scrutiny. Family is a critical structure for individual development, nurture, and self-help. It is a primary, essential social structure that has deep social, political, and economic consequences. Maximizing support for families is essential to valuing privacy, choice, and toleration of diversity. It insuring that the most basic of opportunity structures is equally supported with sufficient resources to safeguard the chance for personal growth and social cohesion. Based on that perspective, it could be argued that any laws or policies with negative or harmful results toward single parents should be struck down as violating liberty, equality, and privacy interests.

But can we get beyond eliminating stigma? The tricky part of restructuring policy toward single parents is identifying legal rationales that go beyond condemning existing policies to a policy which would require affirmative, mandatory support. If the collective political will reorients itself to support children within the families they find themselves in, instead of mythological families that never were, then fundamental legal concepts of insuring equality, while maximizing choice and privacy, could be the premise for a massive reorientation of policy. But those principles would not *require* such support, at least not under existing legal interpretations of their meaning. Articulating a rationale that would mandate support of all families, and particularly the dependents within families, would require a major reorientation of fundamental legal principles.

Why is the law so limited? Constitutional doctrine would seem the natural place to ground and articulate an affirmative, pluralistic view of families and the protection of children, and defeat unsubstantiated stereotypes which affect fundamental rights. Yet existing constitutional doctrine not only makes it difficult to construct an argument that condemns stigma, but also renders it nearly impossible to construct legal entitlement to state action or support.

One of the more serious hurdles is the principle that state action can be challenged but state inaction cannot. The Supreme Court has held that state authorities who mishandled a child abuse case could not be held accountable for the child's injuries, characterizing the state's role as one of inaction rather than of constitutionally defective action (*DeShaney v. Winnebago County Department of Social Services* 1989). Since the state was not required to act, it could not be held responsible for the consequences of its inaction. This was despite the repeated reports, investigations, and monthly visits that exposed abuse over a two-year period prior to the brutal beating that left four-year-old Joshua DeShaney severely retarded.

DeShaney has had a chilling effect on efforts to prod states to live up to their responsibilities for protecting citizens from known potential harms, including both child abuse and other forms of domestic violence. It also stands as a barrier to efforts to impose new obligations as a matter of constitutional entitlement or right. It limits constitutional condemnation of existing policy toward single-parent families in two ways. First, the state's complicity in perpetuating the negative consequences for single-parent families by failing to provide necessary support is unreachable. Second, construction of new support policies such as family benefits and universal childcare is not constitutionally mandated.

Another significant barrier under existing constitutional doctrine is the law's view of state responsibility for poverty. Existing constitutional treatment of poverty ignores wealth distinctions and recognizes no fundamental economic entitlements, making it difficult to argue for economic redistribution or guaranteed minimum support (Cahn 1994). In a series of opinions regarding entitlement to educational opportunity and economic benefits, the Supreme Court has consistently rejected the view that wealth distinctions or limitations on opportunities created by poverty trigger heightened or strict scrutiny of the state's justifications for limiting the opportunities of its citizens.

The Court has also held that although education is a public responsibility, the responsibility is limited to providing some bare minimum of educational opportunity (*San Antonio Independent School District v. Rodriguez* 1973). Equity with respect to opportunity does not require that equivalent resources be spent for all children. In *San Antonio*, the Court did not find it constitutionally offensive that the school financing scheme ranged from $2,000 per child in poor districts to $19,000 per child in rich districts. Since there was no absolute denial of education, the Court reasoned, there was no denial of a fundamental right.

> Whatever merit appellees' argument might have if a State's financing system occasioned an absolute denial of educational opportunities to any of its children, that argument provides no basis for finding an interference with fundamental rights where only *relative differences* in spending levels are involved and where—as is true in the present case—no charge could be made that the system fails to provide each child with an opportunity to acquire the basic minimal skills necessary for the enjoyment of the rights of speech and of full participation in the political process. (*San Antonio Independent School District v. Rodriguez* 1973, 37)

This conclusion totally ignores any notion of equality of opportunity, as well as avoids defining what a meaningful education should be. It also refuses to link the right to equal education to the ability to take advantage of it. At the same time, the Court refused to view the financing structure as one that distinguished or discriminated on the basis of wealth. Claiming that the definition of those who are poor or the class to be evaluated for purposes of equal protection was not well enough defined, the Court then concluded that this "amorphous" class did not have any of the standard indicia of suspectness that would entitle them to strict scrutiny: "the class is not saddled with such disabilities, or subjected to such a history of purposeful unequal treatment, or relegated to such a position of political powerlessness as to command extraordinary protection from the majoritarian political process" (*San Antonio Independent School District v. Rodriguez* 1973, 28). Funny, those criteria rather perfectly describe the characteristics of the poor.

Constitutional treatment of poverty, then, does not require redress of significant class differences, and permits token benefits to act as a sufficient minimum. Even if some level of economic support were mandated (itself unlikely), minimal benefit levels would be unchallengeable.

The Court's jurisprudence on welfare is even less encouraging. While education is conceded to be a fundamental public responsibility, economic support is not. The state is not required to provide support for any of its citizens in need. Nor is the state required to provide reasonable benefits. The Court has adopted a very low level of review of government action with respect to social welfare classifications (*Dandridge v. Williams* 1970). Rather than seeing the provision of benefits necessary to basic needs as triggering the highest scrutiny, the Court placed social welfare policy in the same category as state regulation of business. In case after case, the Court has taken the position that the state is free to dispense its largesse largely as it pleases, or not at all. Because of this, the amount of welfare benefits has gone unchallenged, even when that amount is far below what is necessary to overcome the otherwise nearly inevitable consequences of poverty. The state does not have an obligation to provide meaningful or dignified support that enables the poor to achieve self-sufficiency. Nor are they entitled to support to enable them to do nonwaged, essential work (like caregiving).

If the state provides support, however, it gains the power to intrude into the lives of those families that it "helps." State intrusiveness was sanctioned in *Wyman*, where the Court upheld denial of benefits to a single parent who refused to permit a second home visit subsequent to an initial visit, although the parent was willing to provide any information relevant to her AFDC application (*Wyman v. James* 1971). In that case the Court simply refused to see the visit as a search triggering Fourth Amendment protections. The Court therefore evaluated the state's action under a reasonableness standard and found the visit entirely reasonable. The Court's position has permitted significant regulation of welfare recipients to go constitutionally unchallenged (Williams 1992).

Finally, constitutional analysis thus far has seemed to permit discriminatory, stigmatizing treatment of single parents and their children based on immorality, sexual misconduct, and poor role modeling. When the individual is the focus of constitutional concern, it is all too easy for the state to justify increased regulations and supervision of mothering by acting in its protective capacity for the child against the mother. As noted above, this concern is the basis for intervention in the context of Aid For Families with Dependent Children (*Wyman v. James* 1971).[1] Constitutional notions of privacy, for example, do not protect a woman's refusal to participate in a demeaning paternity proceeding in which sexual history is the central focus (*Allen v. Eichler* 1990).[2]

More sympathetic treatment of illegitimate children, as well as protection of reproductive rights, and decisions regarding marriage and family would seem to be principles that might provide support for single parents. But such alternative grounds for support also seem limited under current doctrine. Under reproductive rights doctrine, if you protect the right to choose, it seems logical to assume that the family you choose to create should be protected as well. Yet the Court has consistently held that as justification for regulations designed to discourage abortion, the state can act in support of particular family forms.[3] Similarly, although the Court has condemned legal structures which punish nonmarital children for the "sins" of their parents, it has not provided independent status and entitlements to children irrespective of parental status. The Court's doctrine with respect to illegitimate children has drawn a wavering, uncertain line with respect to their status. By no means is the status legally insignificant. Rather, the Court has wavered back and forth between the view that children should not be marked by a stigma beyond their control and unrelated to their abilities, and the view that the state should be entitled to uphold the preferred form of childbearing, within marriage, with harsh results to the children born outside of marriage. Ironically (or perhaps not so), the practical consequences of the illegitimacy cases are to deny children certain forms of economic support from their fathers, particularly inheritance support (and theoretically from their mothers as well, but fathers are the dominant actors in the cases). Connecting illegitimacy to economic sanctions is reminiscent of recent welfare reform.

Against this backdrop, there are two alternative strategies. One is to work within existing doctrine and its limitations and to focus on shifting the political consensus on single-parent families. Alternatively, by re-imagining and rethinking doctrine, and in some instances by challenging established doctrine, the legal structure might be proactive in reorienting policy. In the balance of this chapter I explore alternate ways to use both of these strategies.

First, focusing on the definition of family, the goal is to entitle single-parent families to the same or similar benefits as those afforded to two-parent marital families. The more conservative strategy to accomplish this would be simply to include single-parent families as valued families within the definition of "family," while still acknowledging the legitimacy of the preference for the two-parent marital family. The more radical path would challenge the preference.

Even with a reformulated definition of family, the victory would be more ideological than real. In order to expand substantive support and to mandate a minimum threshold of support, we would need to rethink our conception of the relationships of families to community and to the state. This second strategy would focus on insuring equal opportunity for children as well as translating a social commitment and responsibility for children into action. It would focus on principles of race and gender equality for families and children, as well as using the emerging principles of children's rights, to require a re-envisioned relationship between children and the community.

DEFINING FAMILY
Inclusion and Equality

Whenever I have taught a course or seminar on family law, I have asked the students to define "family." The most common answers are emotionally defined: family are the people who love you and whom you love. Love is the basis for emotional, physical, and economic care. It is an emotional commitment that transcends particular circumstances. It has a permanency that transcends other close emotional associations, like friendship or marriage. The permanency is rooted not in formal commitments but rather in intertwined relationships of dependency. My students also commonly visualize and depict family not as singular but as plural: not as family but as families. Finally, while the content of the emotional or psychological bond is often difficult for the students to define more precisely (indeed they often resist such definition), they all are clear about which relationships qualify. They have no difficulty knowing who their family is. This strongly suggests that we should simply let individuals define family. To the extent that it is necessary to identify one family as primary, we should also trust the ability of individuals to do so.

Interestingly, the students commonly remark that their definitions are different from "legal" definitions of family. The conventional legal definitions encompass individuals with whom there is a relationship of blood, marriage, or adoption. The marriage relationship and marital family are valued above all others as the preferred family structure.

The conventional legal definition has the benefit of the ease of determining familial relationships. Family is defined by bright-line concepts: blood, marriage, and/or adoption. But at what cost? The cost is to ignore, stigmatize, or devalue that which does not easily fit into conventional or preferred molds. The traditional definition also tends to focus away from the ways in which these "objective" categories are culturally and legally constructed. Marriage, for example, is limited to heterosexual couples. Adoption is totally a creature of the law, constructed to terminate the familial ties of the child and birthparents, and replace them with a second set of familial ties based purely on emotional ties given legal sanction. Even blood, or genetics, can be overcome by intention and commitment, as in the case of surrogacy. Through conventional definitions we miss the point; that these are signifiers of emotions, but they are not themselves constitutive of "family." They are outward signs of presumed or potential feeling and relationship, but it is the feeling that they memorialize, not the formality of contractual commitment. Relationships of blood and adoption in particular, viewed from the perspective of children, not adults, are relationships of feeling and connection. They are not, as some have pointed out, relationships of ownership and possession (Fitzgerald 1995). The value of an emotionally oriented definition, defined from the perspective of the individual who identifies her family, is that it reflects her lived experience of family. It empowers individuals to define family for themselves rather than having their reality named and constructed by an arbitrary legal structure.

There is some support for an emotional definition and for a definition that honors individual choice in constitutional jurisprudence. The Supreme Court, while stating that marriage is the "basic foundation of the family" (*Smith v. Organization of Foster Families for Equality and Reform* 1977, 843), nevertheless has recognized "the importance of the familial relationship, to the individuals involved and to the society, stems from the emotional attachments that derive from the intimacy of daily association, and from the role it plays in 'promoting a way of life' " (844). This notion of psychological family removes the focus from status or form and focuses instead on the nature and meaning of the relationship, a functional plus emotional/psychological approach.

I don't think there is any serious doubt that single-parent families *are* families. They fit within the Court's acknowledgment of families outside of marital families. The question is, rather, whether they should be included within the circle of preferred families, meaning the circle of families entitled to social and political support because they serve broader social goals as well as individual needs.

By even very traditional definitions of families, single-parent families are entitled to belong. In some respects that is what I have argued: single-parent families are as good as any other kind of family. I have also argued that we implicitly support single parenting within the two-parent family; that is, our dominant model is of a sole or primary nurturing parent. So if we are supportive of families, we should be supportive of single-parent families. Inclusion of single parents as part of the definition of "family" is a strategy consistent with efforts by family law scholars to rethink and redefine concepts of family and parent to be more inclusive and diverse, and to ground the definition less in form and structure than in relationship, function, and emotion. This replaces traditional definitions of family by relationship status. Instead the new definition focuses on what families do, looking to function and connections both within and beyond households.

To the extent that we support two-parent families, single-parent families are entitled to the same support, where same support means equality of result. By requiring inclusion *and* support (with support defined not as the same resources but rather as resources ample enough to achieve the same results), we insure that single parents are supported to the same extent as two-parent families.

The danger in this strategy is that someone defines function. Those who have the greatest power to define may, by this means, exclude families who fail to conform to particular social norms. For example, a single-parent family might be included within the circle of family as long as it acts like a two-parent marital family, by the use of substitutes or stand-ins for the "missing" parent, with due regard to a bottom line of heterosexuality. Single parents with stepparents or *de facto* stepparents, or single parents in a strong coparenting relationship with an ex-spouse or partner would qualify as families; single parents without an opposite-sex parent or parent stand-in would not. Under this view, if function is so defined, the liberating act of inclusion would be defeated by a rigid norm of how one must act once part of the privileged group. The norm of the two-parent marital heterosexual nuclear family dominates if the reason to include other family forms is that they can do the same things as well as that type of family. What is excluded are differences that enrich and expand our understanding of family function, such as the differences and teachings based on the way single-parent families function.

Defining family primarily in terms of emotional relationships, reflected in the individual's naming of his or her family, is the way out of this conundrum. Define family by whom we would include in our picture of family. This definition resonates with our life experiences and permits the greatest range of personal choice. Protected by the traditional reverence for private choices which reaches its apex when valuing choices about intimate relationships, an emotional definition of family honors individuality without imposing any individual definition on the community. The focus is not on function but rather on relationship, on the nature of the emotional ties that bind those we call "family." The definition accords with how we define family for ourselves and how we know family, despite prevailing ideology or legal definitions.

A redefinition of family around emotional, relational meanings and away from structure would move us away from the tempting use of structure or legal formalities such as adoption and marriage as bright-line definitions of family. By focusing away from function, such a definition might avoid the difficulties of reincorporating a particular family model through insistence that families must all perform in particular ways. It might, then, better reflect the pluralistic, complex experience of families in people's lives. The inclusiveness of this definition, as well as a rejection of any preferred family form, would better value all families.

No one definition of family, however, may provide a universal answer to all the difficult questions faced by families, or determine the relative responsibilities and rights of family members to each other and to the state. A relational, emotional definition, for example, does not provide an instant guide for resolving intrafamilial disputes or for allocating responsibilities between individuals and society. I do not mean to suggest a redefinition insures simplicity and universality. Rather, I suggest it as a means to reflect our experience of family in order to move beyond definitions which unnecessarily exclude or subordinate, or privilege a preferred norm. We need flexibility which depends upon the purpose for which we use the definition. By reorienting the overall concept of family toward relational, emotional ties, I mean to insure all families recognition and support. Law has commonly encompassed a range of definitions subsumed under a general understanding of what constitutes a family. It is that general understanding that we need to reorient, while acknowledging the need for more particular definitions to resolve rights and responsibilities. We could begin by recognizing and honoring the social core relationships of all our families.

Challenging Family Privilege

A second, more radical strategy of redefinition of "family" would challenge the priority given to two-parent marital families as unjustified, irrational, and an inequalitarian preference that offends freedom of thought and association, pluralism and tolerance, equality and due process, and privacy. In the alternative, if the priority of two-parent marital families is left untouched or justified, one could challenge the relationship between the most highly valued family and all other families. Honor or privilege need not be coupled with stigma for all others. Instead, a "first among equals" model could be adopted, rather than a model that requires a put-down of all other forms of family.

Challenging the primacy of any family form is an even more radical approach. Current constitutional doctrine permits and even encourages the state to support a particular form or definition of family, thereby frustrating efforts to recognize the value of diverse families. Martha Minow has explored whether First Amendment doctrine could be used to support family diversity under a "free exercise of families" argument (Minow 1991). Under this view single parents would benefit from recognition of the diversity of families and toleration of nontraditional families, akin to the free exercise of religion. Minow acknowledges the serious limitations of this analysis, in particular that "in the absence of a guarantee against governmental establishment of preferred family forms, as is present in the field of religious freedom, free exercise analysis is quite limited" (Minow 1991). But if we concede that the government is entitled to identify and support preferred family forms, then mere toleration of some diversity from that preferred form is not much freedom and virtually no meaningful support.

The argument for displacing the state's glorification of a single-family form has several aspects. First, everything we know about the function of family shows that it has little to do with form. Emphasis on form, therefore, is irrational. Second, elevation of a particular form offends freedom of thought and freedom of association. The structuring of family, of the intimate associations of partners and children, is something that we recognize as the expression of the most fundamental of human freedoms. Privileging one kind of family offends our support of the ability of individuals to maximize their free choices as long as they do no harm to others within or without their family.

The elevation of the nuclear marital family also reinforces a long legal tradition supporting patriarchy. I do not mean to suggest that the two-parent family cannot exist apart from a patriarchal form. Nevertheless, we are far from a marital family that is nonpatriarchal. Under the thin veneer of equality language in family and work law, the realities perpetuate inegalitarian results that replicate patriarchy. It seems far more rational to bring the nuclear family down from its pedestal and encourage other family forms and roles in order to achieve, if possible, a nonpatriarchal marital family. The continued elevation of this family form, in the absence of significant support for egalitarian realities, seems instead to have gotten us only to a modified, or reconstituted, patriarchy. When I ask my students if they can imagine a marital family where one spouse stays at home to nurture children and do household work *with* such an arrangement not creating an imbalance in power and economics, they cannot imagine it. Faced with the realities of gender imbalance, they cannot imagine how to reconstruct interdependency so that it does not require nor is it viewed as hierarchy.

Finally, there is a race component to this argument against privileging the nuclear, marital family. Based both on historical discrimination and current family structures, African Americans in particular have been prohibited or dissuaded from marrying, and currently are economically discouraged from marrying. Any legal structure that privileges nuclear marital families has a disproportionate racial impact. That result alone should disentitle the state from elevating that family form above others.

A direct assault on the ability of the state to privilege *any* family form over all others is not, then, doomed to failure. If such an assualt were to prevail, it might entitle other kinds of families, including single-parent families, to the benefits and privileges accorded to marital families.

A less radical approach would be to argue that while the state may privilege a particular form of family, it cannot stigmatize all others. To stigmatize family form is irrational, again because it is so clear that form does not determine the ability to function as a family, in the most positive sense of functioning. There may be an analogy in freedom of religion doctrine to this "first among equals" principle. Despite the fundamental precepts of tolerance for all religious practices, we nevertheless permit the privileging of Judeo-Christian traditions in holidays, as well as in work and school schedules. But First Amendment doctrine would not permit the stigmatizing of all religions other than Judeo-Christian sects. If this approach were followed with respect to families, it would permit the state to favor a particular form of family but not permit as a corollary the denigration, by policy or effects of policy, of other forms of families.

What is most important about a strategy of inclusion is to connect the viability and support of a wide range of family forms to the construction of a family support policy. As we envision a family support policy, we must decide whether single-parent families would be best served by inclusive family support policies or policies specifically created to deal with the particular issues of single-parent families. A policy of inclusion rather than one of distinction is preferable, but only if single-parent families are explicitly considered, in a nonstigmatizing way, in policy making. Inclusion should not mean invisibility but rather validation of the variety of family forms that function as family, with a generous definition of function.

FAMILY SUPPORT

The Problem of Inadequacy

Regardless of whether current definitions of family can include single parents or if the definition needs to be restructured, inclusion of single parents within the definition of family is a limited strategy. The outcome in terms of concrete support may be little more than symbolic. The support of two-parent families is sorely inadequate. Inclusion of single-parent families, then, within a structure that inadequately serves two-parent families may achieve ideological change, but little in the way of real benefits. Even if benefits are structured to insure that they provide similar consequences, by taking into account differences between single-parent and two-parent families, those consequences will nevertheless be no better than they are for two-parent families.

Support of certain families is accepted and justified as appropriate public support of a critical private social structure which benefits society as a whole. While some families are better supported, none, save the very rich, are adequately supported. This is particularly the case with respect to the crucial allocation of time and energy between work and family responsibilities.

The primary support of two-parent families is through support of marriage. Marriage of course is an imperfect proxy in some respects for the two-parent family, because some couples who have children do not marry, and some married couples do not have children. Nevertheless, it is clear that the strong legal preference for marriage signifies support for the traditional family. The dominant purpose of the intimate relationship protected and valued by marriage is to bear and raise children. The structure of the relationship presumes the traditional family, defined as a family in which there are dependent children and in which mothers and fathers have gender-specific roles, the breadwinner father and the homemaker mother. Women in particular used to be viewed as incomplete, imperfectly developed, unless they married and had children. Support of marriage is therefore equivalent to support of the family, defined as the traditional family.

One of the common myths about the traditional family is that it operates independently and self-sufficiently. Stephanie Coontz has detailed the historical record of family support that flatly contradicts this common belief (Coontz 1992). As she points out, the 1950 suburban (implicitly white) family especially idealized as self-sufficient was highly dependent on government support. The suburban family was subsidized by the benefits of the GI bill, providing educational benefits to primarily male war veterans; by housing loans that enabled families to own their own homes; and by government support of private industry to provide jobs and the building of the infrastructure to support private development. This massive public support named and rationalized in different programs far exceeded any support then or since under the rubric of welfare, yet, as Coontz points out, no one ever feared that this dependency would generate negative social consequences (Coontz 1992, 68–92).

Marriage and family continue to be intertwined in contemporary law. "Family" is a significant category under federal and state law: by one researcher's count, the term alone appears over 2,000 times in the federal code, and from 2,000 to 4,000 times in two states' statutes (Robson 1994, 980). The definition of family, and the preference for the two-parent marital family, is used to distribute resources including financial support, fringe benefits, tax breaks, and housing. Marital status is critical to social security, worker's compensation benefits, intestate succession law, adoption, and the use of reproductive technologies (Jaff 1988). The protection of marital status is also apparent in laws criminalizing cohabitation, adultery, and distinguishing the children born to parents who are not married as "not lawful" or illegitimate.

Perhaps the strongest support of the traditional nuclear family is the tax code. Drafted in the early part of this century when gender roles reflected the accepted ideal of male breadwinners and female homemakers, the code continues to be most strongly supportive of that family pattern. It thus strongly disadvantages the two wage-earner family, by heavily taxing the second wage earner, as well as disadvantaging the single-parent family because household labor continues to be ignored (not taxed, therefore not valued, and not part of the basis for social security benefits) at the same time that income declines (McCaffery 1993b, 617).[4]

Despite the significant support provided for the preferred two-parent family, that support nevertheless has been provided within an ideology of family privacy, family self-sufficiency, and the elevation of the value of work over family. Despite a mythology of care for children and family, the legal support structure as well as the social support structure, is nearly nonexistent. Compared in particular with other postindustrial economies, the United States lacks the family support structures essential to long-term economic and social support of families. Parenting remains a private responsibility carried out as best as possible under workplace structures which largely ignore parental responsibility and at worst impose discipline or discharge for even the most ordinary and common of parental crises: parental leave, childcare, care for ordinary illnesses and extraordinary health conditions, afterschool care, leave to attend conferences and performances, coordination of work and school schedules. The needs of time and space are significant, and the consequences of continuing conflict are evident.

We operated a generation ago with the myth that in the ideal family, one parent would stay at home and provide the parenting for children, while a second parent would provide family income. This ideal worked well for the workplace, because it provided a worker whose family responsibilities insured commitment to the workplace. It worked well for the home, it was believed, because it insured full-time parenting. It was clear that mothers did caregiving and fathers did breadwinning.

Although we have shifted away from this model, we have not yet articulated an alternative model. Our notions of equality no longer allow for presumed gender-based assignment of family roles, nor for the limitation of workplace opportunities. Nevertheless, we continue to operate in a system structured on the assumption of a single nurturing parent at home, and a workplace parent largely limited to workers engaged in only economic parenting. There has been no major restructuring of the workplace, and no significant alleviation of conflict between work and family. Moreover, this conflict is exacerbated by escalating economic needs.

Incorporating single-parent families into the existing structure of family support would be a step forward, because it would potentially eliminate some of the ideological stigma and might increase economic resources to those families. More support, even incremental support, is better than no support and negative stigma. Inclusion into a limited and inadequate structure of family support, however, is not a solution. Just as the enactment of an unfunded, time-limited Family Leave Act covering only 50 percent of the workforce had little impact on the ability of families to bond with newborn or newly adopted children, to care for seriously ill children or other family members, or to tend to their own debilitating illnesses, so too a theoretical expansion of our definition of family and inclusion of single parents within existing support structures is little more than a token, symbolic step with little, real meaning for most single-parent families.

Reconfiguring the Relationship between Family and Community

In order to provide real change in the material circumstances of single-parent families, we must reconceptualize the relationship between family and community. Our individualistic, privatized view of family precludes a collective, communal responsibility for children. There is little sense of social responsibility for children other than one's own, and no mandate for real equality of opportunity. Parents are held responsible for their children, and we fail socially or politically to insure that parents have the resources, and children the opportunities, that would support such a privatized view and make it work for the benefit of individuals and society. Parents lack the wherewithal; they nevertheless are blamed. It is a vicious cycle.

How do you make all children everyone's children? If you can, then assuring benefits, redistributing income, insuring educational and other equality, is a relatively easy step to take. There are several aspects to this. One is redistributive, that is being willing to shift resources to accommodate needs. That willingness should not be blocked by the structure of family within which children reside if the premises for stigmatizing single-parent families are false. The second is reconceiving responsibility for children from exclusive family responsibility to community or social responsibility. Although we in fact provide significant support to certain families, the view that ideally families should be self-supporting as well as self-regulating is very deeply ingrained. It is the basis for arguing that no family or no child within a family has a claim to resources from society as a whole, but rather only, perhaps, from their own family. On the other hand, a reoriented concept of social responsibility would include support for family, in the sense of insuring sufficient resources of time and money for the family to best serve its function, as well as understanding the social or communal role as one of active nurture and support of children.

The importance of community for families and the individuals within families might suggest some accord with communitarianism. This is true in the sense that communitarians critique and balance the notion of autonomous individualism (Mulhall and Swift 1992). The responsibility for families should be social, not solely individual. But the troubling part about communitarianism is the question of who defines and controls the community, who establishes values, who defines morality, and who controls power? At least some communitarians see the two-parent marital family as one of the prime structural premises of their re-visioned society (Etzioni 1993; Anderson and Davey 1995; Coontz 1995).

Even if one could successfully dispute the communitarian fixation with traditional families, it is the understanding of the dynamic and of the place of disadvantaged, stigmatized groups that is most troubling about the theory. This is not to say that there are not those within communitarian schools who are concerned about pluralism and the rights of minorities. The reconfiguration of family and community which I find more persuasive is closest to what Adeno Addis has called "critical pluralism" in the context of rights of ethnic minorities (Addis 1991, 1225; Brown-Scott 1994; Ward 1994). Under that model, disadvantaged subgroups are provided resources in order to flourish, as well as the opportunity and institutional structures to be a dialogue partner with the majority culture. Multiculturalism, either alone or in combination with communitarianism, might yet provide models for family diversity (Taylor 1994; Walzer 1983;

Kymlicka 1995). The combination of cultural, racial, and gender issues complicates the issues of community for single-parent families (Wolf, 1994).

What is required is a reorientation of the state's relationship to families. The basic principles for that reorientation can be found in concepts of equality and children's rights.

Equality and Children's Rights

Support for single-parent families can be argued on the basis of equality principles grounded in thinking about families from gender and race perspectives. Simply put, the argument is that privileging a family form that disproportionately values the majority family structure of white Americans over the family structure most common among African American and Hispanic families constitutes race-based discrimination. The combination of the stark differential in the presence of single-parent families within white and nonwhite communities, in addition to the consequences of single-parent status, should be the basis for an argument that any legal principle which deliberately discriminates either in favor of a particular family form or stigmatizes nonpreferred family forms should be subjected to strict scrutiny. Given the lack of even rational support for preferring particular family forms, and because form does not control or determine outcomes, such an analysis would likely be fatal to any policy seeking to privilege two-parent families at the expense of single-parent families. The affirmative principles would be the support of equality and diversity.

There is a gender component to the equality argument as well. Economic policies or practices which disadvantage single parents disproportionately disadvantage women, particularly with respect to economic benefits or support. Furthermore, those policies which reinforce parenting as an economic role disproportionately disadvantage men, who are treated as if they have no emotional relationship with their children. The policies also disadvantage women who are unable to fulfill an economic role to the same extent as men can, given wage discrimination, sex segregation, and other forms of continuing, pervasive sex discrimination in the workplace.

This understanding of equality within and between families would eliminate significant differences among children, especially economic differences which are derived from their parents. It would be the responsibility of society, through the state, to insure that the accident of birth is not determinative. To use the bootstrap metaphor, this would mean providing boots, as well as teaching the child how to pull, and encouraging each child to reach his or her maximum abilities.

If families are critical to individual growth and development, and also benefit social interests, then families must be supported in order to afford every child this primary, critical social structure in order to maximize individual opportunity as well as social benefit. If equality principles require that gender and race not be determinants of individual accomplishment, then providing support for the most immediate and influential of social structures in order to insure individual development should be required. The role of the state is to safeguard equality of opportunity by insuring that sufficient resources are present for every child to maximize his or her potential. It is at this intersection of equality and freedom, choice and opportunity, that a reorientation of family support and legal conceptions of family has its most powerful appeal.

The explosion of scholarship around children's issues can contribute significantly to this reorientation in at least three ways. First, it can help us define the scope of children's needs. Second, it can provide arguments necessary to refocus our attention on children, rather than on parents, in considering the role and value of families. Third, it can contribute to rethinking the role of community and the state in relation to family.

Our concept of children's rights will define the substance of the opportunities to be provided to all children. Advocates of children's rights have been motivated, to a significant extent, by the goal of better fulfilling children's needs. From what we know about single-parent families, the needs of the children in those families most clearly are for economic support, nurturing support, and access to the opportunity structure, especially education. It is easiest for the legal system to provide for economic needs. It requires redistribution of wealth and recognition of social as well as individual responsibility for, and benefit from, children. There may be debate and uncertainty about defining the outer limit of economic needs, and to what extent compensating for adult inadequacies mandates absolute or near equality with what level of opportunity. However, it is generally agreed that there is such a large gap of basic needs to be closed that surely this supports consensus on a floor of needs which must be met. From that base, we can then argue when we have reached the ceiling that insures equal opportunity.

It is critical that we do not continue to think of needs purely in economic terms. Some may think that nurturing cannot be legislated, so it is not a matter for law. But this assumption is not entirely true. Law can recognize and value single-parent families, and in that way support the nurturing, teaching, and developing which single-parent families do. In redefining family to include and value single-parent families, we support their nurturing, as well as entitle them to economic support if needed. But we can also, by law, provide nurturing support by requiring that work and other structures serve all families, and insure the time to nurture. The scholars who have focused on the importance of nurturing bonds, especially parent-child bonds, in a variety of settings including adoption, step-parenting, grand-parenting, and divorce can contribute to articulating the premise for structures that support nurturing of children, along with those who have advocated for a comprehensive policy of work-family supports.

Second, children's law can help us reorient legal discourse to focus on children, instead of parents. Many advocates for children claim precisely that project as their goal. Whether by advocating for representation, or for means to permit children to be heard by the legal system, or by suggesting a new framework of substantive law that meets children's needs, many of the reforms suggested by children's advocates have the common goal of better concrete assistance for children. For single-parent families, it is essential that policy focus on children, rather than on parents. Family law's traditional focus on parents endangers children in single-parent families, since the stigmatization of parents justifies harshly punitive policies toward their children.

Finally, legal discourse has been influential in constructing our sense of the relationship of individual to family, and to the state. Advocates for children, focusing on bringing children's perspective and experiences to the law, can help suggest a different public role for the community, or communities, that surround, most closely, each family. The law can support those relational, connective ties. Family traditionally was seen as the mediator between the individual and the state. What needs greater focus is shifting the relationship of the community to the family. This requires not only recognizing that caregivers need care and support, but also that the community has both an interest and a responsibility in supporting families. It requires shifting away from the steady movement in support of individualism, autonomy, and contractualism, in favor of connection, support, and social responsibility for families.

The challenge for law, made evident by the function and needs of single-parent families, but an issue for all families, is dependency. As Martha Fineman has pointed out, there are two kinds of dependency, one she calls "inevitable dependency" which is the dependency of children; the second is "derivative dependency" which is the dependency of the caretaker on external supports in order to be a caretaker (Fineman 1992, 8). Law does not recognize the complex characteristics or needs of either kind of dependency, nor does it value caretaking. Yet it is a core attribute of family, which clearly the law has valued, however imperfectly. The understanding of dependency, and support of caretaking, would, in conjunction with concepts of equality and children's rights, provide a basis for family support.

The Problem of Privacy

Privacy is the principle which is most closely associated with family, and privacy operates in ways that permit us as a society to ignore inequality. Under privacy doctrine, family is perceived as an essential, valued social structure which prepares individuals to take advantage of equal opportunity outside the family. Family is the place where one is prepared to assume the benefits of schooling, and eventually, employment. While it is not the only structure that supports these things, family, nonetheless, is viewed as primary— indeed, it is the lack of family or effective family that is commonly cited as the cause of social turmoil. In terms of equality doctrine, family is the place where you learn how to pull up the bootstraps. The opportunity structure is built around the presumption of the equal ability to learn how to do that, centered particularly in family.

Family under conventional privacy doctrine, then, is protected as the quintessential guardian of equality: with family behind you, you can use the opportunity structure. Martha Fineman has explored whether privacy doctrine might be a source of protection for single mothers, particularly against state intrusion or attempts at regulation. She concludes that privacy doctrine cannot be so used, because to do so would require accepting single-mother families within the definition of the "natural" (two-parent, heterosexual) "private" family that is presumed by privacy doctrine (Fineman 1991c, 1992).

What this understanding of privacy leaves out is the consequences of inequality within and between families, and its impact on the life opportunities for children. By seeing privacy as the key to equality, this perpetuates inequality. Equality, from the perspective of children, would mean not only insuring, on the basis of privacy doctrine, the value and validation of their particular family form, but also insuring that the family had the resources to insure the maximal development of the talents of the child. That equality would be measured not only by the availability of economic resources which would permit the optimal use of the opportunity structures, but also equality of noneconomic support.

Dorothy Roberts, in her work exposing the denigration of Black mothers, has argued for a reorientation of constitutional doctrine to provide greater autonomy and support, but points out the heart of the problem, the lack of any affirmative requirement for the state to reallocate and assure resources to achieve meaningful autonomy. "The definition of privacy as a purely negative right serves to exempt the state from any obligation to ensure the social conditions and resources necessary for self-determination and autonomous decision making" (Roberts 1991, 1478). If, however, the right of privacy were viewed as a guarantee of choice making free of race, gender, and class hierarchies, then privacy doctrine would enhance equality rather than reinforce inequality. If autonomy is seen not for the purpose of isolation and individuality, but rather as a means to guarantee control and empowerment that reflects a valuing of *all* individuals to make good choices, then privacy doctrine would be a powerful basis to construct a strong family support policy (Roberts 1991). Roberts sees this connected to due process principles; I would locate it as well in a reorientation of privacy doctrine. As Roberts characterizes it, "the ideal of due process, then, is an individual life free of illegitimate social coercion facilitated by hierarchies of class, gender, or race. The goal is an affirmatively autonomous existence: a meaningfully flourishing, independent, enriched individual life" (1480).

It is clearly important for single-parent families that the conventional role of privacy doctrine should be retained, in order to limit the reach of state regulation and intrusion. Single parents are subject to extraordinarily pervasive control through divorce and welfare. But that need not be the sole understanding of privacy. The protection of diversity, because of the valuing of what families do, can best be accomplished by insuring a threshold of economic and noneconomic support, all consistent with, perhaps even mandated by, a different understanding of privacy.

Family support, then, rather than being blocked by privacy, would be encouraged by privacy. Eliminating this barrier, and reconceptualizing it as part of a mandate, would reinforce the principles of equality and children's rights. Certainly children in single-parent families would not be the sole beneficiaries of this different sense of equality. If meaningful equality were enshrined as a legal principle for children, it would require better support of all parents, as well as better connections between families and other social institutions and the community in general.

Epilogue

Analyzing the social and legal construction of single-parent families not only exposes the fallacies underlying their stigmatization; it also clarifies, once again, the interconnection between work and family in the continuing oppression of women and the increasing impoverishment of children. Work-family relationships as currently constructed also strongly inhibit reconstructing fatherhood as more than being an economic father. Analysis of single-parent families suggests that these families should be the model upon which work and family policy are measured. If the work-family relationship can be improved for these families, then it will be possible to improve the relationship for all families.

Unraveling the stigma attached to single-parent families also exposes the intersection of sexism and racism, and their manipulation to support a color-conscious, color-privileged patriarchy. The reconstructed patriarchy dominates, even to the extent of overriding the welfare of children; patriarchy ignores the increasing impoverishment of children in order to deter racial and sexual independence and equality.

Finally, looking at single-parent families who demonstrate great strength while, nevertheless, clearly needing better support from the legal, social, and economic structures, exposes the price we pay for the elevation of the traditional nuclear family. It also shows us what we lose by failing to see the unique attributes of these families. We think of single-parent families as something to fix. Instead, we should also look to them as creating other paradigms. Single-parent families have something to teach. Most importantly, single-parent families teach us that it is not the form or structure of the family that is important, but what family does.

Single-parent families may represent the frontier of reconstructing family in a nondominating mode. The teachings and understandings derived from the single-parent experience may perhaps contribute to more egalitarian family roles. Indeed, it is ironic, but not far-fetched, to speculate that the increase in single-parent families may ultimately redound to the benefit of two-parent families. Children benefit from single parents as role models, and enhance their self-esteem and independence. Such experience of single parenthood may be the basis for committed, cooperative, nondominating relationships which can be more enduring than those of two-parent families. It may be, however, that it is this very antipatriarchal, egalitarian potential that explains why the attack on single-parent families has been so brutal and unremitting.

I wonder how, as adults, my son and daughter will envision family. My daughter is at the age where the fantasies of marriage and family, intertwined with elaborate costumes and dress up, are part of the texture of popular stories for girls—the happy ending is marrying the prince in an elaborate wedding and living happily ever after. Or maybe not. She has stories that vary the fairy tales—like the Paper Bag Princess, who rejects the ungrateful prince who criticizes the princess's lack of appropriate dress after she saves him from a powerful dragon. And oddly enough, she encounters many single-parent families in popular movies. Many of the Disney tales invariably involve a single-parent father—as in *Beauty and the Beast*, *The Little Mermaid*, and *Aladdin*. So I guess I should not have been surprised when she said, in that way children have of suddenly saying something quite monumental amidst a casual conversation, "Mom, I think I'm not going to get married when I grow up."

My son was recently asked how many people were in his family. He responded with a list that included not only his mother and sister, but also an assortment of grown-ups and children, some of whom he sees nearly every day, some of whom he has not seen for months, one who lives on the other side of the globe. Like his sister, who drew that wonderful picture, his "family" includes the people whom he loves and who love him. The connection is one of the heart. It is the same connection that my students make when I ask them to define family.

My children certainly do not see our family as unusual. I would like them to have choices and then to trust their judgment, their creativity, and their love for themselves and others. I believe all children should have such choices. In order to do so, we must challenge the rhetoric of care for children, which can also justify undermining the families so critical to our children's futures and to our futures. We must challenge rhetoric which discards some children like cheap, unwanted property while continuing to privilege others. It is unconscionable to accept the abandonment of some children because of the structure of their family or to see the poverty of any child as inevitable or insoluble.

Children deserve our support and care. All children. In order for us as a society to provide that support and care, we must value all families which nourish and care for children, regardless of form. While I am not optimistic that we will shift policy in the near future, I am hopeful that if we continue to challenge antifamily policies, we can also envision real support of all families.

Notes

NOTES TO CHAPTER 1

1. On single motherhood see Martha Fineman who states: "Single motherhood represents both the cause and the result of the disintegration of the family and society; it is a demographic category filled with political and moral significance, and as such is viewed as having both explanatory and predictive powers. This is true not only in popular discourse but in more 'reflective' areas of discourse such as the social sciences, policy and law." (Fineman 1991b, 277)

2. "The child is not the mere creature of the state; those who nurture him and direct his destiny have the rights, coupled with the high duty, to recognize and prepare him for additional obligations" (*Pierce v. Society of Sisters* 1925).

3. During the past decade, female-headed households increased dramatically; not all of those households, of course, include minor children. Female-headed households constitute 17 percent of all households; among black households, they are 44 percent; among whites, 13 percent. Children under eighteen are present in 61 percent of all female-headed households (Rawlings 1994, 5–7).

4. Quayle professed the utmost respect for single mothers, citing his sister and grandmothers as among that group (presumably widowed or divorced, and therefore honorable single parents), but targeted out single dads as needing to

act more responsibly toward the children they had fathered (presumably meaning brought into the world, or parented, or both) (Babington 1992).

5. "Many writers claim that father-absence interferes with the boy's development as a healthy male but less with the girl's development as a sound female: 'A boy really needs a father' " (Adams et al. 1984). "Little research has explored the impact of father-absence on female sex-role identification, and the rare papers are often case studies" (168). "It is an interesting comment on our culture that mental health workers worry about a lack of male models for boys, but rarely is concern expressed for the necessity of strong female models for girls" (Bilge and Kaufman 1983, 68). This view has been linked with the assumption that masculine traits, often highly traditionally defined, are the most desirable to acquire, while cross sex traits are devalued (Adams et al. 1984).

NOTES TO CHAPTER 2

1. While the report does not directly *blame* single parents, or single mothers, it nevertheless stigmatizes them: "children do best when they have the personal involvement and material support of a father and a mother and when both parents fulfill their responsibility to be loving providers" (*Final Report* 1991, xix).

2. See also an unpublished paper by David Angel which states that when economic differences are factored in, differences in education, occupation, employment, and happiness between children from two-parent versus single-parent families largely disappear. Angel's research was based on survey data from 1975 to 1990 (Angel 1992).

3. Only about 3.5 percent of those receiving AFDC have a deceased father (Note 1990).

4. See also Maclean who states that a majority of single-parent families in the OECD countries do not rely to any significant extent on private maintenance payments (Maclean 1990, 91, 97).

5. Citing depression-era studies, one author noted that "it can be conjectured that, within the context of the 'traditional family,' children perceive the father's success as an economic achiever and provider to constitute a measure of his effectiveness as a parent" (Siegal 1985, 7). Conversely, the mother's effectiveness is influenced by children's perceptions of their activities inside and outside of the family (97). Interestingly, depression-era studies indicate that when fathers were unemployed and mothers shifted to dominating family decisions, the consequence was not so much damage to the father's image as increased positive evaluations of the mother (10).

6. This term relates to dulia which is the veneration and invocation given by Roman Catholics to their saints as the servants of God. Kittay describes doulia as "nested dependencies," a model of reciprocal, cooperative activity, where "service is rendered to those who become needy by virtue of attending to those in need" (Kittay 1995, 10).

7. In order to meet work and family demands, single employed mothers give up personal time, including sleep and rest (Sanik and Mauldin 1986).

8. Constant care of children can have negative effects on women's well-being, associated with depression and physiological symptoms; also studies of marital happiness show the highest happiness just before a child is born and after their departure ("Feminist Psychology" 1992, 35).

9. See Adams to understand the strongly patrifocal characteristics of Freud's theories (Adams et al. 1984, 19).

10. Culture is a powerful influence and, for young children, so are schools (Snyder 1992, 57).

11. "In short, single mothers face a threefold disadvantage: they are women, they are mothers, and most are formerly married." Each of these factors adds to stress (McLanahan and Booth 1989, 562).

12. This term was coined by Professor Paulette Caldwell, who has used it to analyze the treatment of African American single mothers.

13. In 1993, 17 percent of white single parents were never married, compared to 43 percent of Black single parents; 44 percent of white single parents were divorced, compared to 22 percent of black single parents (Bureau of Census 1994).

14. A similar critique is leveled at research on self-concepts which avoid confronting racism or suggesting ways of constructively helping Black children (Spencer 1988, 59).

15. One researcher has concluded that any indications of children doing better in single-father homes is connected to better economic status (Downey 1994, 132).

16. Many courts remove children from a lesbian parent. For example, paternal grandparents obtained custody based primarily upon the fact that the mother was lesbian (*White v. Thompson* 1990). A father was awarded custody because the court found that the mother's live-in relationship with her lesbian lover tipped the scales in favor of the father (*G.A. v. D.A.* 1987). Another court attached a "presumption of regularity" to the more traditional relationship and placed the burden of proving no adverse effect from the homosexual relationship upon the person advocating it (*Constant A. v. Paul C.A.* 1985). Another court stated that the homosexuality of the mother was an overriding factor in deciding custody in favor of father (*Jacobsen v. Jacobsen* 1981). Finally, a court ordered a change of custody from a lesbian mother to the father, based on expert testimony of a likelihood of social stigma attached to homosexuality and negative role modeling (*S. v. S.* 1980).

17. In September 1993 Family Court Judge John W. Sweeney in Putnam County, New York, denied a request for adoption by a lesbian of her partner's biological child. The court stated that the New York Domestic Relations Law does not provide for adoptions by a same-sex partner. In December 1993, Family Court Judge Anthony J. Sciolino of Rochester, New York, ruled that such an adoption was not prohibited by the New York Law and approved an adoption by a lesbian partner (Anderson 1994). To date, adoption by lesbians of their partner's children has been permitted in New York, Vermont, and Illinois. Although

only Florida and New Hampshire specifically bar homosexuals from adopting children, some states, such as Virginia, deny adoption based on the illegality of homosexual activity. Virginia defines sodomy as oral or anal sex between homosexuals or heterosexuals and makes it a criminal offense. The Virginia Supreme Court has ruled that a parent's homosexuality is grounds for denying custody because homosexual activity is illegal (Campbell 1993, 25).

18. There are an estimated 1.5 million lesbian mothers and one million gay fathers in the United States and six million children with gay or lesbian parents (Gottman 1989, 177).

NOTES TO CHAPTER 3

1. Female single parents did report greater emotional strain and economic strain. The average work burden, between job and home responsibilities, is seventy-five hours per week (Burden 1986, 41).

2. Some studies show that fathers spend, at most, ten minutes daily with newborn infants (Adams et al. 1984, 6). From these studies and others the authors conclude that boys model their behaviors after their mothers, peers, and male instructors, not their fathers (118).

3. If this figure is calculated on the basis of the work women obtain in a highly segregated workplace, then the loss is even greater if it is presumed that childless women have a better chance of obtaining "men's" work.

4. About half of custodial parents are entitled to support under a court order. Of those, awards are small. In 1983 they averaged $1,965 per year for one child, which means that even when support is paid, the family is still impoverished. The remainder of support is paid by the custodial parent. Because women earn less, they have less to share with their children (Czapanskiy 1989).

5. "Today education is perhaps the most important function of state and local governments. . . . It is the very foundation of good citizenship. Today it is a principle instrument in awakening the child to cultural values, in preparing him for later professional training, and in helping him to adjust normally to his environment. . . . Such an opportunity, where the state has undertaken to provide it, is a right which must be made available to all on equal terms" (*Brown v. Board of Education* 1954, 691).

6. The Family and Medical Leave Act of 1993 provides aggregate annual leave of twelve weeks, which may be composed of parental leave, leave to care for a seriously ill immediate family member, and/or leave for the employee's serious illness. The act covers employers of fifty or more employees, and an employee must have worked for twelve months for a minimum of 1250 hours to be eligible for leave. Leave is unpaid, although if an employer provides any form of paid leave, the employer may require the employee to utilize that leave during the period of entitlement to family and disability leave (Dowd 1993, 339).

7. Forty-five percent of entries onto AFDC were due to divorce/separation (Committee on Ways and Means 1993, 725 Table 48).

8. We lack a family support policy beyond very limited unwaged family leave and dominantly middle-class tax support policies. We have moved only slowly toward insuring that child support be paid by all who should and can pay. We continue to place the burden on poor parents to pursue payment of support and provide no backup assurance of support other than welfare benefits which are inadequate to pull a family above the poverty line.

NOTES TO CHAPTER 4

1. Some of the more recent increases may reflect, in part, better collection of data rather than real increases (Saluter 1989).

2. Although two-thirds of all single parents are white, the occurrence of single-parent households is much more common among African Americans. Two-thirds of all African American family groups with children are maintained by single parents, compared to one-quarter among whites. Among Hispanics, single parents constitute 35 percent of family groups with children (Bureau of Census 1994). According to one report, less than half (44 percent) of Black adults are now married, a drop of one-third from 1970. By the age of thirty to thirty-four, 44 percent of Black men and 43 percent of Black women had never married in 1991. For whites, the proportions were 25 percent for men and 15 percent for women; for Hispanics, 27 percent for men and 19 percent for women. Among Black teenagers, the rate of teenage pregnancy and unwed motherhood remains high but is not rising; white teenagers are closing the race differential by an upward trend in unwed parenthood. Black teenagers nevertheless are four times more likely to have children than white teenagers (Bureau of Census 1994).

3. The same pattern exists for other women of color. Divorce does not mean a dramatic economic change, because they too begin from lower economic levels than do most white women (Wagner 1993, 121).

4. For a fascinating article comparing the development of nineteenth-century family law and southern law of the slave family, see "An Impossible Marriage: Slave Law and Family Law" (Burnham 1987). Burnham's description of the legal definition of the slave family has some eerie resonances to how we view children as disconnected pieces of property, rather than as embedded in families of whatever form:

> The slave family . . . was constructed outside of legal developments governing family relationships . . . the slave family could be an organic unit of permanently linked, interdependent persons. In the eyes of the law, each slave stood as an individual unit of property, and never as a submerged partner in a marriage or family. (Burnham 1987, 189).

The rationale was that slaves were different, licentious, dumb, childish, and therefore undeserving of legal recognition and value. How this resonates with today's views of single-parent families!

5. Harris argues that resistance to affirmative action is tied to the threat to

whiteness and does an extensive analysis of how this operates (Harris, C. 1993).

6. As one single mother stated: "[the system is] set up to help you fail and if you fail it's not there to help you—so what is the purpose in it? I don't understand it" (Polakow 1993, 79).

7. The most common test, the Human Leukocyte Antigen (HLA) test, is generally administered at its highest, most reliable level, Level III, and tests for 90 genetic markers. DNA testing is even more reliable, but more expensive.

8. These costs were quoted in a phone conversation on July 27, 1995, with a representative from Cellmark Diagnostic (1–800–872–5227) located in Germantown, Maryland.

9. Procedural requirements include the indigent father's right to appointed counsel; the requirement that indigent fathers be provided blood tests at state expense when the state initiates the proceeding (Little v. Streater 1981); the requirement of clear and convincing evidence standard (instead of a preponderance of the evidence standard); and the right to a jury trial.

10. For practical difficulties in obtaining information about paternal patterns, see an interesting article written by Nichols-Casebolt and Garfinkel (1991).

11. For a description of the favored status of widows and the history of widows benefits as compared with welfare benefits, see Steven Sugarman's (1993) article. As the system presently operates, it distinguishes between young widows with dependent children and older widows, especially displaced housewives; the system pays greater benefits to the older widows if one ignores the benefits paid to the young widow on behalf of the dependent child.

12. For an excellent summary of the bills, see the article authored by Matthew Diller (1995).

NOTES TO CHAPTER 5

1. It is interesting to note that until recently virtually all research on unemployment and its effects on family and especially on parental dynamics was focused exclusively on men. To the extent women are now being studied, Black women are studied the least, despite their longer work history. The consequences for parenting of unemployment and for women generally follow the consequences for men, that is, depression and more authoritarian discipline (McLloyd 1994).

2.

> For the most part, young Black mothers are not demoralized about their future; in fact, they are more likely to have high educational expectations, greater school attachment, and access to child care. . . . We find that young white mothers tend to marry earlier and to drop out of school at higher rates than Blacks. White females are most likely to experience accelerated adult role entry by becoming not only mothers but wives. Young Black mothers are willing to postpone marriage and accept the low-income Black community norm that the role of mother is more important than wife, particularly when an unstable marriage is foreseen. . . . This

research suggests that young white women suffer more immediate educational handicaps from counternormative role transitions than young Black women (Peters et al. 1981, 222).

3. There is a similar pattern among Mexican American families of a less dramatic economic shift, because two-parent families also are poor, but have a stronger support structure (Wagner 1993).

4. For divorced women, this translates into a higher sense of satisfaction after divorce, less depression, and fewer adjustment difficulties.

5. Children of single-mother families have a significant degree of contact with adult males. This study shows the benefit of another adult in the household of the same sex. It also underscores the importance of support networks for positive outcomes for children of single-parent households (Stolba and Amato 1993).

NOTES TO CHAPTER 6

1. The widow/widower's benefit continues until the youngest child reaches sixteen years of age. Children's benefits continue until the each child reaches the age of either eighteen or nineteen.

2. As Sugarman notes, such a system would not simply replace AFDC, since the entitlement would run to all single parents, so single parents not on AFDC would also qualify (Sugarman 1995). What I suggest here is a more modest proposal that would target nonmarital single parents first, although ideally it would include all single parents, including those where no father can be found or identified, or where there is good cause not to do so.

3. This is reflected in terminology and presumptions of custody statutes. See, for example, Florida's scheme of a primary residential parent and liberal visitation for the other parent (Fl.St. §61 et seq.).

4. This study compares single mothers' net disposable income to average net disposable income. The ratio in Sweden is .8422; in the United States .5381; and in Australia .5486. The lowest echelon countries studied are the United States, Canada, and Australia. Public transfers are an inescapable portion of a single mothers' income. It is interesting to note that in the United States, on average single mothers are younger, have more children, and have the youngest children compared to other countries studied (Garfinkel, et al. 1993, 180).

NOTES TO CHAPTER 7

1. The Supreme Court relied on the rights of the child as against the mother to uphold the state's power to send social workers into the homes of benefit recipients, unannounced and without consent (*Wyman v. James* 1971).

2. The plaintiff named several men as possible fathers of her child, but they were either excluded by blood tests or could not be located. The agency then required her to turn over a calendar on which she supposedly had written the

names of her sexual partners. When she refused, her benefits were cut (Fineman 1991c, 964).

3. There are many cases on reproductive rights and the sanctity of private decision making regarding family (*Griswold v. Connecticut* 1965; *Eisenstadt v. Baird* 1972; *Roe v. Wade* 1973; *Planned Parenthood v. Casey* 1992).

4. According to McCaffery, this pattern occurs because tax law aggregates incomes of husband and wife, because there is no taxing of self-supplied services which may serve as an incentive to stay at home, because social security contributions and benefits protect stay-at-home spouses while penalizing secondary earners, because there is inadequate coverage for mixed business/pleasure expenses, and because the taxation of noncash benefits encourages single earners to provide health, pension, and related benefits to the entire family (McCaffery 1993b).

References

BOOKS AND ARTICLES

Aaron, Henry A., and Cameran M. Lougy. 1986. *The Comparable Worth Controversy.* Washington D.C.: Brookings Institute.

Adams, Paul L., Judith R. Milner, and Nancy A. Schrepf. 1984. *Fatherless Children.* New York: Wiley.

Addis, Adeno. 1991. "Individualism, Communitarianism, and the Rights of Ethnic Minorities." *Notre Dame Law Review* 66:1219.

Allen, Charlotte. 1994 "Federalization of Child Support: Twenty Years and Counting." *Michigan Bar Journal* 73:660.

Allessandri, Steven M. 1992. "Effects of Maternal Work Status in Single-Parent Families on Children's Perception of Self and Family and School Achievement." *Journal of Experimental Child Psychology* 54:417.

Amar, Akhil R., and Daniel Widawsky. 1992. "Commentary: Child Abuse as Slavery: A Thirteenth Amendment Response to DeShaney." *Harvard Law Review* 105:1359.

Amato, Paul R., and Bruce Keith. 1991. "Separation from a Parent during Childhood and Adult Socioeconomic Attainment." *Social Forces* 70:187.

Amott, Teresa. 1988. "Working for Less: Single Mothers in the Workplace." In *Women as Single Parents: Confronting Institutional Barriers in the Courts, the Workplace and the Housing Market,* edited by Elizabeth A. Mulroy. Dover, Mass.: Auborn House Publishing.

Anderson, Cerisse. 1994. "Recent Rulings Divide on Lesbian Adoptions." *New York Law Journal* (January 25).

Anderson, Paul, and Devin Davey. 1995. "Communitarianism." *New Statesman and Society* (March 3).

Angel, David. 1992. "The Declining Significance of Biology." Presented at Critical Network Conference, Boston, Massachusetts (unpublished manuscript, on file with the *Harvard Women's Law Journal*).

Austin, Regina. 1989. "Sapphire Bound." *Wisconsin Law Review* 1989:539.

Babington, Charles. 1992. "Trying to Redefine Debate, Quayle Denounces Hollywood, Praises Single Mothers." *Washington Post* (September 2).

Barber, Bonnie L., and Jacquelynne S. Eccles. 1992. "Long-Term Influences of Divorce and Single Parenting on Adolescent Family and Work Related Values, Behaviors and Aspirations." *Psychological Bulletin* (January).

Belchman, Elaine A. 1982. "Are Children with One Parent at Psychological Risk? A Methodological Review." *Journal of Marriage and Family* 44:179.

Belsky, Jay. 1990. "Parental and Nonparental Child Care and Children's Socioemotional Development: A Decade in Review." *Journal of Marriage and Family* 52:885.

Bennett, Claudette E. 1995. *The Black Population in the United States March 1994 and 1993.* Washington, D.C.: United States Department of Commerce, Bureau of the Census.

Bergmann, Barbara R. 1986. *The Economic Emergence of Women.* New York: Basic Books.

Besharov, Douglas. 1992. "Beyond Murphy Brown: We're Ignoring the Fact That All Single Mothers Aren't Alike." *Washington Post* (September 27).

Bilge, Barbara, and Gladis Kaufman. 1983. "Children of Divorce and One-Parent Families: Cross-cultural Perspectives." *Family Relations* 32:59.

Blankenhorn, David. 1995. *Fatherless America: Confronting Our Most Urgent Social Problem.* New York: Basic Books.

Bowlby, John. 1988. *A Secure Base: Parent-Child Attachment and Healthy Human Development.* New York: Basic Books.

Bowman, Cynthia G. 1993. "Street Harassment and the Informal Ghettorization of Women." *Harvard Law Review* 106:517.

Boyle, Jacqueline. 1994. "Mom Appeals Judge's Custody Ruling." *Detroit Free Press* (August 2) sec. B.

Bradley, David. 1990. "Equality for Children of Unmarried Parents in Swedish Law." *Journal of Social Welfare Law* 5:341.

Bray, Rosemary. 1992. "So How Did I Get Here?" *New York Times Sunday Magazine* (March 5) §6 p. 35.

Brewer, Rose M. 1988. "Black Women in Poverty: Some Comments on Female-Headed Families." *Signs* 13:2.

Bronstein, Phyliss, JoAnn Clauson, Miriam Frankel Stoll, and Craig L. Abrams. 1993. "Parenting Behavior and Children's Social, Psychological, and Academic Adjustment in Diverse Family Structure." *Family Relations* 42:268.

Brown-Scott, Wendy. 1994. "Symposium: Changing Images of the State: The Communitarian State: Lawlessness or Law Reform for African-Americans." *Harvard Law Review* 107:1209.

Buckley, William F. 1992a. "Blame Illegitimate Births, Too." *San Diego Union Tribune* (May 15) sec. B.

———. 1992b. "The Murphy Brown Law." *Baltimore Evening Sun* (May 27) 15A.

Burden, Dianne S. 1986. "Single Parents and the Work Setting: The Impact of Multiple Job and Homelife Responsibilities." *Family Relations* 34:215.

Bureau of Census. 1989. *U. S. Department of Commerce, Studies in Marriage and the Family, Singleness in America.* 16.

———. 1992. *U. S. Department of Commerce, Who's Supporting the Kids?* (January 29).

———. 1994. *U.S. Department of Commerce, Statistical Abstract of the United States.* 114th edition: 471.

Burnham, Margaret. 1987. "An Impossible Marriage: Slave Law and Family Law." *Law and Inequality* 5:187.

Burtless, Gary. 1992. "When Work Doesn't Work: Employment Programs for Welfare Recipients." *Brookings Review* 10:26.

Cahn, Edgar S. 1994. "Reinventing Poverty Law." *Yale Law Journal* 103:2133.

Campbell, Linda P. 1993. "Custody Ruling Fuels Gay Rights Discussion." *Chicago Tribune* (September 12) p. 25.

Carbone, June R., and Margaret F. Brinig. 1991. "Rethinking Marriage: Feminist Ideology, Economic Change, and Divorce Reform." *Tulane Law Review* 65:953.

Carlson, Cindy. 1987. "Children and Single-Parent Homes." In *Children's Needs: Psychological Perspectives,* edited by Alex Thomas and Jeff Grimes. Washington, D.C.: National Association of School Psychologists.

Cashion, Barbara C. 1982. "Female-Headed Families: Effects on Children and Clinical Implications." *Journal of Marital and Family Therapy* 8:77.

Chamallas, Martha. 1986. "Women and Part-time Work: The Case for Pay Equity and Equal Access." *North Carolina Law Review* 64:709.

Chambers, David L. 1990. "Step Parents, Biological Parents, and the Law's Perception of 'Family' after Divorce." In *Divorce Reform at the Crossroads,* edited by Steve Sugarman and Herma H. Kay. New Haven: Yale University Press.

Claude, Judy. 1986. "Poverty Patterns for Black Men and Women." *The Black Scholar* September/October.

Committee on Ways and Means, House of Representatives. 1992. "Overview of Entitlement Programs." 102d Congress, 2d Session. Washington, D.C.: U.S. Government Printing Office.

———. 1993. "Overview of Entitlement Programs." 103d Congress, 1st Session. Washington, D.C.: U.S. Government Printing Office.

Coontz, Stephanie. 1992. *The Way We Never Were: American Families and the Nostalgia Trap*. New York: Basic Books.

———. 1995. "The American Family and the Nostalgia Trap: Attributing Americans' Social Problems to the Breakdown of the Traditional Family." *Phi Delta Kappan* 76:K1.

Creno, Cathryn. 1995. "The Custody Crunch Demands of Courts, Workplace Play Havoc with Mom's Lives." *Arizona Republic Phoenix Gazette* (June 27).

Crockett, Lisa J., David J. Eggebeen, and Alan J. Hawkins. 1993. "Father's Presence and Young Children's Behavioral and Cognitive Adjustment." *Journal of Family Issues* 14:355.

Czapanskiy, Karen. 1989. "Child Support and Visitation: Rethinking the Connections." *Rutgers Law Journal* 20:619.

———. 1991. "Volunteers and Draftees: The Struggle for Parental Equality." *University of California at Los Angeles Law Review* 38:1415.

"Dateline." 1994. *NBC News* (September 13).

DeParle, Jason. 1994. "Welfare Mothers Find Jobs Easy to Get But Hard to Hold." *New York Times* (October 24) A1:10.

Dickson, Janet Hopkins. 1991. "The Emerging Rights of Adoptive Parents: Substance or Specter?" *University of California at Los Angeles Law Review* 38:917.

Diller, Matthew. 1995. "What's Doing in Federal Welfare Reform: Here Come the Block Grants." *Newsletter of the American Association of Law Schools, Poverty Law Section, Gillis Long Poverty Law Center, Loyola University School of Law*, Vol. 28 (September).

Dolgin, Janet L. 1994. "The Family in Transition from Griswold to Eisenstadt and Beyond." *Georgetown Law Journal* 82:1519.

Dolkart, Jane L. 1994. "Hostile Environment Harassment: Equality, Objectivity, and the Shaping of Legal Standards." *Emory Law Journal* 43:151.

Dowd, Nancy E. 1989a. "Work and Family: The Gender Paradox and the Limitations of Discrimination Analysis in Restructuring the Workplace." *Harvard Civil Rights-Civil Liberties Law Review* 24:79.

————. 1989b. "Envisioning Work and the Family: A Critical Perspective on International Models." *Harvard Journal on Legislation* 26:311.

————. 1990. "Work and Family: Restructuring the Workplace." *Arizona Law Review* 32:431.

————. 1993. "Family Values and Valuing Family: A Blueprint for Family Leave." *Harvard Journal on Legislation* 30:335.

————. 1994. "Book Review: A Feminist Analysis of Adoption." *Harvard Law Review* 107:913.

————. 1995. "Stigmatizing Single Parents." *Harvard Women's Law Journal* 18:19.

Downey, Douglas B. 1994. "The School Performance of Children from Single-Mother and Single-Father Families: Economic or Interpersonal Deprivation." *Journal of Family Issues* 15:129.

Duffy, May E. 1993. "Social Support: The Provider's Perspective." *Journal of Divorce and Remarriage* 19:57.

Duncan, Greg J., and Willard Rodgers. 1990. "Lone-Parent Families and Their Economic Problems: Transitory or Persistent?" In *Lone-Parent Families: The Economic Challenge*, edited by Elizabeth Duskin. Washington, D.C.: Organization for Economic Co-operation and Development Centre.

Duskin, Elizabeth. 1990. "Overview." In *Lone-Parent Families: The Economic Challenge*, edited by Elizabeth Duskin. Washington, D.C.: Organization for Economic Co-operation and Development Centre.

Ellman, Ira Mark, Paul M. Kurtz, and Katherine T. Bartlett. 1991. *Family Law: Cases, Text, Problems*. 2nd edition. Charlottesville, VA.: Michie.

Ellwood, David T. 1988. *Poor Support: Poverty in the American Family*. New York: Basic Books.

Epstein, Richard A. 1992. *Forbidden Grounds: The Case against Employment Discrimination Laws*. Cambridge, Mass.: Harvard University Press.

Ermisch, John. 1990. "Demographic Aspects of the Growing Number of Lone-Parent Families." In *Lone-Parent Families: The Economic Challenge*, edited by Elizabeth Duskin. Washington, D.C.: Organization for Economic Co-operation and Development Centre.

Estin, Ann Laquer. 1993. "Maintenance, Alimony, and the Rehabilitation of Family Care." *North Carolina Law Review* 71:721.

Etzioni, Amitai. 1992. "Responsive Communitarian Platform: Rights and Responsibilities." *Responsive Community* Winter 1991/1992.

————. 1993. *The Spirit of Community: Rights, Responsibilities, and the Communitarian Agenda*. Southbridge, Mass.: Crown Publishing.

Evans, Sara M., and Barbara J. Nelson. 1989. *Wage Justice: Comparable Worth and the Paradox of Technocratic Reform*. Chicago: University of Chicago Press.

Family and Medical Leave Act, 1993. 29 U.S.C.A. §§2601–54.

"Feminist Psychology." 1992. In *Feminist Perspectives in Therapy: An Empowerment Model for Women*, edited by Judith Worell and Pam Remer. Chichester, N.Y.: Wiley.

Ferree, Myra Marx. 1990. "Beyond Separate Spheres: Feminism and Family Research." *Journal of Marriage and Family* 52:866.

1991. *Final Report of the National Commission on Children, Beyond Rhetoric: A New American Agenda for Children and Families*. Washington, D.C.: United States Government Printing Office.

Fine, Mark A., and Andrew I. Schwebel. 1988. "An Emergent Explanation of Differing Racial Reactions to Single Parenthood." *Journal of Divorce* Vol. II.

Fineman, Martha L. 1983. "Implementing Equality: Ideology, Contradiction and Social Change: A Study of Rhetoric and Results in the Regulation of the Consequences of Divorce." *Wisconsin Law Review* 1983:789.

———. 1991a. *The Illusion of Equality: The Rhetoric and Reality of Divorce Reform*. Chicago: University of Chicago Press.

———. 1991b. "Images of Mothers in Poverty Discourses." *Duke Law Journal* 1991:274.

———. 1991c. "Intimacy Outside of the Natural Family: The Limits of Privacy." *Connecticut Law Review* 23:955.

———. 1992. "The Neutered Mother" *University of Miami Law Review* 46:653.

Fitzgerald, Wendy A. 1994. "Maturity, Difference, and Mystery: Children's Perspectives and the Law." *Arizona Law Review* 36:11.

———. 1995. "Children, Property and Capital: A Strategy for the Legal Recognition of Children" (unpublished work in progress).

Ford, Donna Yvette, Florida Statute 61.001 et seq., J. John Harris, III, and William L. Turner. 1991. "The Extended African American Family: A Pragmatic Strategy That Blunts the Blade of Injustice." *Urban League Review* 14:71.

Free, Marvin Davis, Jr. 1991. "Another Look at the Relationship between the Broken Home and Juvenile Delinquency." Society for the Study of Social Problems.

Funiciello, Theresa. 1990. "The Poverty Industry: Do Government and Charities Create the Poor?" *Ms.* (November/December).

Furstenberg, Frank F., Jr., and Andrew J. Cherlin. 1991. *Divided Families: What Happens to Children When Parents Part*. Cambridge: Harvard University Press.

Garfinkel, Irwin, and Patrick Wong. 1990. "Child Support and Public Policy." In *Lone-Parent Families: The Economic Challenge*, edited by Elizabeth

Duskin. Washington, D.C.: Organization for Economic Co-operation and Development Centre.

Garfinkel, Irwin, and Sara S. McLanahan. 1986. *Single Mothers and Their Children: A New American Dilemma*. Washington, D.C.: Urban Institute Press.

Garfinkel, Irwin, Yin-Ling Wong, and Sara S. McLanahan. 1993. "Single-Mother Families in Eight Countries: Economic Status and Social Policy." *Social Science Review* (June).

————. 1994. "Child Support Orders: A Perspective on Reform, In the Future of Children." *Children and Divorce* 84.

Gilbert, Lucia A., and Vicki Rachlin. 1987. "Mental Health and Psychological Functioning of Dual-Career Families." *Counseling Psychologist* 15:7.

Gongla, Patricia A. 1982. "Single Parent Families: A Look at Families of Mothers and Children." In *Alternatives to Traditional Family Living*, edited by Harriet Gross and Martin B. Sussman. New York: The Haworth Press.

Gottman, Julie Schwartz. 1989. "Children of Gay and Lesbian Parents." *Marriage and Family Review* 14:34.

Graham, Hilary. 1987. "Being Poor: Perceptions and Coping Strategies of Lone Mothers." In *Give and Take in Families: Studies in Resource Distribution*, edited by Julia Brannen and Gail Wilson. London: Allen and Unwin.

Greif, Geoffrey L. 1985. *Single Fathers*. Lexington, Mass.: Lexington Books.

Guttman, Joseph. 1989. "The Divorced Father: A Review of the Issues and the Research." *Journal of Comparative Family Studies* 20:247.

Hamner, Tommie J., and Pauline H. Turner. 1985. *Parenting in Contemporary Society*. Englewood Cliffs, N.J.: Prentice-Hall.

Handler, Joel. 1994. "Ending Welfare As We Know It: A Wrong and Pernicious Idea." Presented at Law and Society Annual Convention, Phoenix, Arizona (on file with the *Harvard Women's Law Journal*).

Handler, Joel, and Y. Hasenfeld. 1991. *The Moral Construction of Poverty: Welfare Reform in America*. Newbury Park: Sage Publications.

Harris, Cheryl I. 1993. "Whiteness as Property." *Harvard Law Review* 106:1707.

Harris, Kathleen Mullan. 1993. "Work and Welfare among Single Mothers in Poverty." *American Journal of Sociology* 99:317.

Hartmann, Heidi I., Patricia A. Roos, and Donald J. Treiman. 1985. "An Agenda for Basic Research on Comparable Worth." In *Comparable Worth: New Directions for Research*, edited by Heidi I. Hartmann. Washington, D.C.: National Academy Press.

Hawthorne, Nathaniel, 1850. *The Scarlet Letter*. New York: W. W. Norton.

Heath, Phyllis A., and Kathleen Cavanaugh. 1993. "Divorced Mother's Gender Role Ideology, Locus of Control, and Disciplinary Patterns." *Sex Roles: A Journal of Research* (December) 781:29.

Hill, Robert Bernard. 1971. *The Strengths of Black Families*. New York: Emerson Hall Publishers.

Hilton, Jeanne M., and Virginia A. Haldeman. 1991. "Gender Differences in the Performance of Household Tasks by Adults and Children in Single-Parent and Two-Parent, Two-Earner Families." *Journal of Family Issues* 12:114.

Hochschild, Arlie. 1989. *The Second Shift: Working Parents and the Revolt*. New York: Viking.

Hogan, Dennis P., Ling-Xin Hao, and William L. Parish. 1990. "Race, Kin, Networks, and Assistance to Mother-Headed Families." *Social Forces* (March) 68:797.

Holden, Karen C., and Pamela J. Smock. 1991. "The Economic Costs of Marital Dissolution: Why Do Women Bear a Disproportionate Cost?" *Annual Review of Sociology* 17:51.

Holmes, Gilbert A. 1994. "The Tie That Binds: The Constitutional Right of Children to Maintain Relationships with Parent-Like Individuals." *Maryland Law Review* 53:358.

House Report 4. 1995. 104th Congress, 1st Session (June 11).

Jacobsen, R. Brooke, and Jerry J. Binger. 1991. "Black Versus White Single Parents and the Value of Children." *Journal of Black Studies* 21:302.

Jaff, Jennifer. 1988. "Wedding Bell Blues: The Position of Unmarried People in American Law." *Arizona Law Review* 30:201.

Jehl, Douglas. 1992. "Quayle Deplores Eroding Values: Cites TV Show." *Los Angeles Times* (May 20) sec. A.

Jencks, Christopher. 1992. "Hold Off on Welfare Change." *Christian Science Monitor* (November 16).

Jones, Jacqueline. 1985. *Labor of Love, Labor of Sorrow: Black Women, Work, and the Family from Slavery to Present*. New York: Basic Books.

Kamerman, Sheila B., and Alfred J. Kahn. 1988. *Mothers Alone: Strategies for a Time of Change*. Dover, Mass.: Auburn House Publishing.

Kaus, Mickey. 1986. "The Work Ethic State: The Only Way to Break the Culture of Poverty." *New Republic* (July 7).

Kay, Herma H. 1987. "Equality and Difference: A Perspective on No-Fault Divorce and Its Aftermath." *University of Cincinnati Law Review* 56:1.

Kessler-Harris, Alice. 1982. *Out to Work: A History of Wage-Earning Women in the United States*. New York: Oxford University Press.

King, Jeanne. 1995. "Judge Tells Wealthy Dad to Pay Child Support." *Reuters North American Wire Service*. (August 18).

Kissman, Kris. 1991. "Feminist Based Social Work with Single Parent Families." *Families in Society: Journal of Contemporary Human Services* 23.

Kittay, Eva Feder. 1995. "Taking Dependency Seriously: The Family and Medical Leave Act Considered in Light of the Social Organization of Dependency Work and Gender Equality." *Hypatia* 10:7.

Krause, Harry D. 1990. *Family Law: Cases, Comments and Questions,* third edition. St Paul, Minn.: West Publishing Company.

Kymlicka, Will. 1995. *Multicultural Citizenship: A Liberal Theory of Minority Rights.* Oxford: Clarendon Press.

Lerner, Gerda. 1986. *The Creation of Patriarchy.* New York: Oxford University Press.

Leslie, Leigh A., Elaine A. Anderson, and Meredith P. Branson. 1991. "Responsibility for Children: The Role of Gender and Employment." *Journal of Family Issues* 12:197.

Lewis, Edith A. 1989. "Role Strain in African-American Women: The Efficacy of Support Networks." *Journal of Black Studies* 20:155.

Li, Jiang Hong, and Roger A. Wojtkiewicz. 1992. "A New Look at the Effects of Family Structure on Status Attainment." *Social Science Quarterly* 73.

Lino, Mark. 1994. "Income and Spending Patterns of Single Mother Families." *Monthly Labor Review* (May).

Littleton, Christine A. 1987. "Equality and Feminist Legal Theory." *University of Pittsburgh Law Review* 48:1043.

Lupu, Ira C. 1994. "The Separation of Powers and the Protection of Children." *University of Chicago Law Review* 61:1317.

Maccoby, Eleanor E., and Robert H. Mnookin. 1992. *Dividing the Child: Social and Legal Dilemmas of Custody.* Cambridge: Harvard University Press.

Maclean, Mavis. 1990. "Lone-Parent Families, Family Law and Income Transfers." In *Lone-Parent Families: The Economic Challenge,* edited by Elizabeth Duskin. Washington, D.C.: Organization for Economic Co-operation and Development Centre.

Mahoney, Martha. 1991. "Legal Images of Battered Women: Redefining the Issue of Separation." *Michigan Law Review* 90:1.

Malin, M. 1994. "Fathers and Parental Leave." *Texas Law Review* 72:1047.

Malson, Michelene R. 1986. "Understanding Black Single Parent Families: Stresses and Strengths." The Stone Center, Wellesley College, Work in Progress No. 25.

Marks, Nadine F., and Sara S. McLanahan. 1993. "Gender, Family Structure, and Social Support Among Parents." *Journal of Marriage and the Family* 55:481.

McCaffery, Edward J. 1993d. "Slouching towards Equality: Gender Discrimination, Market Efficiency and Social Change." *Yale Law Journal* 103:595.

———. 1993b. "Taxation and the Family: A Fresh Look at Behavorial Biases in the Code." *University of California at Los Angeles Law Review* 40:983.

McCormick, Harvey L. 1995. *Social Security Claims and Procedures*. Fourth edition pocket part. St. Paul, Minn.: West Publishing.

McKenry, Patrick C., and Mark A. Fine. 1993. "Parenting Following Divorce: A Comparison of Black and White Single Mothers." *Journal of Comparative Family Studies* 24.

McLanahan, Sara, and Karen Booth. 1989. "Mother-Only Families: Problems, Prospects and Politics." *Journal of Marriage and the Family* 557.

McLanahan, Sara, and Gary Sandefur. 1994. *Growing Up with a Single Parent: What Hurts, What Helps*. Cambridge: Harvard University Press.

McLoyd, Vonnie C., and Leon Wilson. 1990. "Maternal Behavior, Social Support, and Economic Conditions as Predictors of Distress in Children." *New Directions for Child Development* 46:49.

McLoyd, Vonnie C., Toby Epstein Jayaratne, Rosario Ceballo, and Julio Borquez. 1994. "Unemployment and Work Interruption among African American Single Mothers: Effects on Parenting and Adolescent Socioemotional Functioning." *New Directions for Child Development* 65:562.

Mead, Lawrence M. 1988. "Jobs for the Welfare Poor: Work Requirements Can Overcome the Barriers." *Heritage Foundation Policy Review* (Winter) 60.

Measell, Richard F. 1992. "The Impact of Coming from a Single Parent Household on the Labor Force Plans of College Females: Some Economic and Counseling Implications." *Journal of Divorce and Remarriage* 18:219.

Mednick, Martha. 1987. "Single Mothers: A Review and Critique of Current Research." *Applied Social Psychology Annual* 7:184.

Meucci, Sandra. 1992. "The Moral Context of Welfare Mothers: A Study of U.S. Welfare Reform in the 1980's." *Critical Social Policy* 12:52.

Meyer, Daniel R., and Steven Garasky. 1993. "Custodial Fathers: Myths, Realities, and Child Support Policy." *Journal of Marriage and the Family* 55:73.

Millar, Jane. 1989. *Poverty and the Lone-Parent: The Challenge to Social Policy*. Brookfield, Vt.: Gower Publishing.

Minow, Martha. 1986. "Rights for the Next Generation: A Feminist Approach to Children's Rights." *Harvard Women's Law Journal* 9:1.

———. 1991. "The Free Exercise of Families." *University of Illinois Law Review* 1991:925.

———. 1994. "The Welfare of Single Mothers and Their Children." *Connecticut Law Review* 26:871.

Mnookin, Robert H., Eleanor E. Maccoby, Catherine R. Albiston, and Charlene E. Depner. 1990. "Private Ordering Revisited: What Custodial Arrangements Are Parents Negotiating?" In *Divorce Reform At the Crossroads*, edited by Stephen D. Sugarman and Herma H. Kay. New Haven, Conn.: Yale University Press.

"Mother Wins Custody after Losing It Because of Daycare." 1995. *The Tennessean* (November 9).

Mott, Frank L. 1994. "Sons, Daughters and Fathers' Absence: Differentials in Father-Leaving Probabilities and in Home Environments." *Journal of Family Issues* 15:97.

Moynihan, Daniel P. 1988. "Forward." In *Welfare Reform: Consensus or Conflict?* edited by James S. Denton. Lanham, Md.: University Press of America.

———. 1994. "The Tangle of Pathology." In *The Black Family: Essays and Studies*, 3rd edition, edited by Robert Staples. Belmont, Calif.: Wadsworth Publishing.

Mulhall, Stephen, and Adam Swift. 1992. *Liberals and Communitarians.* Oxford: Blackwell Publishers.

Murray, Charles. 1993. "The Coming White Underclass." *Wall Street Journal* (October 29).

———. 1995. "On Welfare, A Worse Sky Is Falling." *New York Times* (November 16) A24.

National Research Council. 1990. *Who Cares for America's Children?* 27.

———. 1991. *Work and Family.* 31.

Nichols-Casebolt, Ann, and Irwin Garfinkel. 1991. "Trends in Paternity Adjudications and Child Support Awards. *Social Science Quarterly* 72:83.

Norton, Arthur J., and Paul C. Click. 1986. "One Parent Families: A Social and Economic Profile." *Family Relations* 35:9.

Note. 1990. "The Child Support Enforcement Provisions of the Family Support Act of 1988." *Journal of Legislation* 16:191.

———. 1991. "Looking for a Family Resemblance: The Limits of the Functional Approach to the Legal Definition of Family." *Harvard Law Review* 104:1640.

O'Connell, Mary E. 1993. "On the Fringe: Rethinking the Link between Wages and Benefits." *Tulane Law Review* 67:1421.

Olson, Myra R., and Judith A. Haynes. 1993. "Successful Single Parents." *Families in Society* 74:259.

Olson, Sheryl L., Elizabeth Kieschnick, Victoria Banyard, and Rosario Ceballo. 1994. "Socioenvironmental and Individual Correlates of Psychological Adjustments in Low-Income Single Mothers." *American Journal Orthopsychiat.* (April) 64.

Omnibus Budget Reconciliation Act of 1993, 42 U.S.C. S666.

Parker, Louise. 1994. "The Role of Workplace Support in Facilitating Self-Sufficiency among Single Mothers on Welfare." *Family Relations* 43:168.

Pearson, Jessica, and Nancy Thoennes. 1988. "Supporting Children after Divorce: The Influence of Custody on Support Levels and Payments." *Family Law Quarterly* 22:319.

Peters, Marie F. 1981. "The Solo Mother." In *Black Families,* edited by Harriett Pipes McAdoo. Beverly Hills: Sage Publications.

Pettit, Jeffrey R. 1993. "Help! We've Fallen and We Can't Get Up: The Problems Families Face Because of Employment-Based Health Insurance." *Vanderbilt Law Review* 46:779.

Polakow, Valerie. 1993. *Lives on the Edge: Single Mothers and Their Children in the Other America.* Chicago: University of Chicago Press.

Polatnick, M. Rivka. 1984. "Why Men Don't Rear Children: A Power Analysis." In *Mothering: Essays in Feminist Theory,* edited by Joyce Trebilcot. Totowa, N.J.: Rowman and Allanheld.

Polikoff, Nancy D. 1982. "Why Mothers Are Losing: A Brief Analysis of Criteria Used in Child Custody Determinations." *Women's Rights Legal Reporter* 7:235.

Popenoe, David. 1988. *Disturbing the Nest: Family Change and Decline in Modern Societies.* New York: Aldine de Gruyter.

Posner, Hon. Richard A. 1989. "Conservative Feminism." *University of Chicago Legal Forum* 1989:191.

Rawlings, Steve W. 1994. *U.S. Department of Commerce, Series P-20, No. 477 Household and Family Characteristics March 1993* xv:xviii.

Renwick, Trudi, and Barbara R. Bergmann. 1993. "A Budget-Based Definition of Poverty with an Application to Single-Parent Families." *Journal of Human Resources* 28:1.

Rexroat, Cynthia. 1990. "Race and Marital Status Differences in the Labor Force Behavior of Female Family Heads: The Effect of Household Structure." *Journal of Marriage and the Family* 52:591.

Rhode, Deborah. 1988. "Occupational Inequality." *Duke Law Journal* 1988:1207.

———. 1992. "Sexual Harassment." *Southern California Law Review* 65:1459.

———. 1993. *The Politics of Pregnancy: Adolescent Sexuality and Public Policy,* edited by Annette Lawson. New Haven, Conn.: Yale University Press.

———. 1994. "Feminism and the State." *Harvard Law Review* 107:1181.

Rich, Adrienne C. 1986, *Of Woman Born: Motherhood as Experience and Institution.* New York: Norton.

Risman, Barbara J. 1986. "Can Men 'Mother'? Life as a Single Father." *Family Relations* 35:95.

Roberts, Dorothy E. 1991. "Punishing Drug Addicts Who Have Babies." *Harvard Law Review* 104:1421.

———. 1994. "The Value of Black Mothers' Work." *Connecticut Law Review* 26:871.

Roberts, Paula. 1991. "Child Support Enforcement: An Introduction." *Clearinghouse Review* (November).

Robson, Ruth Ann. 1994. "Resisting the Family: Repositioning Lesbians in Legal Theory." *Signs* 19:975.

Rodman, Hyman, and Constantina Safilios-Rothschild. 1984. "Weak Links in Men's Worker-Earner Roles: A Descriptive Model." In *Family and Work: Comparative Convergences,* edited by Merlin B. Brinkerhoff. Westport, Conn.: Greenwood Press.

Rosenthal, Andrew. 1992. "After the Riots: Quayle Says Riots Sprang from Lack of Family Values." *New York Times* (May 20) sec. A.

Rosenthal, Marguerite G. 1994. "Single Mothers in Sweden: Work and Welfare in the Welfare State." *Social Work* 39:270.

Russell, C. Denise, and Jon G. Ellis. 1991. "Sex-Role Development in Single Parent Households." *Social Behavior and Personality* 19:5.

Saluter, Arlene F. 1989. *Singleness in America, Studies in Marriage and the Family.* Washington, D.C.: United States: Bureau of Commerce, Bureau of Census Series P-23, No. 162.

Sanik, Margaret Mietus, and Teresa Mauldin. 1986. "Single Versus Two Parent Families: A Comparison of Mother's Time." *Family Relations* 34:53.

Schamess, Gerald. 1990. "Toward an Understanding of the Etiology and Treatment of Psychological Dysfunction among Single Teenage Mothers: Part I, A Review of the Literature." *Smith College Studies in Social Work* 60:153.

Schultz, Vicki. 1990. "Telling Stories about Women and Work: Judicial Interpretations of Sex Segregation in the Workplace in Title VII Cases Raising the Lack of Interest Argument." *Harvard Law Review* 103:1749.

Segal, David. 1992. "Motherload." *The Washington Monthly* (October) 31.

Siegal, Michael. 1985. *Children, Parenthood, and Social Welfare in the Context of Developmental Psychology.* New York: Oxford University Press.

Sigel, Irving E. et al. 1984. "Psychological Perspectives of the Family." *Review of Child Development Research* 42.

Simons, Ronald L., Les B. Whitbeck, and Rand D. Conqer. 1990. "Husband and Wife Differences in Determinants of Parenting: A Social Learning and Exchange Model of Parental Behavior." *Journal of Marriage and the Family* 52:375.

Singer, Jana B. 1992. "The Privatization of Family Law." *Wisconsin Law Review* 1992:1443.

———. 1993. "Divorce Obligations and Bankruptcy Discharge: Rethinking the Support/Property Distinction" *Harvard Journal on Legislation* 30:43.

Snyder, Margaret C. 1991. "Letters on Poverty: Growth of Mother Centered Families." *New York Times* (December 28).

———. 1992. "Socialization for Womanhood: A Sex-role Analysis." In *Feminist Perspectives in Therapy: An Empowerment Model for Women,* edited by Judith Worell and Pam Remer. Chichester, N.Y.: Wiley.

Social Security Bulletin. 1983. 46:5.

Spencer, Margaret Beale. 1988. "Self-Concept Development." In *Black Children and Poverty, A Developmental Perspective New Directions for Child Development,* edited by D. T. Slaughter. San Francisco: Jossey-Bass.

Stacey, Judith. 1994. "The New Family Values Crusaders." *The Nation* (July 25).

Stack, Carol B. 1974. *All Our Kin: Strategies for Survival in a Black Community.* New York: Harper and Row.

Stanfield, Rochelle L. 1994. "Bridging the Gap." *National Journal* (January 15).

Starnes, Cynthia. 1993. "Divorce and the Displaced Homemaker: A Discourse on Playing with Dolls, Partnership Buyouts and Dissociation under No-Fault." *University of Chicago Law Review* 60:67.

Steinbach, Alice. 1995. "Career vs. Children: Women Face Difficult Choice; Custody Wars." *Baltimore Sun* (March 13).

Stier, Max. 1992. "Corruption of Blood and Equal Protection: Why Sins of the Parents Should Not Matter." *Stanford Law Review* 44:725.

Stolba, Andrea, and Paul R. Amato. 1993. "Extended Single-Parent Households and Children's Behavior." *Sociological Quarterly* 34:543.

Strauss, David A. 1989. "Discriminatory Intent and the Taming of Brown." *University of Chicago Law Review* 56:935.

Sugarman, Steven D. 1993. "Reforming Welfare through Social Security." *University of Michigan Journal of Law Review* 26:817.

———. 1995. "Financial Support of Children and the End of Welfare As We Know It" (unpublished paper presented at the University of Virginia College of Law).

Taylor, Charles. 1994. "The Politics of Recognition." In *Multiculturalism: Examining the Politics of Recognition,* edited by Amy Gutmann. Princeton, N.J.: Princeton University Press.

Taylor, Robert Joseph, Linda M. Chatters, M. Belinda Tucker, and Edith Lewis. 1990. "Developments in Research on Black Families: A Decade Review." *Journal of Marriage and the Family* 52:1001.

"Teen Pregnancy Study, Dads Often Older." 1995. *Times Picayune* (September 12).

Thomas, Susan L. 1994. "From the Culture of Poverty to the Culture of Single Motherhood: The New Poverty Paradigm." *Woman and Politics* 14:65.

Thompson, Linda, and Alexis J. Walker. 1989. "Gender in Families: Women and Men in Marriage, Work, and Parenthood." *Journal of Marriage and Family* 51:845.

Turner, Rebecca A., et al. 1991. "Family Structure, Family Processes, and Experimenting with Substances during Adolescence." *Journal of Research on Adolescence* 1:93.

Uniform Parentage Act §4. 1973.

Van Buren, Abigal. 1995a. "Dear Abby." *Gainesville Sun* (August 15).

———. 1995b. "Dear Abby." *Gainesville Sun* (October 2).

Vogejda, Barbara. 1992. "Single Parents' Double Bind: Multi-Generational Households Need Help with Economics, Child Care." *Washington Post* (April 26).

Vosler, Nancy R., and Enola Proctor. 1991. "Family Structure and Stressors in a Child Guidance Clinic Population." *Families in Society* 72:164.

Wagner, Roland M. 1993. "Psychosocial Adjustments during the First Year of Single Parenthood: A Comparison of Mexican-American and Anglo Women." *Journal of Divorce and Remarriage* 19:121.

Walzer, Michael. 1983. *Spheres of Justice: A Defense of Pluralism and Equality.* New York: Basic Books.

Ward, Cynthia V. 1994. "A Kinder, Gentler Liberalism? Visions of Empathy in Feminist and Communitarian Literature." *University of Chicago Law Review* 61:929.

Warshak, Richard A. 1986. "Father-Custody and Child Development: A Review and Analysis of Psychological Research." *Behavioral Sciences and the Law* 4:185.

Washington, Valora. 1988. "Historical and Contemporary Linkages between Black Child Development and Social Policy." In *Black Children and Poverty, A Developmental Perspective: New Directions for Child Development,* edited by D. T. Slaughter. San Francisco: Jossey-Bass.

Wattenberg, Esther. 1993. "Paternity Actions and Young Fathers." In *Young Unwed Fathers: Changing Roles and Emerging Policies,* edited by Robert Lerman and Theodora Ooms. Philadelphia: Temple University Press.

Watts, David S., and Karen M. Watts. 1991. "The Impact of Female-Headed Single Parent Families on Academic Achievement." *Journal of Divorce and Remarriage* 17:97.

Weisner, Thomas S., Helen Garnier, and James Loucky. 1994. "Domestic Tasks, Gender Egalitarian Values and Children's Gender Typing in Conventional and Nonconventional Families." *Sex Roles* 30:23.

Weitzman, Lenore J. 1981. "The Economics of Divorce: Social and Economic Consequences of Property, Alimony and Child Support Awards." *University of California at Los Angeles Law Review* 28:1181.

———. 1985. *The Divorce Revolution: The Unexpected Social and Economic Consequences for Women and Children in America.* New York: The Free Press.

Weitzman, Lenore J., and Ruth B. Dixon. 1979. "Child Custody Awards: Legal Standards and Empirical Patterns for Child Custody, Support and Visitation after Divorce." *University of California at Davis Law Review* 12:471.

White, Lucie E. 1993. "No Exit: Rethinking Welfare Dependency from a Different Ground." *Georgetown Law Journal* 81:1961.

Williams, Joan. 1989. "Deconstructing Gender." *Michigan Law Review* 87:797.

Williams, Joan. 1991. "Gender Wars: Selfless Women in the Republic of Choice." *New York University Law Review* 66:1559.

Williams, Lucy A. 1992. "The Ideology of Division: Behavior Modification Welfare Reform Proposals." *Yale Law Journal* 102:719.

Williams, Victoria Schwartz, and Robert G. Williams. 1989. "Identifying Daddy: The Role of the Courts in Establishing Paternity." *Judges' Journal* 28:2.

Wolf, Susan. 1994. "Comment." In *Multiculturalism: Examining the Politics of Recognition*, edited by Amy Gutmann. Princeton, N.J.: Princeton University Press.

Woodhouse, Barbara Bennett. 1993. "Hatching the Egg: A Child-Centered Perspective on Parents' Rights." *Cardoza Law Review* 14:1746.

Wright-Carozza, Paolo. 1993. "Organic Goods: Legal Understandings of Work, Parenthood, and Gender Equality in Comparative Perspective." *California Law Review* 81:531.

Younger, Judith T. 1992. "Light Thoughts and Night Thoughts on the American Family." *Minnesota Law Review* 76:891.

CASES

Allen v. Eichler. 1990. No. 89A-FE-4, W.L. 58223 (Del. Super. Ct. April 3).

Andrews v. Drew Municipal Separate School District. 1975. 507 F.2d 611.

Asdourian v. Ogden Food Service. 1987. 816 F.2d 678.

Bowers v. Hardwick. 1986. 478 U.S. 186.

Brown v. Board of Education. 1954. 347 U.S. 483.

Caban v. Mohammed. 1979. 441 U.S. 380.

Cameron v. Board of Education. 1991. 795 F.Supp. 228.

Chambers v. Omaha Girls Club. 1987. 834 F.2d 697.

Clark v. Hamilton Community Schools. 1985. WL 383 Slip Opinion (N.D. Ind.)

Constant A. v. Paul C.A. 1985. 496 A.2d 1.

Dandridge v. Williams. 1970. 397 U.S. 471.

DeBoer v. Schmidt (In re Clausen). 1993. 502 N.W.2d 649.

DeShaney v. Winnebago County Department of Social Services. 1989. 489 U.S. 189.

Eckmann v. Board of Education. 1986. 636 F.Supp. 1214.

Eisenstadt v. Baird, 1972. 405 U.S. 438.

G.A. v. D.A. 1987. 745 S.W.2d 726.

Grayson v. Wickes. 1979. 607 F.2d 1194.

Griswold v. Connecticut. 1965. 381 U.S. 479.

Gubernat v. Deremer. 1995. 140 N.J. 120.

Harvey v. YWCA. 1982. 533 F.Supp. 949.

In re Adoption of Baby E.A.W. 1995. 658 So.2d 961.

In re Kirchner. 1995. 649 N.E.2d 324.

Jacobsen v. Jacobsen. 1981. 314 N.W.2d 78.

Lalli v. Lalli. 1978. 439 U.S. 259.

Lehr v. Robinson. 1983. 463 U.S. 248.

Lewis v. Delaware State College. 1978. 455 F.Supp. 239.

Little v. Streater. 1981. 452 U.S. 1.

Loving v. Virginia. 1967. 388 U.S. 87.

Maynard v. Hill. 1988. 125 U.S. 190.

Michael H. v. Gerald D. 1989. 491 U.S. 110.

Parham v. Southwestern Bell Telephone. 1970. 433 F.2d 421.

Parris v. Parris. 1995. 460 S.E.2d 571.

Perry v. Grenada Municipal Separate School District. 1969. 300 F.Supp. 748.

Pfeifer v. Marion Center Area School District. 1988. 700 F.Supp. 269.

Pierce v. Society of Sisters. 1925. 268 U.S. 510.

Planned Parenthood v. Casey. 1992. 112 S. Ct. 2791.

Prost v. Greene. 1995. 652 A.2d 621.

Roberts v. United States Jaycees. 1984. 468 U.S. 609.

Roe v. Wade. 1973. 410 U.S. 113.

S. v. S. 1980. 608 S.W.2d 64.

San Antonio Independent School District v. Rodriguez. 1973. 411 U.S. 1.

Shull v. Columbus Municipal Separate School District. 1972. 338 F.Supp. 1376.

Skinner v. Oklahoma. 1942. 316 U.S. 535.

Smith v. Organization of Foster Families for Equality and Reform. 1977. 431 U.S. 816.

Terre v. Boraas. 1974. 416 U.S. 1.

White v. Thompson. 1990. 569 So.2d 1181.

Wyman v. James. 1971. 400 U.S. 309.

Index